IN SEARCH OF THE GOOD LIFE

Rebecca Todd Peters

In SEARCH of the GOOD LIFE

The Ethics of Globalization

2010

The Continuum International Publishing Group
80 Maiden Lane, New York, NY 10038

The Continuum International Publishing Group Ltd.
The Tower Building, 11 York Road, London SE1 7NX

COVER ART: *Poverty in Moscow* (Corbis)

COVER DESIGN: Wesley Hoke

Library of Congress Cataloging-in-Publication Data
A catalog record for this book is available from the Library of Congress.

ISBN: PB: 978–0–8264–1858–6

Printed in the United States of America

To Jeff Hatcher,
my partner and friend

Contents

Preface

This project arose out of my participation in the ecumenical movement through the Presbyterian Church (USA), the World Council of Churches, and the World Student Christian Movement. My worldview was transformed through my own global experiences and the lives of young women from disparate parts of the world who I came to know. As we discussed globalization at conferences around the world through the 1990s, it seemed that we needed more concrete and nuanced ways to discuss both the positive and negative effects and experiences of globalization. And so, this project arose out of my experience of seeking to understand God's call to justice and sustainability in the midst of the ecumenical movement, feminist organizing and leadership development, and studying liberation theology and ethics at Union Theological Seminary. I hope that the typology that I offer here will help to educate some, to help clarify a confusing mess for others, and perhaps help others to see that there are alternatives to the dominant forms of globalization that currently hold sway in our world.

Typologies, however, are tricky things. On the one hand their very purpose—to simplify a complex problem and help make it more easily understood—is their very weakest point. In the process of simplifying, generalizing, and categorizing what is inevitably compromised is attention to the complexity of each position and the nuanced aspects of each body of discourse. In the end, we must remember that lived experience is open to more possibility than a rigid typology can allow and there is greater variation within each position than can be adequately represented in these pages. Nevertheless, I believe that the four theories of globalization presented in these pages can help bring clarity to the confusing topic of globalization for many people. Simply by understanding the extent to which globalization is a human construct, I hope that people will be empowered to enter into the discourse and debate about where our society is headed so that we may consciously build a world rooted in a value system that cares for people and the planet.

This project began as a dissertation at Union Theological Seminary in New York where I was blessed with a wonderful group of colleagues working on issues of economics and justice. I am deeply indebted to many friends, colleagues, teachers, and mentors whom I encountered during my years at Union. My work is stronger and richer because of the conversations with many of these people, but particular thanks for helping me think through the ideas in this book go to Janet Parker, Cynthia Moe-Lobeda, Maylin Biggadike, and Gary Matthews. The support, assistance, and critique of my teachers and mentors Beverly Harrison and Larry Rasmussen have helped to shape this project from its initial stages as an idea in a graduate seminar into its current form. Thanks are also due to Randall Styers who served with Bev and Larry on my dissertation committee.

I wrote the dissertation while living in Nashville, Tennessee, and thanks go to the gracious women in the Dissertation Support Group at Vanderbilt Women's Center who invited me into their midst, and to the Vanderbilt Divinity School Library. I would also like to thank Jeff Hatcher, Stacy Rector, Drew Henderson, Nibal Petro Henderson, Melinda Bray, and Nathaniel Bray, who came to a proofreading dinner to help me clean up the text before submitting it to Union and also for their friendship and support over the years. Many thanks also to the staff of Burke Library at Union who were always willing to help.

I had the opportunity to receive feedback on the manuscript in various forms over the past couple of years and the critiques and questions that I received from many people who seriously engaged my work have contributed to the development of my ideas. Special thanks are due to the faculty of the Jepson School of Leadership Studies at the University of Richmond for awarding my dissertation the 2002 Jepson Dissertation Award and for the ideas, thoughts, and critiques shared in a colloquium discussion of the manuscript. Portions of this manuscript were presented at the 2001 American Academy of Religion meeting and the 2003 Society of Christian Ethics meeting and I am grateful for the feedback and questions received on those occasions. Thank you, also, to the members of the Society of Christian Ethics writer's group on economics, Pamela Brubaker, Larry Rasmussen, Carol Robb, Janet Parket, Doug Hicks, Cynthia Moe-Lobeda, and Laura Stivers, for discussion of one of the chapters at our 2004 meeting.

I am also grateful for the support I have received from Elon University through an endowed position as the Distinguished Emerging Scholar in

Religious Studies. The release time has been invaluable to me in rewriting and editing this manuscript and the research funds have supported my scholarship in numerous ways. Thanks to the Belk Library staff at Elon, but especially to interlibrary loan coordinator Lynn Melchor, without whose help my research would have been much more time consuming. I have also been blessed with a number of departmental colleagues who have been very supportive and helpful in too many ways to mention—Juliane Hammer, Jim Pace, Jeffrey Pugh, and J. Christian Wilson—and dear friends who have supported me academically and personally—Brooke Barnett, Ann Cahill, Cindy Fair, Laura Roselle, and Sharon Spray.

My deep gratitude goes to the selection committee for the 2003 Trinity Prize for their support of this book and to my editor Henry Carrigan, whose excitement about the book has made it a pleasure to work with him. Thanks also to editor Amy Wagner for her work on the production of the book and to copyeditor Lauren Weller, whose editing greatly improved the readability of the book. I am also deeply grateful to Robin Lane who read the manuscript in its entirety and offered helpful feedback at the end stages of the process.

Finally, as a feminist scholar I am very grateful and attentive to the family and friends who enrich my life and support me in my professional work. I began this project when my daughter Sophia was eight weeks old and I am especially thankful for the numerous loving and caring people who have helped to care for her over the past five years at childcare centers at Vanderbilt, First Presbyterian Church in Burlington, and the University of North Carolina at Greensboro (Curry 205)—yeah Kanika and Stradley! I am deeply indebted to dear friends, colleagues, and communities who sustain me in my personal and professional work—Liz Bounds, Pam Brubaker, Cindy Cushman, Marilyn Legge, Laura Stivers, Kris Thompson, the Young Mom's Group, Second Presbyterian Church in Nashville and Guilford Park and Epiphany Presbyterian churches in Greensboro; and to my family whose love supports and nurtures me—Sophie Hatcher Peters and Becky Peters. Finally to my dear husband who helps to keep me grounded and sane, this book is dedicated to you for your support of my professional work, for your partnership in marriage and parenting, and for your friendship and love.

PART 1

SETTING THE STAGE

1

A Cacophony of Voices

Situating the Conversation

Situating Globalization

We live at the forefront of the era of globalization. Simply put, the idea of globalization is a concept that is still being defined. Different constituencies who use the term often have very specific ideas about what they mean by it, but these ideas are not necessarily shared by other groups. This discrepancy can lead to public discourse in which people appear to be talking about the same subject, but end up talking past one another. One version lauds the success and progress that globalization has made as technology increasingly draws the world closer together. Another blames globalization for destroying cultures, promoting the dependency of so-called "developing" countries, and decimating the environment.[1] The disagreement among "experts" about the definition and moral value of globalization confuses most people who witness the debate.

Our encounter with the practice of globalization is unavoidable. On a daily basis we are called upon to make decisions as corporate customers and global consumers. Do we shop at Wal-Mart when we know that the lower prices are a result of predatory pricing and low-wage labor from the "two-thirds" world?[2] Do we drink Coke or hold stock in the company when we know that products like this are part of the promotion of an already expanding global monoculture that reflects U.S. sensibilities? Every day, "first" world citizens make consumer decisions that have remarkable ramifications regarding the shape of commerce, labor, and culture in our world. What we buy and where we buy it are important ethical choices that affect the pathways that globalization will take in our world.

Many people are disempowered by the international scope and scale of globalization. This alienation can contribute to two differing responses to the phenomenon. One group, the essentialists, uncritically accept the dominant rhetoric that the current model of economics or globalization is just the way it is, while another group, the determinists, acquiesce to the belief that globalization is part of an evolutionary process that is happening to our world and there is not much we can do about it anyway. Both of these responses are a result of uncritically allowing others to define problems as well as solutions and can become dangerous and defeatist positions for people living through enormous shifts in society.

They also are not the only choices people have in responding to the changes taking place in the world around us. Understanding that we have agency in addressing the contradictions of globalization can help us to see that it is within our power to shape globalization in response to God's call for justice. This study seeks to make clear the moral differences embedded in the globalization debates as a way of helping people gain deeper insight into the importance of these ideological positions and their ramifications for all of creation.

We live in a world in which the traditional boundaries of time and space that have separated peoples, cultures, countries, and continents are rapidly disintegrating. Globalization is happening. The burning moral question must be much more nuanced than whether globalization is "good" or "bad." We must examine the differing moral visions of different versions of globalization with an eye toward seeking justice. What is often overlooked in the debates is the fact that globalization was created by humanity and that we bear responsibility—to ourselves, to each other, to future generations, and to God—to ensure that globalization is constructed in a socially responsible and just way. We have the power, authority, and responsibility to participate in the current political and social discourses and processes that continue to shape the face of globalization in our world. God does not afford us the luxury of opting out of moral responsibility. One of the defining factors of our humanity is that we are moral creatures. It is incumbent upon us, as historical agents participating in the formation of globalization, to understand that the process of globalization is a human creation and that humanity bears responsibility in defining and shaping the future pathways of globalization.

The contribution of this study to the globalization debates is to identify and analyze theories of globalization based on the perspectives of their differing moral visions. I will argue that there are four distinct globalization theories operating in our world today and that these positions hold vastly different ethical norms for what constitutes "the good life." The value centers of these theories offer us an important vantage point from which to view the epistemological reality of each position. From these vantage points the reader will be able to see the dialectical relationship that exists between ideology and practice and how the values promoted by each position work together to promote a particular social reality.

The present study aims to bring the resources of Christian ethics to bear on the phenomenon of globalization. The goals of this study are threefold. The first is to provide some orientation to the complicated debate about globalization that enables clarification of the positions. Careful reading of the cacophony of views on globalization unearths four identifiable streams of discourse within the debates, each offering a different moral vision for the world. The policy questions that drive the debate (e.g., how much governmental intervention in markets is acceptable, whether or not to forgive "the debt") merely reflect a deeper division between differing moral orders for our world. Policy debates about which direction globalization should move are morally serious debates about what values humanity will choose to privilege in the post-Cold War world. At heart, these debates are about what kind of world we will build for our children and our children's children.

In addition to mapping some of the ethical terrain of these debates, this study also will provide specific moral analysis of these four models of globalization. Differing sets of moral values affect particular interpretations of globalization by leading in different public-policy directions. The second goal of this study is to explore the moral values that are both explicit and implicit in the differing models of globalization and to assess how these values affect the subsequent public-policy directions of the various positions.

While the descriptive task of mapping the terrain of the globalization debates and the critical task of investigating the moral order of each position are important, they do not go far enough in providing an assessment of the future of globalization in our world. What remains is asking the normative question, What ought to be the case in our world? The third goal of this study is to argue that our moral task is to ensure that globalization proceeds in ways that honor creation and life and that any theory of globalization ought to be grounded in values that prioritize a democratized understanding of power, encourage care for the planet, and enhance the social well-being of people. These three values form the normative grid I use to evaluate the competing claims of the different streams of discourse. These values, which represent a feminist ethical response to the question of what constitutes "the good life," form the cornerstone of my analysis and will be more fully elaborated in the next chapter. Before we take up the task of examining what is meant by "the good life," it is necessary first to examine the social theoretical assumptions that inform this study.

Situating the Study

A major premise of this study is that people understand and encounter globalization in different ways. This premise reflects a postmodern approach to the globalization debates that recognizes that differing experiences of similar globalizing processes yields different definitions of what globalization is to different people.

Recognizing these different epistemological positions regarding globalization allows deeper insight into the contentious nature of the globalization debates. Oftentimes, people simply are not talking about the same "thing" even when using the same words. Given this postmodern predicament, bringing clarity to the globalization debates is not simply a matter of settling on common definitions. What must be recognized is that there are actually numerous different theories of globalization competing for dominance. Some of these theories highlight the economic integration of nation-states, others emphasize the stress on material culture and expression that faces many marginalized communities, while others focus on the increasing technological sophistication and integration that is changing our world.

The resources of critical theory offer some tools for making sense of the "cacophony" of voices that currently constitute the globalization debates. Critical theory refers to that branch of philosophy that is concerned with exploring issues raised by postmodern theory. Broadly speaking, postmodern thought is characterized by a loss of confidence in objective perspectives and a skepticism toward the use of meta-narratives as explicatory tools.[3] Standpoint theory provides an alternative to the traditional notion of "objectivity" that presumes the ability to access a pristine and identifiable truth or position. In its place, standpoint theorists offer particular knowledge rooted in subjective experience as an important vantage point for social analysis.

Situated Knowledge as a Starting Point

This study is shaped by certain assumptions about how knowledge is formed and developed; namely, that knowledge is "situated" within particular social locations.[4] In other words, what we know is shaped by those factors that have formed our identity. It is from particular social locations that people develop epistemologies, or theories of knowledge. Differently said, it is through personal, lived experience that we each come to know the world and how it works. Fredric Jameson describes a standpoint as

> the presupposition . . . that, owing to its structural situation in the social order and to the specific forms of oppression and exploitation unique to that situation, each group lives the world in a phenomenologically specific way that allows it to see, or better still, that makes it unavoidable for that group to see and to know, features of the world that remain obscure, invisible, or merely occasional and secondary for other groups.[5]

Understanding social location as yielding distinct and particular knowledge sheds some light on the debates about globalization by forcing us to acknowledge that our individual experience of the effects of globalization contributes to particular assessments of its strengths and weaknesses. Our standpoint also affects what we are able to think and dream about the future. Differing perspectives on globalization exist because people experience the world in different ways. Consequently, social location shapes the way that people approach the topic of globalization and causes them to reflect differently on their obligations, values, and decisions. In many ways the different theoretical standpoints addressed in this study represent not just four different viewpoints and voices, but four manifestly different social worlds that are marked and separated by particular values, some of which may be irreconcilable.

Examination of these differing views of globalization may enable people to understand better that globalization is a historical process, one being molded and shaped by individual and institutional choices and decisions that are undergirded by particular cultural, theological, and social values. In order to get a sense of how the different positions are constructed and to understand the differences between them, it is necessary to examine a second assumption about knowledge that informs this study.

Grounding Theory in Praxis

While knowledge arises in and is informed by lived experience, knowledge is more than just theoretical abstraction or mere information about a given subject. From the perspective of historical materialism, theoretical work should not remain at an abstract level disassociated from the material lives of actual people, but should possess within it the tools that can help people in creating justice.[6] This kind of theoretical inquiry is content not with merely explaining the world, but with developing a kind of theory rooted in transformative praxis. In other words, this model of knowledge is more than merely cognitive; it is a knowledge that arises from an engaged effort to change the world. As a fundamentally socially transformative form of knowledge, historical materialism is a form of knowledge that grows out of an engaged and intentional struggle to enable social transformation.

The materialist perspective argues that different theoretical positions are inextricably bound up in shaping the social realities they attempt to describe. At the same time, materialists believe that knowledge arises from practice. At the epistemological level, theory and practice form a dialectical relationship in which our beliefs function to help create the social reality in which we live, while at the same time, our engagement in the world generates a new level of cognitive awareness. The critical knowledge that emerges from this dialectical crucible, in which belief and theory are ground together with a praxis that actively seeks out social transformation, is an understanding of the world as change.

In any complicated debate, such as the one surrounding globalization, it is important to examine the underlying theory and the accompanying practices together because they can help us gain a deeper understanding of the dialectical complexity of different positions. This deeper understanding will provide a context within which a comparison of the moral priorities of different positions in the debates about globalization will help us to grasp the contradictory nature of the different theoretical interpretations of globalization.

This interrogation of differing interpretations of globalization is concerned with more than just defining and explaining globalization. The theoretical analysis of this study is shaped and corrected by particular normative claims that arise through engaging in the development of emancipatory critical knowledge. The desire to pursue genuine critical social transformation gives rise to normative claims of a democratized understanding of power, care for the planet, and the social well-being of people. While a model of globalization based on these norms reflects a Christian ethical perspective that these values will promote social transformation and justice in our world, it also requires a shift away from the model of globalization that dominates our world today.

From a materialist perspective, it is also necessary to pay particular attention in this study to the historical conditions of early twenty-first century capitalism and the effects of those conditions on the material lives of all people, rich and poor. Historical contextualization is important because "the starting point of any theory has consequences."[7] While the different theories of globalization presented here may not necessarily share the same starting point, or even tell the same historical story, acknowledging the differences between the positions will help us clarify the values of each position. Employing a materialist historical perspective in this analysis of globalization primarily shifts the standard focus of questions about globalization from economic concerns to concern for the material conditions of life: from profit to sustainability, from centralized wealth and power to democratized power and eco-justice.

Methodologically, these sorts of shifts require locating particular social realities within their historical contexts. In this study, attention to historical contexts takes the form of reading each particular theory about globalization within the context of its adherents' interpretation of history. Paying attention to the differences in the starting points of each position as well as to their interpretations of history is significant because different ways of seeing the world enable different responses. Careful attention to historical memory helps illuminate the political priorities of different positions. While we will see that the dominant models of globalization often focus primarily on economic questions, this study seeks to transform the debates by putting the earth community at the center of our analysis of globalization. This shift of the starting point from neoclassical economic theory to the earth community provides us a new way of viewing the social reality of globalization that offers the possibility of new and different responses to the problems embedded in contemporary processes of globalization.

Situating the Globalization Debates

The subject of globalization has been addressed in a number of academic fields, including international relations, political science, sociology, economics, philosophy, anthropology, and religious studies. In international relations, political science, and sociology, the questions regarding globalization have dealt with the theoretical conundrum of conceptualizing the entire world, in Roland Robertson's terms, as a "single place."[8] In economics, globalization is largely approached as the integration of all national economies into a single global economy.[9] In philosophy, theorists have mainly focused on the cultural aspects of globalization.[10] Anthropologists focus on documenting local communities' experiences of globalization.[11] Finally, in religious studies, the debate regarding globalization has revolved around the central question of how globalization is affecting the practice of religion around the world.[12] While the study of globalization is truly a diverse and interdisciplinary area, there remains a gap in the literature addressing the phenomenon of globalization.

Much of the discourse in globalization studies revolves around attempts to try to define, explain, and theorize what globalization "is" or to examine differing accounts of its history and development. Unfortunately, this approach assumes a universal quality to the phenomenon of globalization. It assumes that globalization represents a single reality that can be debated. Globalization represents different realities to different people. For those connected to the World Trade Organization, it has meant increased trade and capital flows; for the development community, it has provided an avenue for fighting poverty and disease; for anti-globalization protestors, it has been seen as an exploitation of the poor by the wealthy; and for many in the "two-thirds" world, it has served as a new form of colonialism.

Aside from debating the relative merits of globalization, there is another way to approach the topic; namely, to acknowledge that the lived material realities of differing people around the globe provide a variety of competing epistemological positions from which to define, explain, and understand globalization. The typology proposed here is aimed at bringing specificity and clarity to the confusing debates about globalization in the fields of economics, popular culture, politics, and international relations, to name just a few.[13] Any presentation of varied positions necessarily requires delimiting the wide variation of voices and perspectives that are represented in the discourse to be studied. Nevertheless, the choice of the positions in this study represents serious moral reflection on both the breadth and depth of the literature pertaining to globalization. The perspectives presented in this study represent the four most prominent ideological readings of globalization as they are articulated and manifested, not only in contemporary discourse, but also in action and mobilization around the development of public policy on the national and international levels.[14] The choice to focus on the players most directly involved in shaping public policy reflects the overriding concern of this study that the issue of globalization is first and foremost an issue of survival—planetary, cultural, and human. While all four positions concur that there are threats to the planet, to human culture, and to a large portion of humanity, they differ in their assessment of the severity of these threats and in their moral response.

Simply stated, the version of globalization that we embrace—as people, as countries, as institutions, as businesses—has profound implications for how planetary, cultural, and human survival will take place in the twenty-first century.

Since the four positions represent distinct ideological orientations, each signifies divergent understandings and interpretations of the meaning and value of globalization. Beverly Harrison has argued that understanding the different ways that ideology functions in the development of social theory can aid in our ability to comprehend and make sense of complex theoretical problems.[15] More specifically, she offers a twofold definition that illuminates two very different effects that ideology can have on the development of social theory. On the one hand, ideology can be understood as a worldview or "cultural gestalt" that functions to set limitations and boundaries on the subjects' ability to "see" beyond their own social location or life experience. On the other hand, ideology in a more dangerous sense can function to mask aspects of reality as a defense mechanism in support of its own position. This type of mystification clouds the ability of its subjects to gain a complete picture of the situation at hand. Clearly, an important part of the present task is to examine the ideological biases of each position as a way to differentiate their theoretical visions of globalization.

The categorizations I use in this study have emerged from and draw together groups of like-minded individuals, institutions, and organizations, which I designate with a few umbrella terms. I will use the following terms—*neoliberal*, *development*, *earthist*, and *postcolonial*—to help illustrate the four theories of globalization highlighted here. These distinctions represent large categories of people, groups, businesses, and agencies whose boundaries are more permeable than set; nevertheless, to argue the point that there are fundamentally different ways of understanding globalization, I offer these categories as a starting point for the sake of discussion. Specific difficulties associated with the naming of the individual positions will be addressed in each chapter.

Outline of Chapters

Chapter 2 frames the theological questions and interests that will guide this examination of theories of globalization. It provides a brief introduction to the task of feminist liberation ethics that, along with the critical social theory introduced in this chapter, serves as the epistemological framework for this study. This chapter also serves to develop the theological and methodological frameworks that form the evaluative grid of this study by examining what each position considers to be "the good life."

While globalization is often reduced to an economic paradigm characterized by increased trade among nations and the creation of a single global economy, as we will see in chapter 3, this represents just one theory of globalization. This position, known as neoliberalism, is informed by an ideology that promotes growth and profits through increased external trade between nations and is largely associated with corporate or big business. The leaders of this position are the most outspoken champions of the "free market"; they represent the World Trade Organization, multinational and transnational corporations, the Organisation for Economic Co-operation and Development, and the International Chamber of Commerce, to name just a few of the players.

Chapter 4 examines the development community, which represents the second stream of discourse and is associated with the World Bank,[16] the United Nations Development Programme, the United States Agency for International Development, and a host of similar organizations. Within the field of development studies, there are a number of different ways of defining what constitutes "development." From the big business perspective, development is synonymous with economic growth and a concern that "underdeveloped" countries focus on their private sector. The grassroots perspective is described by Indian professor John Mohan Razu in this way:

> Development means development of the people. People ought to be the core and essence of development. Multi-storeyed buildings [*sic*], infrastructural facilities, increase in GNP, GDP, per capita income, industrial and agricultural production are not development; they are tools of development.[17]

This study will focus on those voices within the development community that are influenced by social equity liberalism[18] and will follow Razu's definition of development as primarily focused on social development.

Chapter 5 features the third position in this typology, which is associated with the ideology of earthism.[19] Specifically, the focus will be on the ideology shared by people and organizations that can broadly be defined as adhering to a growing grassroots principle alternately called "globalization from below," "bioregional model," and "localization." This principle is rooted in the belief that local communities need once again to become the center of economic, cultural, and social activity rather than continuing the trend of recent decades toward transnational corporations and what has been termed the "McDonaldization" of culture.[20] The chapter focuses specific attention on relatively small grassroots organizations that are working on issues of environmental justice as well as developing alternative economic paradigms.

The final position on globalization, taken up in chapter 6, is a reflection of the activities of local communities of people who are mobilizing to address the powers of globalization that are destroying life for the already poor and marginalized people of the world.[21] This position is designated as postcolonial because most of its adherents share an identification of the current expression of globalization as neocolonialism. While most people who hold this position are from the global South, there are an increasing number of marginalized people in the so-called "developed" world whose relative social and economic positions align them more with "the poor" in other countries than with the majority of people in their own. In this chapter we will see how the postcolonial model offers resistance to the constraints of a form of globalization that disallows marginalized people the possibility of meaningful participation in the decision-making processes that affect their lives.

The four chapters delineating these varied theories of globalization follow a similar format. Each begins by locating its perspective within the historical framework most commonly accepted by that position, followed by a presentation of the ideological assumptions that inform each perspective. Each chapter then moves to an articulation of the position's understanding of what globalization should look like, including the strengths and weaknesses of present forms of globalization as viewed from that particular standpoint. Each chapter concludes with a presentation of the position's vision of the good life as expressed through the values most closely associated with human moral agency, teleology, and human flourishing.

Chapter 7 uses the normative moral criteria of the democratization of power, care for the planet, and the social well-being of people to evaluate the moral standing of the four positions on globalization presented in this study. While all four models recognize globalization as a historical process in which the world is already engaged, this study holds as a basic assumption that it is within the power of human agency to shape the direction globalization will take in the future. To this end, the final chapter is interested in mapping out some future pathways for globalization that honor and respect creation and that engender a moral agency that enables people to find strength and power in working toward a more morally accountable and responsible form of globalization.

Notes

1. The terms "developed" and "developing," commonly used to distinguish countries in the global North from countries in the global South, will appear in this study in quotation marks to indicate the contestability of the notion of "development." Challenges to the concept of development are taken up more fully in chapter 6.

2. For a detailed account of Wal-Mart's business philosophy and practices, see Bill Quinn, *How Wal-Mart Is Destroying America and the World: And What You Can Do about It* (Berkeley, CA: Ten Speed Press, 2000).

In this study, the phrase "'two-thirds' world" will be used instead of the more traditional "'third' world" in recognition of the fact that the majority of the world's people live in the "two-thirds" world. This is in defiance of the pejorative implications in the terminology that the "first" world is somehow more important or of a higher status or value than the so-called "third" world. The term "'first' world" will be used to denote the countries that were the "first" to industrialize and thus gain power in the world of global trade, namely Western Europe, North America, and

Japan. These terms are used in this study for convenience but appear in quotation marks to signify their insufficiency in adequately representing these groups of nations and their complex relationships.

3. Some postmodern theories, such as structuralism, repudiate notions of objective perspectives altogether. In its most extreme form, postmodernism can lead to a theoretical position of moral nihilism that I reject. The specific version of feminist theory that I explicate below represents reformulations of critical theory, not a total repudiation of the task of theorizing. For more detailed reading of postmodern and critical theories that have influenced this study, see Walter Truett Anderson, ed., *The Truth about the Truth: Deconfusing and Re-constructing the Postmodern World* (New York: J. P. Tarcher, 1995); Bruno Latour, *We Have Never Been Modern*, trans. Catherine Porter (Cambridge, MA: Harvard University Press, 1993); David Harvey, *The Condition of Postmodernity: An Enquiry into the Origins of Cultural Change* (Cambridge, MA: Blackwell, 1990); and Linda J. Nicholson, ed., *Feminism/Postmodernism* (New York: Routledge, 1990). For an introduction to postmodern theory that rejects meta-narratives see Jean-Francois Lyotard, *The Postmodern Condition: A Report on Knowledge*, trans. Geoff Bennington and Brian Massumi (Minneapolis: University of Minnesota Press, 1984).

4. Social location refers to the set of identity-forming circumstances—such as race, ethnicity, culture, and class—that affects and influences one's experience of the world. The feminist standpoint theory that has influenced me shares or appropriates aspects of Marx's critique of capitalism, his theory of labor, and his thesis that capitalism produces intrinsically class-stratified social relations.

In Marx, the standpoint of the proletariat is the central epistemological concern. Marx argued that the material life structures one's knowledge and that the disadvantaged position of the proletariat allows them to see the world in a different way from the bourgeoisie. Furthermore, Marx argued that the epistemological position of the proletariat offers not just a different but also a more correct vision of class society, as the proletariat is able to see the inherent problems and flaws of capitalism, which the bourgeoisie is unable to see. Feminist standpoint theory builds on Marx's insight that the disadvantaged possess an epistemological privilege, but standpoint theorists expand that claim by focusing on the vantage point of women and the subsequent epistemological insights this provides into patriarchal society.

For in-depth feminist discussions of standpoint theory, see Nancy C. M. Hartsock, "The Feminist Standpoint: Developing the Ground for a Specifically Feminist Historical Materialism," in *Feminist Social Thought: A Reader*, ed. Diana Tietjens Meyers (New York: Routledge, 1997); Sandra Harding, "What Is Feminist Epistemology?" in *Whose Science? Whose Knowledge? Thinking from Women's Lives* (Ithaca, NY: Cornell University Press, 1991); and Patricia Hill Collins, "Toward an Afrocentric Feminist Epistemology," in *Black Feminist Thought: Knowledge, Consciousness, and the Politics of Empowerment* (New York: Routledge, 1990).

5. Fredric Jameson as quoted in Nancy C. M. Hartsock, *The Feminist Standpoint Revisited and Other Essays* (Boulder: Westview Press, 1998), 239.

6. Rosemary Hennessy and Chrys Ingraham define historical materialism as emancipatory critical knowledge. Rosemary Hennessy and Chrys Ingraham, *Materialist Feminism: A Reader in Class, Difference, and Women's Lives* (New York: Routledge, 1997), 4.

7. Ibid., 5.

8. See Ian Clark, *Globalization and International Relations Theory* (Oxford: Oxford University Press, 1999); Ankie Hoogvelt, *Globalisation and the Postcolonial World: The New Political Economy of Development* (London: Macmillan Press Ltd., 1997); Eleonore Kofman and Gillian Youngs, *Globalization: Theory and Practice* (London: Pinter, 1996); Roland Robertson and William Garrett, *Religion and Global Order* (New York: Paragon House Publishers, 1991); Saskia Sassen, *Globalization and Its Discontents* (New York: The New Press, 1998); Caroline Thomas and Peter Wilkin, eds., *Globalization and the South* (New York: St. Martin's Press, 1997); and Malcolm Waters, *Globalization* (London: Routledge, 1995).

9. See Dean Baker, Gerald Epstein, and Robert Pollin, *Globalization and Progressive Economic Policy* (Amherst, MA: Cambridge University Press, 1998); and Michel Chossudovsky, *The Globalisation of Poverty: Impacts of IMF and World Bank Reforms* (London: Zed Books, 1997).

10. See C. Fred Alford, *Think No Evil: Korean Values in the Age of Globalization* (Ithaca, NY: Cornell University Press, 1999); Fredric Jameson, *Postmodernism, or, The Cultural Logic of Late Capitalism* (Durham, NC: Duke University Press, 1991); Fredric Jameson and Masao Miyoshi, eds., *The Cultures of Globalization* (Durham, NC: Duke University Press, 1998); and Ray Kiely and Phil Marfleet, *Globalisation and the Third World* (London: Routledge, 1998).

11. See Marc Edelman, *Peasants against Globalization: Rural Social Movements in Costa Rica* (Stanford, CA: Stanford University Press, 1999).

12. See Dwight N. Hopkins et al., *Religions/Globalizations: Theories and Case Studies* (Durham, NC: Duke University Press, 2001); Max L. Stackhouse with Peter J. Paris, eds., *God and Globalization: Religion and the Powers of the Common Life* (Harrisburg, PA: Trinity Press International, 2000); Max L. Stackhouse, ed., *Christian Social Ethics in a Global Era* (Nashville: Abingdon Press, 1995); Peter Beyer, *Religion and Globalization* (London: SAGE Publications, 1994); and Enoch H. Oglesby, *Born in the Fire: Case Studies in Christian Ethics and Globalization* (New York: Pilgrim Press, 1990).

13. The simplification of the globalization debates into four distinct paradigms is not intended to imply that the debate itself is in any way simple. On the contrary, my intention is to provide a different lens, a moral lens, through which to view the complexity of the debate.

14. *Ideology* is a tricky word these days. It is a word often used to dismiss or undermine someone else's position. For instance, if someone is accused of making an "ideological argument," the intended implication is that the argument is simplistic and reductionistic, reflecting a rigid, predetermined narrow position. Perhaps the term *ideology* has acquired this negative connotation because it is also a term that is closely aligned with Marxian theory, an ideology that is currently out of vogue in

academia. For our purposes an ideology is a particular belief system that informs and shapes a political, economic, or, in this study, globalizing system or perspective.

15. Beverly Wildung Harrison, *Making the Connections: Essays in Feminist Social Ethics* (Boston: Beacon Press, 1985), 56.

16. The World Bank is a multilateral banking institution set up after World War II to aid in European reconstruction. While historically it has upheld both a neoclassical and, most recently, a neoliberal ideology, the current president, James Wolfensohn, and former senior economist Joseph Stiglitz have criticized the Washington Consensus model and are publicly seeking to alter both the Bank's image and its practices. Time will tell whether they are successful in truly challenging neoliberalism, but for now I will give them the benefit of the doubt and include them in the "development" community.

17. I. John Mohan Razu, "Transnational Corporations (TNCs) as Vehicles of Globalisation Process: A Critique from Development Perspective," *Bangalore Theological Forum* 30, nos. 3–4 (1998): 67.

18. Carol Johnston uses the phrase "social equity liberalism" in chapter 6 of her book, *The Wealth or Health of Nations: Transforming Capitalism from Within* (Cleveland, OH: Pilgrim Press, 1998). I have chosen to adopt this phrase in my work because the term "welfare liberal" has become exceedingly pejorative over the years.

19. This ideology will be defined more explicitly in chapter 5.

20. George Ritzer, *The McDonaldization of Society: An Investigation into the Changing Character of Contemporary Social Life* (Thousand Oaks, CA: Pine Forge Press, 1996).

21. While most of the people who support this position are poor and marginalized people themselves, there are also people who stand in solidarity with the poor through their own advocacy and work, privileged people who stand in resistance to the kind of future promoted by the dominant paradigm of globalization.

2

The Ethics of Globalization

Developing a Normative Christian Ethical Approach to Globalization

Refocusing Christian Ethics

Chapter 1 identified the social theoretical framework of historical materialism as a methodological foundation for the present study. As the Christian materialist-feminist standpoint of this study has not been widely developed or assumed within Christian discourse, it warrants further explanation.[1] Bringing materialist-feminism together with Christian ethics grounds the normative claims of this study within a concrete moral discourse that provides a platform to engage the predominantly secular discussions regarding globalization and to challenge Christian churches and people to reconsider the role we currently play in uncritically reproducing dominant forms of globalization.

The historical dualism between spirit and matter within the Christian tradition has been marked by a separation of the physical, material side of human existence from that which is considered spiritual or transcendent. When this kind of rift deems "spiritual" issues as the only ones worth pursuing, it often dismisses critical moral questioning in relation to the political and economic order. Under these circumstances, the primary questions raised regarding globalization are spiritual in nature: To what extent does one's wealth impede relationship with God? How do we fulfill our obligation to care for the poor and marginalized in our midst? A spiritualistic approach to economic and political ethics is concerned not with the material relationships and circumstances that create wealth and poverty, but rather with the spiritual effects that wealth and poverty have on the individual believer. This approach emphasizes "taking care of" the poor rather than changing the material circumstances that have created their poverty.

A feminist-liberationist position, while acknowledging that the way in which wealth is created, produced, and shaped is a spiritual issue, is simultaneously concerned about the way the political economy is structured. This particular standpoint regards social transformation as a crucial element of justice-making and is rooted in a critical social theoretical perspective that finds its starting point in the historical reality of people's lives, with particular attention to the lives of the marginalized. Attention to the concrete material realities of globalization and a commitment to justice shape the normative approach to globalization found in this study in ways that speak directly to the secular debates regarding globalization.

Rereading the Reformed Tradition in Light of a Feminist Liberation Standpoint

Those of us who embrace Reformed hermeneutics have long believed that God works through humanity to help bring about God's purpose in the world. Reformed Christianity understands that part of the responsibility of faith is to live differently in the world. The Reformed calling is to live a life of service toward God and others and to strive toward a just moral order. In other words, the Reformed tradition is radically oriented toward inclusivity, representation, and an active God working through the Holy Spirit in our communities. This is the theological hermeneutic that informs the present study. While historical churches have not always lived up to this conviction, this study is shaped by the seeds of justice-oriented community buried deep within the Reformed tradition. This study also presumes a historically socially conscious method that has a history of combining personal and communal spiritual nurturance with justice-seeking social reform.

In many ways, the goals of materialist-feminism parallel the historic goals that have guided churches that are a part of the Reformed tradition. In seeking to make the faith and the church more relevant to the common folk in the Middle Ages, Protestant Reformers emphasized that liturgy and worship should take place in the common vernacular so that the people could follow along. In a similar vein, the prominence of the dictum *sola scriptura* led to new translations of the Bible as well as an increase in literacy among commoners. More contemporary developments in the Social Gospel tradition of Protestantism witness to the importance of the role of social justice in the Reformed tradition.

A Reformed theological hermeneutic understands the process of theological work to be a continually evolving task. In other words, our knowledge about God and our understanding of faith are always in a process of growing, changing, and renewing our lives. This approach is capable of responding to the changing world and the insights that it can bring to bear on our knowledge of God and our relationship with God. It also allows for a contemporary examination of globalization that rigorously investigates the various positions with an eye to discerning what they can help us learn about our faith and about the divine.

The analysis presented here also assumes a praxis epistemology that believes moral truth is something that human beings enact. No abstract moral truth exists outside of concrete, historical human communities. Those moral practices that we embody become the moral truths for our communities. The way we live in the world is a testimony to our moral vision and our values. People who cling to moral absolutes will argue that this sort of epistemology opens the door to a cultural relativism in which anything goes.[2] Such accusations confuse relativity with arbitrary subjectivism and obscure the role of ethics in moral conversation. The choice, however, is not between an arbitrary subjectivism (in which "anything goes") and moral absolutism (there is a "right" and a "wrong" choice). There is a third way.

A process of tested normativity allows for a moral complexity absent in the two previous approaches. The fact is that there are better and worse moral choices and that this assessment is based on communally negotiated moral norms. A tested normativity requires the creation of ethical standards that are developed through the kind of public debate that requires persuasiveness, commitment, and inclusivity. This type of praxis epistemology is challenging because it forces communities to develop their own ethical standards and does not provide any easy answers. It requires that we pay detailed attention to the consequences of our actions and that we continue to correct our limited understandings of morality when we are faced with new information. A praxis epistemology is open to correction and recognizes that morality is not static but ever growing and changing.

The materialist-feminism position developed here shares the conviction with more traditional ethical standpoints that theology is important. Theology is the process by which the community discusses and comes to understand its faith and what its members believe together. It is the critical side of faith. All thinking, questioning Christians are engaged in "doing" theology; this is the only way to have intelligible faith. Christianity has traditionally taught that what we believe about our faith and about the world has moral implications and that we as Christians are to enact our beliefs in the living out of our daily lives. This teaching has been reinforced by the notion that it is the mark of a hollow faith to proclaim liberty for the captives on Sunday and then do nothing to help free those same people in our daily actions and routines Monday through Saturday. As Beverly Harrison points out, social ethics has traditionally been "conceived as subservient and deducible from theological tradition."[3]

A liberationist epistemology describes different roles for theology and social ethics. The model of a "spiral of praxis" is rooted in the materialist epistemology described earlier. This model holds that knowledge is both formed and changed in the concrete action of struggle (which represents our social ethic) and our reflection on that struggle (which represents our theology). The model is a spiral instead of a circle because it is impossible to come full "circle" and exit a praxis model without being changed—the spiral represents the forward movement enacted by the struggle for social justice. Understood in this way, our theological beliefs exist in a dialectical interaction with our moral norms as each is forever being shaped and reshaped by our active engagement in the struggle for social justice.

In contrast to traditionalist methods, here it is presumed that there is an intimate dialectical interaction between theological beliefs and moral norms. The call to engage the world as Christians is so strong that our faith requires corresponding moral behavior and activity. This behavior is not required for forgiveness of sins or for salvation; it is required because anything less would be to misunderstand humanity's responsibility to walk the walk of our faith. Praising God and claiming Jesus as our Savior are empty acts of piety if our very lives are not transformed by the radical call of justice that echoes through Christian Scripture, tradition, and experience. These three sources—Scripture, tradition, and experience—form the methodological foundation for the theological approach of this study.

The Bible remains a critical foundational resource for the intellectual and spiritual development of numerous Christians. Biblical authority means that Scripture is a living document that continues to bear witness to how God is calling humanity to live in the face of a changing world. The study of the Bible in community becomes an integral part of helping us discern how to interpret God's message to us. The living witness of the Bible is evident in the broad recurrent themes that continue to resonate in the lives of people who are seeking answers to the hard questions that life poses: Why can I not feed my family? Why do people fly planes into buildings? Where is God in the midst of war, famine, poverty, death? In response to these questions, Scripture offers the themes of liberation, justice, reconciliation, and peace as ways forward for our future as an earth community.

In addition to Scripture, theological and moral norms are also embedded in Christian history and tradition. The faith and lives of our ancestors are always present as ways of reminding us where we have come from, even as we seek to understand where God is calling us to go in the future. Our ancestral traditions should provide a link to our past rather than a chain that binds us. One of the reasons that Christianity has remained a living faith is its ability to continue to help guide people on their journeys of faith by growing and changing as creation has grown and changed. A vibrant and meaningful religion is one that is rooted enough in its past to be able to pass along the stories and meaning of the faith while still being open to receive God's continued revelation and growing into the new challenges and opportunities that the future holds.

God is engaged in our world, and consequently we experience God's inbreaking Spirit in the day-to-dayness of our lives. The continued revelation of God that occurs in the ordinary lives of God's people today must be recognized and affirmed as part of the ongoing unfolding of our theological history. Women and men, children and adults, Africans, Asians, North and South Americans, Europeans, gay and straight, rich and poor—people of faith everywhere have experiences of God that help to broaden our understanding of God, our faith, and the moral life. The sharing of the Word of God through preaching, teaching, discussion, prayer, and dialogue is another example of how theological beliefs and moral norms are shaped in the Christian tradition. Because humans are rational, thinking creatures, the use of human reason is also recognized as an important element of theological and moral reflection.

This Study as an Exercise in Public Theology

The task of public theology in an era of globalization and pluralism is increasingly difficult. Part of the task of recognizing and acknowledging the multicultural and diverse gifts that various communities have to offer is to be open to the wisdom and insight that many of the world's religions offer to these debates. In this process, the historic hegemonic power of Christianity to define and determine public policy and debate about moral issues is necessarily being challenged. This does not mean that Christian ethics is no longer a valid and important resource for moral inquiry and conversation. It means that the role that Christian ethics (and ethicists) plays is necessarily being rethought as it relates to the task of public theology.

Postmodern critiques of the inadequacy of objectivist and universalist assumptions made in the name of Christianity have unmasked the biased assumptions of much of what passes as "public" discourse on religion. The Republican "Contract with America" from the early 1990s offers an excellent example of a very particularized theological ideology that was touted as representing the "Christian" point of view. U.S. citizens quickly voted many of these "Christian" representatives out of Congress in the next election in a public outcry against the domination of one sectarian vision of society that was not shared by the majority. Generally speaking, the ideological biases of distinct religious voices are now more clearly identified and acknowledged within the realm of public policy and debate in democratic societies. In democratic states in which communities no longer share confessional and/or theological bonds, the voice of the theologian can be suspect.

Nevertheless, at least two important tasks remain for the theological ethicist. First, we need to realize that considered reflection on the pressing moral and theological problems of the day that draws on the resources of particular faith traditions can serve an important prophetic role. The spiritual resources of varied faith traditions can often offer new insights into seemingly intractable social problems and moral conflicts. This is particularly the case when the language and discourse focus on engagement with material social problems and invite thoughtful reflection on the issues at hand.

Second, we must recognize that our public discourse and attitudes are already deeply theological and ideological. Ethicists can help demystify the entrenched public debates surrounding controversial topics by unmasking the ideological and theological biases embedded within various positions. This contribution to the task of public theology can offer clarity to public policy debates by illuminating the ideological biases that are often invisible to the participants.

Establishing "the Good Life" as a Normative Framework for Evaluating Competing Positions on Globalization

We have already encountered the fear of moral relativity raised by the praxis epistemology that grounds this study. Along similar lines, some scholars argue that postmodernism's attack on the notion of a singular universal truth has rendered the globalization debates morally neutral.[4] These scholars fear that acknowledging a variety of different epistemological positions as interpretations of globalization may lead to a postmodern position of moral relativity.[5] This study, however, does not concede that the four theories of globalization presented herein are morally and practically equivalent. To the contrary, the fact that globalization has consequences in the material reality of people's lives is evidence that these debates are morally significant. I join ethicist Elizabeth Bounds in her assessment that postmodernism has brought about "a turn against the definition of ethics as a set of abstract and universalizable principles which exist outside of any given historical framework."[6] This way of thinking demands that globalization be examined within the broader historical framework of the early twenty-first century. Bounds also believes that there has been "a corresponding turn toward notions of morality as social, embedded, particular."[7] The task before us is how to compare and evaluate globalization positions that originate from different standpoints and to understand these positions as social, embedded, and particular.[8]

This difficult task requires that we establish reasonable standards that will allow us to adjudicate between competing claims in the globalization debates. As Sandra Harding points out with regard to similar concerns that feminist theory relativizes our capacity to make judgments about "better" and "worse" theories, "Women do not have the problem of how to accommodate intellectually both the sexist claim that women are inferior in some way or another and the feminist claim that they are not"[9]—the point being that not all ways of knowing represented by different epistemological perspectives are necessarily equally valid.

Examining the value claims and moral world of each of the four theories of globalization presented here requires that we develop the kind of tested normativity discussed earlier. That will be accomplished in this study by interrogating each position with a common question or set of questions. These common questions can serve as adjudicatory standards among theories of globalization that differ greatly. From a Christian ethical perspective, the reason to examine the ethics of each of these globalization positions is so that we can compare what they value—what vision of life they offer to humankind and to the earth. In order to assess the answers to these questions, this study will evaluate the positions with a set of standards aimed toward determining how each position envisions "the good life." Since this is one of the quintessential questions of Christian ethics, it is appropriate to ask how each of these theories of globalization answers the question of what constitutes the good life. Posing this question necessarily makes certain assumptions that are anthropocentric. After all, we are making this inquiry from the perspective of what constitutes the good life for human beings. As we will see in the unfolding of these different perspectives, not all of their corresponding answers are equally anthropocentric.

But what exactly do we mean by "the good life," and how are we to determine what this looks like within each position? In order to provide more specificity to this broad theo-ethical inquiry, this study will be informed by the following questions: What is this position's understanding of moral agency? What is humanity's purpose—our end, or telos? What constitutes human flourishing? These three questions represent an approach to the topic that will allow the examination of a number of philosophical and theological questions.

What Is Our Context for Moral Decision-Making?

Within the context of Christianity, the idea of human moral agency is often traced back to the creation narratives found in the book of Genesis. The story of Eve, Adam, and the serpent provides us with a mythical account of how human beings became moral agents. This story, which is set in the prehistory of the Israelite people, is meant to help explain an aspect of human nature—to help the people understand who they are and how they came to be that way. It is an early theological attempt to infuse material perceptions of the way things are with sacred meaning. Confronted with the confusing reality that moral decisions are often ambiguous and complex, the intention of this myth is to explain how moral agency came to be a part of human nature. In examining the story, we can see that it is not primarily about human sexuality or even human shame; rather, it tells the story of how human beings came to know the difference between good and evil, right and wrong.

Feminist interpretations of this story have reclaimed Eve as not only the mother of all living, but as the mother of wisdom, a seeker of knowledge.

Rather than live in a paradisiacal setting without knowing the difference between good and evil, Eve sought "wisdom"; she chose to "know." Her actions symbolize human acknowledgment of the complexity of our situation as moral agents; for, quite simply, to be a moral agent is to make difficult judgments and decisions about what is right and wrong and to modify our behavior accordingly.

By examining how individuals make decisions in each of these paradigms of globalization, we gain critical insight into how each position envisions the good life. How we identify what is right and wrong, good and evil, has grave consequences for what the good life will look like. Moral agency is at the heart of ethical practice. Inherent in human nature is the capacity to make rational decisions about our behavior and actions in accordance with particular norms about what is right and wrong. In examining moral agency in this study, we will pay particular attention to how those moral norms are constructed and how they influence the exercise of moral agency by individuals. We will examine the context in which decisions are made and pay particular attention to who is involved in the decision-making process. Who has voice, influence, power and why? And, on a deeper level, we will ask the question, What does this tell us about the core values that undergird and support each of these globalization theories? By looking at how each particular position understands the exercise and role of moral agency, we gain deeper insight into the core values of that position and how it envisions the good life.

Democratized Understanding of Power as the Context for Moral Agency

The standpoint of this study is to argue that a democratized understanding of power ought to serve as the context for exercising moral agency. This is critically important because questions of power—where it is located, who has it, how it is used and abused—are some of the most crucial aspects of globalization from a moral perspective. With the rise of corporate power (e.g., marketing, media campaigns, the World Trade Organization) and financial power (e.g., the stock market, multilateral banking institutions, speculators), the democratic gains that accompanied modernity are slipping away as nation-states are ceding their own power to corporations in sometimes frantic efforts to secure industrial plant facilities, attract investment, and otherwise promote economic growth.

The traditional understanding of power in Western culture is a quantitative one.[10] In this analysis, power is understood as a limited resource to which only a small number of people are allowed access. This model is played out in the corporate world in the hierarchical decision-making models that vest the most power in CEOs, CFOs, boards of trustees, and upper management personnel. Under these kinds of circumstances, this zero-sum understanding of power becomes self-fulfilling. When power is structured in such a way that few people have access to it, then it does become a limited resource and one person's gain results in someone else's corresponding loss.

When power is defined by a hierarchical process that is rooted in controlled decision-making, that element of power that exists and functions as a human resource is denied. The implications of this model become evident when decisions are made, when money is allocated, when access is granted to information, knowledge, systems, people. When decision-making processes are structured in such a way that decisions are made by a limited number of people, then we turn power into a limited resource by controlling who has access to power via the human activity of isolated decision-making. When power is quantified, when it is a factor in accessing resources, or when access to power is severely limited, power becomes the ability or capacity to control; under these circumstances, power becomes abusive.

Though there are elements of this understanding of power that operate to inform the dominant notions of power in our culture, the theoretical understanding of power in this study is different. Power as a human resource is the ability or capacity to function effectively as well as the capacity to function as an agent of change. Christian social ethicist Larry Rasmussen has observed that theories of power and theories of community are intimately connected. As he puts it, "To analyze power is to see how communities have been shaped and legitimized."[11] While it is true that power can become finite when it is structured that way in particular historical situations, it is also true that human institutions and parties can generate positive and new forms of power. This study insists on a radically different model of understanding power, one that involves a deliberate increase in participation in decision-making and includes access to and the sharing of resources.

The notion of sharing power with others has led to the concept of empowerment, a process in which people are supported in ways that allow them to develop a personal sense of their own capacity to function effectively, whether in their jobs, in their homes, as parents, or in other areas of their lives. The notion of sharing power is based on a fundamentally different conception of power. In a relational model, power is understood as an unlimited resource that actually expands as it is given away.[12] Of course, most organizations—businesses, committees, churches, agencies—function with some kind of mixed model of power incorporating elements of both hierarchical and relational power. From a moral perspective, the important thing is to be aware of the attitudes toward power and the way power is distributed in an organization. This kind of power analysis can help to make transparent what a particular group or organization values.

Given this understanding of power, the call to democratize our exercise of power is based on a relational model of power centered on the concept of power-sharing. A democratized understanding of power requires that the voices of the marginalized—women, indigenous peoples, the poor, people of color, minorities, gays and lesbians, disabled peoples—are not just listened to, but that representative voices of all peoples are included in meaningful ways in the decision-making bodies of all the engines of globalization. Integrating this kind of moral norm into extant globalization practices would mean a radical reorientation for the organizational and decision-making structures of such institutions as the World Trade Organization, the International Monetary Fund (IMF), and the World Bank as well as the creation of new mechanisms to monitor and regulate the overweening power and authority of corporations.

What Is the Telos of Human Life?

Determining the purpose for our lives is at once a spiritual, theological, and philosophical inquiry. For some the inquiry is played out in terms of one's individual spiritual journey and personal sense of relationship with the divine. For others the question is primarily about trying to discern God's plans and intentions for our lives, our communities, and our world. Finally, for others it is strictly a philosophical pursuit related to maximizing one's own deeper sense of placement and meaning in the world. In various ways and in different degrees of depth and self-reflection, all people must confront the question of how we are to live our lives. Interpreting the meaning of our lives is wholly related to decisions that we make about our vocation, our family, our community, and our interactions in the world around us. One of the primary themes of the Hebrew Bible is the attempt to discern the answer to this question.

In the Exodus stories we see Moses and the Hebrew people struggling with their lives of servitude and marginalization as they seek insight into new possibilities for what their lives could be like. As the monarchy is being established we see tensions between what the people claim as their vision for their lives and their future and God's vision for the community. In the voices of the prophets, we hear the voice of God calling the people back to their responsibilities for justice and caring for the community. Finally, in the exilic period God's relationship to the Hebrews shifts once again, as God responds to their experience of alienation and marginalization and calls them back into relationship as a community. In different social locations and in changing social contexts, the Hebrew people struggle with making meaning of their lives and discerning what God is calling them to do and be.

One of the insights that we gain from the story of the Hebrew people is that there is no single, "right" way or path of life. In different times and in different places, God calls out to the people with different messages of hope, challenge, and faithfulness. While their moral calling to justice, integrity, and community may remain the same, the path toward achieving these goals shifts depending on their circumstances. In this sense, the task of faith can be understood to be the task of discerning what God is calling us to do—here and now. While God's teleological vision for the human community remains consistently one of justice for the entire creation, the specific message or task at hand may shift as new expressions of injustice unfold in the life of the community.

There is quite a wide range of self-reflection related to this question on the part of each of the positions examined in this study. Some positions are guided by the desire to understand God's call and to respond faithfully to it. Other positions understand the challenge of "living well" on more individualistic terms. Answering the question of what makes one happy and what gives meaning to life offers deep insight into what each position's vision for the world might be.

Caring for the Planet as Humanity's Telos

The normative principle proposed here is that at this place and at this time, humanity's purpose or teleological calling is to care for the planet. Threats to planetary survival have been thoroughly researched and documented repeatedly over the last few decades. Beginning with Rachel Carsen's *Silent Spring* in 1962, human beings have been faced with the knowledge that we are perpetrating violent damage to our ecosystem and yet "first" worlders often feel incapable of turning things around. Our lives have become so dependent on fossil fuels, fast food, and electricity that we often feel powerless to affect real change, change that will slow global warming, reduce emissions, conserve energy. The task seems too enormous, so beyond any individual's capacity to affect change, that people are often immobilized by their insignificance in the face of the looming catastrophe.

It is true that the threat of ecological destruction is an enormous problem that will not be transformed solely by the voluntary lifestyle changes of individual people. What is required is a radical reorientation of our priorities. In a country where most people are comfortable in their consumptive lifestyle choices, this will not be a popular proposal. But the situation is grave enough that we must be realistic about what is required. At the same time, collective action depends on the behavior of individual members of society, and thus individual responsibility and action should not be dismissed as insignificant.

Adopting the value and practice of caring for the planet as a normative moral condition for globalization requires a radical reorientation of our moral universe. The selfish anthropocentric focus on human beings as the primary concern in social, environmental, and economic decision-making is simply untenable. Those of us who are enculturated in Western perspectives must expand our narrow frameworks to recognize that our moral universe extends beyond the boundaries of the human population. In a world where climate change is threatening to alter radically not only the earth's temperature, but also its physical constitution, where animal and plant species are disappearing at unprecedented rates, and where desertification is destroying formerly abundant land, we are clearly morally responsible for the human actions that are generating the destruction of our planet.

Many of these actions are rooted in a Western consciousness that promotes a subject-object relationship between humanity and the rest of creation that has served to justify human exploitation and the abuse of the planet and its resources. It is critical for Western human society to work toward a transformation of our worldview that will allow us to see other species, as well as the natural resources of our ecosystem, not as objects, but as subjects that possess an intrinsic value that qualifies any instrumental value they might hold for human purposes. Before we can even begin to start thinking about the reparations that are essential for the earth's continued survival, we must transform the very way we think about ourselves in relation to the larger earth community.

We must move toward acknowledging that our moral universe includes all living creatures and the earth as well as humanity.[13] God created the entire earth community as good, and it therefore has intrinsic value, not merely instrumental value. Scripture repeatedly tells the story of God's love for creation. This story is so theologically fundamental to the Jewish and Christian faiths that the opening words of the Hebrew Scripture begin with the story of God's creation. This story unfolds day by day and night by night. God's care and concern for each aspect of creation are apparent as God carefully completes each task in turn, separating light from darkness, separating waters from waters, and bringing order into the preexisting chaos. By the third day, the refrain "And God saw that it was good" enters the text like a mantra repeated by God as a blessing and as a prayer both recognizing and establishing the goodness of the new creation all in the same breath. The breath of God utters this incantation that binds God forever to this new creation: "And God saw that it was good." The role of intrinsic versus instrumental value is monumental in the context of the globalization debates, as this study will make clear.

Human beings were created as relational beings, and our position as part of a larger earth community is an essential element of our humanity. This insight serves as a corrective to a more traditional Augustinian theological anthropology that views humanity within a hierarchical order of creation. In this more traditional view, angels are placed just below God and are followed by men, women, animals, and then the rest of creation. In such a hierarchical theological anthropology, our very humanity is defined in opposition to the rest of creation; it is that which not only separates us from the rest of creation, but also elevates us above everything on earth. In contrast, the theological anthropology supported here holds that our very humanity is defined by how well we are able to understand and respect our place within God's larger creation; namely, the entire earth community. Of course, challenging a hierarchical ordering of nature does not deny the fact that there are inherent differences, significant differences, within the earth community. Humanity's capacity as moral creatures means that we bear a particular responsibility and moral accountability for our actions. Once we embrace a theological anthropology that understands that our very humanity is defined by our relationship with the larger world, it becomes clear that human beings have moral obligations that extend to the entire earth community.

Based on these theological foundations, caring for the planet becomes humanity's teleological calling; thus the sacredness of life is recognized as a fundamental moral concern undergirding the normative criteria of this study. In the context of the globalization debates, this means that all moral claims regarding globalization must be attentive to the entire earth community. In other words, there are no other criteria—profit, growth, stockholders—that can provide any mitigating circumstances in which the well-being of the earth community is not approached as the primary moral consideration in any decision-making process.

What Constitutes Human Flourishing?

Finally, in examining the question of what constitutes the good life from the human perspective, we must examine differing notions of what constitutes human flourishing. This question is particularly important from the point of view of Christian social ethics, which has historically concerned itself with seeking a vision of human flourishing in which all God's children are cared for.[14] There is a certain irony inherent in the fact that the possibility of concerning ourselves with human flourishing rather than mere human survival is a luxury afforded us by many of the very aspects of globalization investigated in this study. The fact that farmers the world over produce enough food to provide for the material needs of all the world's people combined with the fact that we possess the technological capabilities of transporting these resources where they are most needed raises deep and disturbing ethical questions about our collective priorities as a human community.

Critical inquiry into disparate visions of what constitutes human flourishing presupposes an intrinsic value to human life that is deeply rooted in the Christian tradition. While there are tensions in the biblical representation of this value, God exhibits a concern and care for humankind that are consonant with God's care for the whole of creation noted above.[15] As we examine the question of what constitutes human flourishing in each of the positions, we will pay particular attention to who will actually flourish in each of these visions of the good life and how each of these theories addresses the material, social, and spiritual needs of the world's poor and marginalized peoples. From the perspective of Christian ethics, a vision of the good life that does not adequately account for the well-being of all God's creation is not morally tenable.

The Social Well-Being of People as What Constitutes Human Flourishing

Ultimately, we are called by God to strive for social justice for the entire earth community. One of the most prominent and challenging themes of the biblical witness and the Christian tradition is to seek to live in this world as if we were already in the kingdom.[16] One of the dangers of Christianity is spiritualizing the hardships of this world; poverty, disease, and death can be perversely denied, dismissed, or ignored by Christians who are focused on enduring this world as if it were a mere steppingstone to the next. Our spirituality should not call us out of this world; rather, it should fill us with strength and fortitude to fight for change and justice within this world. Differently said, God calls humanity to reconciliation and justice in *this* world.

The social well-being of people, then, must be a central moral norm for what constitutes human flourishing. While the social well-being of people begins with taking care of basic needs, it does not stop with the argument that all people have a right to adequate food, clothing, and shelter. In addition to our basic physical needs, all human beings are deserving of respect and dignity; these are markers of our very humanity. Often when we reduce our understanding of people's well-being to their physical needs alone, we are able to busy ourselves with providing for others without seriously questioning what people need to acquire these basics for themselves. The argument here is that it is not enough merely to provide for people's basic needs, for example, through creating food and clothing banks, air-dropping food supplies, or providing cots at a local homeless shelter. One element essential for building up personhood is the satisfaction that comes with being able to meet one's own needs.[17] While it is important to ensure continually that our societies are equipped with back-up plans to help those who fall through the cracks or who experience life traumas or catastrophes, the provision of people's basic needs cannot be sustained in the long haul through Band-Aid efforts. Attention to the social well-being of people requires that society address the structural barriers that prevent all of God's people from having access to such essentials as affordable safe shelter, nutritious and reasonably priced food, and decent clothing.

While caring for one's self and one's family happens in a variety of ways, one aspect of the social well-being of people that cannot be forgotten is access to education and vocational training. In a world that is in the midst of a technological revolution, we are, in many ways, in a situation similar to that of the industrial revolution. In the late eighteenth and early nineteenth centuries, largely rural and farm-oriented societies in Europe and North America were thrust into a situation in which jobs were located in cities and the work was different from anything people had ever done before. The opening of the twenty-first century shows a world in much the same state of occupational disarray. Technology is changing familiar forms of work and creating whole new sectors of employment. Farming is now inundated with biotechnology and massive equipment that have all but eliminated the family farm. Education, at all levels, is in a process of transformation as a result of both the changed attention spans and learning processes of "tech kids" as well as the technological resources available for classroom and pedagogical use. E-commerce is beginning to make inroads into the commercial markets and is shaking up the world of the retail market. Mechanization, robots, and computers are making manufacturing jobs virtually obsolete. Literally no job sector has been left untouched by the technological revolution.

Concern for the social well-being of people requires that we think deeply and broadly about these changes that are transforming the very nature of work in our society. The social well-being of people requires that they experience meaning and value in their work. In a country where the fastest-growing job sector is the service industry and people in general are stricken with malaise and meaninglessness in their lives, issues of meaning and value in the workplace must rise to the fore in any ethical conversations pertaining to globalization. Additionally, access to education, vocational training, and retraining must be made a priority in all areas of the world.

Issues of malaise and meaninglessness lead us to the next critical area of the social well-being of people. As stated earlier, human beings were created as relational beings; we long for community, relationships, and meaningful interaction with others. While the Western philosophical tradition since Kant has focused primarily on individual well-being, it is the communal aspect of human existence that is currently under fire.[18] Rasmussen argues that community is itself the matrix in which the moral life is created, developed, and lived.[19] The moral health of our world depends on the continued existence of communities of moral formation and accountability. Our communities can provide us with a place of integrity and respect where we are able to struggle with life dilemmas, build relationships, and foster understanding. This does not mean that communities are necessarily homogenous, nor are they places of refuge from conflict. Rather, communities are places where we are able to disagree, to challenge, to question, and to wrestle with moral issues within an environment of integrity and respect. The moral health of individuals depends on our ability to continue to sort out our responses to the world within the context of a community of dialogue and accountability.

A number of factors currently threaten the health and well-being of our communities. In the "first" world, the technological revolution also has been synonymous with the creation of a virtual media world that has replaced community and community activity for many people. Record numbers of people gathered to watch the CBS television show *Survivor*, which pitted two artificial "tribes" of people against one another for cash prizes.[20] This show epitomized the trend in recent years toward escapism in television, movies, the Internet, video games, and other media outlets that function to separate people rather than building community and relationships. The rise in popularity of "reality TV" shows illustrates a new level of community disintegration in which people passively choose to spend time watching strangers build relationships, climb mountains, and camp out rather than actively seek out community or actively create or participate in their own entertainment. In the media-dominated culture of the twenty-first century, any examination of the social well-being of people must focus seriously on issues of community life and personal relationships.

Finally, the social well-being of people is often reflected most profoundly in the cultural expressions of art, music, dance, and theater. There are many communities in the "two-thirds" world who fear the loss of their traditional cultural practices to the marketed "Americanization" of their cultures through the engines of globalization. Whole generations of global youth sway to the beat of a new genre of music called "global pop" while their elders look on, dismayed at their youth's lack of interest in traditional forms of song and music.[21]

Conclusion

These three questions—What is our context for moral decision-making? What is the telos of human life? What constitutes human flourishing?—will be used to interrogate the moral vision of each of the four theories of globalization examined in this study. These questions are an important aspect of critical inquiry, as any theoretical perspective must be held responsible for answering the question, What does this theory teach us about living in the world? If people are dying because of a theory, then we must bring a moral judgment against that theory. If we choose a theory without paying attention to its moral consequences, then we get the unexamined morality of that theory. In other words, our actions in the world do matter. We get the world that we enact. If we do not pay attention to the morality of the theories governing our world, then we get a world that does not pay much attention to morality either. The ethical arguments examined in these pages are primarily about discerning how we can live well, a struggle that is fundamentally theological as well as ethical. As co-creators with God, we must recognize that how we live our values shapes the world around us for good or ill. Values are not abstract ideals that we hold up as banners of righteousness; they are not separable from our actions. In fact, it is the other way around: Our actions and interactions in the world are often clearer expressions of what we value than our words are. For this reason it is never good enough to examine a theory or a group's purported values; we must examine their practices as well.

Notes

1. For a more detailed explanation of materialist feminism, see Rosemary Hennessy and Chrys Ingraham, *Materialist Feminism: A Reader in Class, Difference, and Women's Lives* (New York: Routledge, 1997).

2. See the discussion of postmodernism in note 3 in chapter 1; as well as Sandra Harding, *Whose Science? Whose Knowledge? Thinking from Women's Lives* (Ithaca, NY: Cornell University Press, 1991), esp. chap. 6; and Donna J. Haraway, *Simians, Cyborgs, and Women: The Reinvention of Nature* (New York: Routledge, 1991), esp. chap. 9.

3. Beverly Wildung Harrison, *Making the Connections: Essays in Feminist Social Ethics*, ed. Carol S. Robb (Boston: Beacon Press, 1985), 248.

4. Sandra Harding describes the dilemma posed by postmodernism: "From the perspective of [the] conventional notion of objectivity—sometimes referred to as 'objectivism'—it has appeared that if one gives up this concept, the only alternative is not just a cultural relativism (the sociological assertion that what is thought to be a reasonable claim in one society or sub-culture is not thought to be so in another) but, worse, a judgmental or epistemological relativism that denies the possibility of any reasonable standards for adjudicating between competing claims." Harding, *Whose Science? Whose Knowledge?* 138–39.

5. For a more nuanced treatment of this intellectual concern see Harding, *Whose Science? Whose Knowledge?* esp. chap. 6; and Haraway, *Simians, Cyborgs, and Women*, esp. chap. 9.

6. Elizabeth M. Bounds, *Coming Together/Coming Apart: Religion, Community, and Modernity* (New York: Routledge, 1997), 15.

7. Ibid.

8. This is the type of standpoint that Donna Haraway describes as a "partial perspective." In challenging the traditional academic notion that there is an objective vantage point that yields absolute truth, Haraway argues that "objectivity turns out to be about particular and specific embodiment, and definitely not about the false vision promising transcendence of all limits and responsibilities. The moral is simple: only partial perspective promises objective vision." For a detailed development of this position, see Haraway, *Simians, Cyborgs, and Women*, chap. 9.

9. Harding, *Whose Science? Whose Knowledge?* 154.

10. For more detailed and nuanced analyses of power, see Christine Firer Hinze, "Power in Christian Ethics: Resources and Frontiers for Scholarly Exploration," *The Annual of the Society of Christian Ethics* 12 (1992): 277–90; and Larry Rasmussen, "Power Analysis: A Neglected Agenda," *The Annual of the Society of Christian Ethics* 11 (1991): 3–17.

11. Rasmussen, "Power Analysis," 7.

12. For example, if I start an organization and I structure the decision-making process in such a way that I must approve all decisions that are made, I have created a hierarchical model of governance. If I structure the organization so that decisions are made collectively or different people are empowered to make different kinds of

decisions, then the organization can be said to be using a power-sharing model of governance. Power exists in both models, but who has access to it and how it is utilized play out very differently.

13. For a more thorough theological development of this argument, see Larry Rasmussen, *Earth Community, Earth Ethics* (Maryknoll, NY: Orbis Books, 1996). In this book, Rasmussen moves Christian ethical discourse from its traditional focus on humanity to a broader understanding of *earth community*. He counters the anthropocentric orientation that has dominated Christianity with the challenge that humanity must begin to understand that we are part of a larger community, an earth community that encompasses all of God's creation.

14. See John Atherton, *Christian Social Ethics: A Reader* (Cleveland, OH: Pilgrim Press, 1994).

15. While there are many stories that witness to God's concern for the human community (e.g., the exodus, the parable of the lost sheep, Jesus' passion for the poor and marginalized), there are also deeply disturbing "texts of terror" that eviscerate the intrinsic value of female human life in ways that belie misogynist tendencies in the text and the tradition (e.g., Hagar, Tamar, the unnamed woman of Judges, the daughter of Jephthah). See Phyllis Trible, *Texts of Terror: Literary-Feminist Readings of Biblical Narratives* (Philadelphia: Fortress Press, 1984).

16. I embrace Ada Maria Isasi-Diaz's transformation of the concept of "kingdom" and its patriarchal, hierarchal connotations to the concept of "kindom," which represents the "kinship" of all creation and the promise of a just future. See Ada Maria Isasi-Diaz, *Mujerista Theology: A Theology for the Twenty-first Century* (Maryknoll, NY: Orbis Books, 1996), 103n8.

17. This does not necessarily mean that each *individual* must be responsible for meeting *all* of his or her own needs; there are some needs that are best met collectively and some situations in which communal care for others is appropriate and provided without guilt or shame. The point is that structural barriers to self-sufficiency and the importance of self-respect are often overlooked in charitable models of aid.

18. For recent treatment of the importance of "community" in the moral life, see Larry Rasmussen, *Moral Fragments and Moral Community: A Proposal for Church in Society* (Minneapolis: Fortress Press, 1993); and Bounds, *Coming Together/Coming Apart.*

19. Rasmussen, *Moral Fragments*, 12.

20. The idea behind the show is that strangers must form alliances and relationships in order to "survive" on a desert island. Each week one person from each "tribe" was voted off the show. The last survivor on the island won one million dollars.

21. While the advent of rock and roll in the United States shares some parallels with the generational rift over music preferences mentioned here, the most alarming difference is the power and dominance of U.S. influence over the creation of cultural trends and icons around the world.

PART 2

THE DOMINANT THEORIES OF GLOBALIZATION

Neoliberalism and Development

For most people the term "globalization" is synonymous with some form of economic globalization. The two dominant models of globalization that are examined in this study are indeed visions of the future that are rooted in a shared economic theory. While each position nuances it in different ways, neoclassical economic theory is the engine that is currently driving the global economy. While neoclassical economics has developed over a period of several hundred years, this field of thought has itself split into two different theoretical branches designated in this study as "laissez-faire" and "social equity." Though both branches of neoclassical economics lay their roots in such quintessential economic thinkers as Adam Smith and David Ricardo, their modern permutations allow for a considerable amount of discrepancy over how globalization will develop in the future. The following elaboration of basic elements of neoclassical economics serves as the theoretical starting point for the examination of the neoliberal and development models of globalization in the next two chapters.

Growth

The fundamental preoccupation of growth in neoclassical economics can be traced to Adam Smith (1723–1790). Smith was, if not the first, at least the most well-known early theorist of capitalism. Writing in the late eighteenth century, Smith chronicled the economic activity that was transforming Europe—the rise of machines (e.g., looms, spinning wheels), the increase of the division of labor, and the growing emphasis on trade. His work *An Inquiry into the Nature and Causes of the Wealth of Nations* became the prototype for the development of subsequent economic theory. *The Wealth of Nations* was an articulation of an economic theory that was conceived as part of a larger social world. Smith knew that economics is an element of human society, not a type of human society, and he did not view it as an abstract science. As Rasmussen points out, "[Smith] did not . . . envision a capitalist society. He envisioned a capitalist economy within a society held together by noncapitalist moral sentiments."[1] Smith's economic theory was consciously located within a moral framework.

Carol Johnston credits Smith's focus on economic growth as the primary economic goal as a way to escape the land constraints that dominated England in the late eighteenth century.[2] She sums up Smith's goal in *Wealth of Nations*: "to show that it is indeed this process of economic production and consumption, not the hoarding of metals, that ensures and increases wealth."[3] Smith's second theoretical move related to growth was to assign the source of value to labor rather than to land.[4] By focusing on labor, Smith's theory promoted a second vital neoclassical economic assumption that growth primarily occurs through increased productivity. His famous example of the pin factory illustrates how production can be exponentially increased through the efficient division of labor.[5]

Economics as a "Science"

When David Ricardo (1772–1823), who was part of the "classical" school of economics, established the deductive method as the best means for achieving clarity and effectiveness in economics, he began the move toward establishing economics as a "science." The real turning point, however, came when a group of economists known as the marginalists gave economics its disciplinary method—mathematics. Johnston explains, "[The marginalists] set out to make economics as much like a science as possible—particularly like Newtonian mechanics—and this meant concentrating on mathematics. Their tool, marginal analysis,[6] remains the most powerful tool of economics and has had considerable influence in Western culture in general."[7]

One of the marginalists, Leon Walras (1834–1910), asserted that the "primary concern of the economist is not to provide a plentiful revenue for the people or to supply the State with an adequate income [Adam Smith], but to pursue and master purely scientific truths."[8] The rise of the marginalists split economic theory in two directions, one focused on the "demand side" of the economics (marginalists) and the other focused on the "supply side" (classical school).[9] Alfred Marshall (1842–1924), a masterful mathematician, provided the economic tools for calculating marginal analysis that succeeded in pulling the two theoretical camps back together into a "neoclassical synthesis."[10] This neoclassical approach, which has dominated mainstream economics for the last one hundred years, defines itself as a "scientific" methodology.

The "Economic Man"

The notion of *Homo economicus*, or "economic man," is attributed to John Stuart Mill (1806–1873). Building on the deductive reasoning of the marginalists, Mill defined consumers as self-interested wealth maximizers, a definition that inherently supports the previous economic assumptions of individualism and growth.[11] In describing political economy, Mill argues that it is concerned with

> man . . . solely as a being who desires to possess wealth, and who is capable of judging of the comparative efficacy of means for obtaining that end. It predicts only such of the phenomena of the social state as take place in consequence of the pursuit of wealth. It makes entire abstraction of every other human passion or motive; except those which may be regarded as perpetually antagonizing principles to the desire of wealth, namely aversion to labour, and desire of the present enjoyment of costly indulgences.[12]

It is important to note several of the value judgments that are implicit in this definition. First, the study of political economy is defined as the study of the activity of people who desire to gain wealth. Johnston points out that this definition automatically excludes other potential motives such as "achieving a healthy level of community subsistence, engaging in types of work that are more satisfying because more interesting or personal, [or] working with others to build something needed, such as housing."[13] A second value judgment in Mill's definition is one that has become a significant problem in contemporary society; namely, that people have a natural aversion to labor. Underlying this value judgment are the assumptions that people would prefer not to work if this were a financial possibility and that the primary function of work is to maximize wealth. The first assumption has contributed largely to the marginalization and condemnation of financially secure women who have chosen to work while raising children.[14] The second assumption has led to a decreasing concern for the inherent meaning and value of work in a globalizing economy. As Swedish ethicist Göran Collste notes, "[The neoclassical view of work] has little support among those psychologists and sociologists who have studied the value of work. It seems to be a fairly unanimous view that work is extremely important for the well-being and self-image of the human being."[15] Finally, Mill's definition of *Homo economicus* is also the basis for the notion of the "rational man" or the "rational actor" in economic theory. The value judgment underlying this assumption is that profit maximization is the only "rational" behavior in the marketplace, an assumption that has yet to be substantiated.

The Role of Government

When discussing the role that governments should play in relating to the markets, economists often use the term "free market," by which they mean an economic arena that is not restricted by governmental intervention. The assumption underlying the free market is that competition is a sufficient control for supply and demand and that it ensures the efficient allocation of resources. From this perspective government involvement in market affairs is viewed as constraining to trade and is commonly referred to as "fettering" the market.

From a critical perspective, we should recognize that a functioning "free market" is in fact a fiction. In reality the government is active in multiple ways ensuring that markets are able to function at all. It is important to remember that regardless of their professed support for a "free market," conservatives and liberals in the United States both expect and rely on some level of government involvement in the economic realm. From a standardized system of weights and measures, to safety guidelines for workplaces, to the law enforcement and legal systems that enforce these "interventions," the marketplace simply is not an abstract entity that exists outside the political sphere of involvement. The political and economic spheres differentiate between distinct aspects of society, but clearly economic matters affect political activity and vice versa. So while both the conservative and liberal standpoints recognize the necessity of some role for government in the marketplace, they differ on their position of the degree of that involvement. Conservatives favor as little governmental intervention as possible while liberals usually advocate a stronger role for government.

Economics as Value-free

The final assumption of neoclassical economics that bears noting is related to the prior assumption that the economy can be separated from politics and exist as an independent field of scientific inquiry. Implicit in the positioning of economics as a science is the perspective that science is value-free, so economics must be as well. As John Neville Keynes put it: "Political economy is . . . a science, not an art or a department of ethical inquiry. It is described as standing neutral between social schemes. It furnishes information as to the probable consequences of given lines of action, but does not itself pass moral judgments."[16]

It is this assumption that has freed the consciences of economists, businesspeople, and politicians around the globe who have repeatedly denied the ethical responsibilities of economics, business, and corporations. It is perhaps this assumption that has played the strongest role in the development of the branch of neoclassical economics known as neoliberalism, which will be examined in the next chapter.

Notes

1. Rasmussen, *Moral Fragments and Moral Community* (Minneapolis: Fortress, 1993), 41–42.
2. Carol Johnston, *The Wealth or Health of Nations: Transforming Capitalism from Within* (Cleveland, OH: Pilgrim Press, 1998), 11.
3. Ibid., 12.
4. Ibid., 6.
5. Adam Smith, *An Inquiry into the Nature and Causes of the Wealth of Nations* vol. 1, ed. R. H. Campbell and A. S. Skinner (1775; Indianapolis: Liberty Fund, 1981), 14–15.
6. Marginal analysis is based on the law of satiety, which states that when a buyer reaches a certain point, rather than buy another unit of the same thing, something else is preferred over that next unit. This last unit, the point at which the buyer ceases buying the one thing and chooses something else, is the "margin." Johnston, *Wealth or Health of Nations*, 78.
7. Ibid., 77.
8. Ibid., 86.

9. Ibid., 77.
10. Ibid.
11. Ibid., 46.
12. John Stuart Mill, "On the Definition and Method of Political Economy," as quoted in ibid., 47.
13. Ibid., 47
14. The implication from this line of reasoning is that women who *choose* to work under these circumstances either have poor maternal instincts and do not care enough about their children to stay home with them, or they are greedy and would prefer to make more money to support a grander lifestyle.
15. Gören Collste, "Value Assumptions in Economic Theory," *Studies in Ethics and Economics* (Uppsala, Sweden: Uppsala University, 1998), 16.
16. John Neville Keynes (father of John Maynard Keynes) as quoted in Johnston, *Wealth or Health of Nations*, 5.

3

Globalization as New World Order

Neoliberalism as the Reigning Economic Paradigm

"Big Business" as the Force behind Economic Globalization

The dominant form of globalization in our world today is built on an ideology known as "neoliberalism" and is supported by the engines of big business; namely, transnational and multinational corporations, corporate business leaders and bankers, and the institutions and agencies that they have created, such as the Organisation for Economic Co-operation and Development, the International Chamber of Commerce, and the World Trade Organization. Most supporters of this position fall into the socioeconomic category of "owners of capital." Whether this capital is in the form of land, stocks and bonds, or factories, proponents of this perspective can be classified as members of a propertied class. A second characteristic of neoliberalism that often goes hand in hand with wealth is an emphasis on education. This factor is particularly important in specifying the social location of big business, because it is often within the institutions of higher education that the proponents of this position first learned the economic ideology, including the theory that guides their conception of globalization. Since most proponents of big business are among the world's social elites whether from England or India, the United States or Zimbabwe, such persons have constructed their world in such a way that they are able to exist with little contact with the social reality of the majority of the world's people.

Neoliberal ideology is designated by a variety of names, including the Washington Consensus, laissez-faire, structural adjustment, and trickle-down or supply-side economics, but here I will primarily use the terms "big business" and "neoliberalism" to refer to this position. Proponents of neoliberal ideology promote privatization on the grounds that markets are more efficient at providing services than governments. They seek deregulation based on the argument that governmental regulations inhibit economic growth, expansion, and trade. Supporters also promote trade liberalization based on Ricardo's law of comparative advantage. In short this means that countries should focus on producing those products that they can produce most efficiently, and they should use those goods to trade on the market for all other necessities.

This position, theorized most prominently by Milton Friedman and the Chicago school, developed the label "neoliberalism" in the "two-thirds" world where its assumptions are deeply questioned. As the hegemonic economic model in the "first" world, it has become synonymous with capitalism for many people. Uncritical acceptance of neoliberalism masks the reality that this model is a particular form of capitalism that has gained sway in recent years. A more critical perspective acknowledges that market economies have existed throughout history in a variety of forms and that the particularities of a market society distinguished by neoliberalism bear some examination. The task of this chapter will be to analyze the ideological assumptions of neoliberalism with an eye toward discerning the core values of this position.

Contemporary Political and Economic Change as Background

Neoclassical economists identify the post-World War II period as inaugurating a new economic era that focused on supporting and encouraging the growing economic interdependence of nation-states. After a half century of war and occupation, Europe was in shambles. Many countries had fallen far behind the industrial and technological advances that had propelled American business forward. Furthermore, the infrastructures and productive capabilities of Germany, France, Britain, Italy, and several other nations had been severely compromised by the ravages of war.

It was in this postwar period that significant financial plans and decisions were set into place by world leaders to guide the process of European and Japanese recovery. As a result, neoclassical historical accounts of globalization frequently begin with the conference at Bretton Woods, New Hampshire, in 1944. Here world leaders established the World Bank and the International Monetary Fund as multilateral economic institutions with the mandate to aid in postwar reconstruction.[1] United States' control of 70 percent of the world's gold and foreign exchange reserves and 40 percent of industrial output had prompted domestic adoption of free trade, and the U.S. position of power in the Bretton Woods negotiations assured the adoption of similar policies on a global level.[2] While the prevailing wisdom of neoclassical laissez-faire policies won the day at Bretton Woods, the Marshall Plan embraced a more Keynesian approach by infusing nearly $12 billion in grants and low-interest loans into war-torn western European countries.[3]

With the Marshall Plan supplying most of Europe's financial needs in the postwar period, the Bretton Woods institutions soon found that their aid was not necessary for postwar reconstruction. The international leaders of these newly created institutions turned the attention of the IMF and the World Bank toward the perceived backwardness and relative poverty of the so-called "underdeveloped" world. Most of these formerly colonized countries had achieved their formal independence in the 1940s and '50s, but they had yet to achieve economic independence.

Colonial policies had affected the economic development of the "two-thirds" world in two ways. First, the colonial governments and their corporations had used their colonies as sources of raw materials, labor, and trade. These policies and practices served an extractive function for the colonial governments and as such they did not emphasize or enable a productive independent economy to develop in most of these countries. Second, decades of "foreign" political control and the imbalance of trade in the direction of selling raw materials and buying goods from the colonial master had prevented indigenous development of industry or trade that was capable of facilitating the move to self-determination and independent statehood. Consequently, these former colonial states now had formal political recognition of their independence by the international community but were unable to interact on a par with their former colonizers in the political and economic realm.

In the 1950s and '60s "development" became the name of the game in international finance, and billions of dollars were lent to countries in Africa, Asia, and Latin America to assist them in becoming more "like" Western economies. Partly this lending was necessary for the IMF and World Bank to stay in business, but it was also a "logical" next step to the economists and business leaders who were behind the promotion of "development." The postwar period had seen tremendous leaps forward in transportation and communication that had enabled increased trade and global economic integration; and to neoliberals, this was progress. The perspectives of capitalist economic activity that shaped the practices of business and industries developed during this period of global economic integration made them unable to ignore the trade potential (and billions of consumers) represented by the "two-thirds" world. To the neoclassically trained economic mind, the continued economic dependence of many of these countries on their formal colonizers could most readily be "solved" by helping these countries develop market economies, like the economies of the nations that colonized them, that could ensure their prosperity.

In the 1970s the oil crisis that raised oil prices from thirteen to thirty-four dollars a barrel generated an enormous amount of "petrodollars" that left unprecedented capital reserves in banks the world over.[4] Since neoclassical economic theorists believe that money sitting in banks is inefficient, they urged commercial banks to find ways of investing the rapid increase in bank deposits that the oil crisis generated. This led to lower interest rates and easier credit ratings for the former colonies. Additionally, the World Bank infused billions of dollars in loans into the global South as director Robert McNamara attempted to redefine the institution's mission as the eradication of poverty. The abandonment of the gold standard by the United States in 1971 in favor of floating exchange rates led to increased currency speculation and increased economic liquidity for corporate dollars. Prior to Nixon's abandonment of the gold standard, the value of currencies of other countries existed in a fixed rate of exchange with U.S. dollars. Because the exchange rates were now subject to change, speculators began to bet on the economic stability of various countries and their currencies.

Significant challenges to development theory began in the 1980s as the increasing indebtedness of the "two-thirds" world generated alternative discourses and theories. Bankers and government officials who subscribed to neoclassical economic models required an economic reordering of individual governmental budgets in line with an even more austere version of laissez-faire theory being promoted by the Reagan and Thatcher governments that came to be known as "neoliberalism." This reordering of governmental budgets was done through the implementation of structural adjustment programs that were linked to new and refinanced IMF loans. Also known as the Washington Consensus, this set of economic assumptions resulted in reduced social welfare spending and focused on creating an unfettered export-oriented marketplace. In the early Reagan years, there was often talk of "trickle down" economics as a way of justifying continued economic benefits for the wealthy. The new ideology coincided with increased direct foreign investment from the corporate world and a growing capitalist elite within countries now drawn into this growing global network of transnational capitalism. This ideology grew stronger in the 1990s as an unprecedented bull market continued to amaze and astound economists, investors, and the business world. To these folks the profitability of the market was sufficient proof that neoliberalism was working. In contrast, those who had only their labor to sell in the economic arena were to discover that what had actually trickled down was a longer work week for less real wages for many of the world's workers.

How a Neoliberal Ideology Shapes the Economy

The neoliberal position is the legacy of the laissez-faire tradition of neoclassical capitalism. This position languished in the postwar economy as the ascendancy of Keynesian economics allowed for broader support of social safety net measures and policies regulating worker, environmental, and health safety. The Reagan/Thatcher era of the 1980s began a shift toward supply-side economics. Supporters of the supply-side model argued that investment in the business sectors of economies (i.e., the owners of capital) would eventually "trickle down" to the rest of the population through increased job opportunities and better social services provided by a stronger economy. Simultaneously in the 1980s the IMF and the World Bank imposed strict structural adjustment policies on debtor nations in the "two-thirds" world—policies that followed similar economic reasoning to what was occurring in the "first" world. These structural adjustments were aimed toward making these economies more "efficient," which translated into cutting back on expenditures in the social service and educational sectors as a way to "trim fat" out of budgets and promoting export-oriented programs of growth. In the 1990s, as former Eastern bloc countries and debt-ridden "two-thirds" world countries began searching for ways to ease their economic straits, neoliberalism was promoted to foreign governments by policy analysts and financial institutions, in the form of the Washington Consensus, as a remedy for poor economic performance. The Washington Consensus was a set of policy directives (including trade liberalization, privatization, and deregulation) that promoted a neoliberal economic ideology.

Trade Liberalization as a Global Panacea for Economic Woes

The issue of trade liberalization is at the heart of the neoliberal policy agenda. In fact, it is this issue that defines the "neo" in neoliberal. As we have seen in our review of neoclassical economics, trade has consistently been an important part of the capitalist paradigm; but it was not until the debt crisis of the 1980s that trade began to be touted as the panacea for troubled economies. The end of the Cold War and the breaking down of traditional trading blocs in the early 1990s further opened the door to the structuring of a new economic paradigm, one that was more global in focus than ever before. Given that transnational corporations are the engines of growth and trade in the new global economy, a brief overview of the development of the corporation over the last several decades is illustrative of the neoliberal emphasis on increased trade.

A number of distinct developments in the 1970s led to major shifts in the economic role that corporations play in the political economy. After twenty years of "recovery" from WWII and the longest period of sustained growth in capitalist history, several things became apparent. First, the increased competition of European and Asian business and industry was challenging American economic hegemony and rates of profit. This happened as the European countries became stronger after their initial recovery and reconstruction phase and as the newly industrializing countries of southeast Asia were able to introduce lower-priced goods into markets in which U.S. companies had traditionally had a stronghold.

Second, capitalist markets in the "first" world were becoming saturated as the majority of the population who could afford luxury consumer items had already purchased them. This saturation necessitated new strategies for lifting sagging profits, particularly in the United States. When two-driver families already owned two cars, new advertising strategies had to be developed to convince them they needed a third, and likewise for other consumer products. People who had achieved a certain level of success and self-satisfaction were transformed from "citizens" into "consumers" through the relentless efforts of the advertising industry.

Let us recall that this was also the era of the oil crisis and the abandonment of the gold standard. Both of these events created increased capital that was available for investment. The speculation caused by abandoning the gold standard led to the transfer of large amounts of capital to offshore accounts and the beginning of an era of high finance that has resulted in the creation of profits from nonproductive economic activity and an overinflated stock market.[5] However, while the funds available for corporate investment increased, the stagflation of the period decreased the purchasing power of the typical consumer.[6]

Finally, the appearance of Robert McNamara as president of the World Bank and his dedication to the eradication of poverty infused billions of dollars in loans into the "two-thirds" world. McNamara's bank threw billions of dollars at hundreds of projects without understanding the difference between quality and quantity.[7] In the end many of the projects displaced whole communities of people, destroyed environmental resources, or were so mismanaged they had to be abandoned.

The results of these developments led to a dramatic increase in the direct foreign investment of a number of corporations into various parts of the "developing" world. The accumulated value of U.S. direct foreign investment more than doubled between 1970 and 1978, and that of non-U.S. foreign direct investment more than tripled.[8] This move enabled transnational corporations to take advantage of drastically reduced wages and the abundance of petrodollars that were flowing through the global South. These countries provided the additional benefit of untapped market potential to replace the decreased consumer spending practices in the global North.[9] This era marked the beginning of the "multinationalization" of many large corporations. David Korten makes a helpful distinction between "multinational" and "transnational" corporations:

> A multinational corporation takes on many national identities, maintaining relatively autonomous production and sales facilities in individual countries,

> establishing local roots and presenting itself in each locality as a good local citizen. Its globalized operations are linked to one another but are deeply integrated into the individual local economies in which they operate, and they do function to some extent as local citizens.
>
> The trend, however, is toward transnationalism, which involves the integration of a firm's global operations around vertically integrated supplier networks. . . . Although a transnational corporation may choose to claim local citizenship when that posture suits its purpose, local commitments are temporary, and it actively attempts to eliminate considerations of nationality in its efforts to maximize the economies that centralized global procurement makes possible.[10]

While some of the massive influx of money into "developing" countries in the 1970s came in the form of direct foreign investment, much of it was in the form of loans, both from the World Bank and from commercial banks hoping to cash in on the industrial growth in the "two-thirds" world.[11] By the early 1980s, as the winds of progress blew in a different direction, the currencies of many "developing" countries began to devalue, making it difficult to service the interest payments on those same loans. The World Bank and the IMF came to the rescue by providing a new class of loans to many debtor nations. We have already made note of these loans, called "structural adjustment loans." While they allowed countries to continue to pay interest on their commercial loans, they did not get the countries out of debt.

Structural adjustment loans were conditional loans that required member governments to adhere to a strict set of structural adjustment programs that reflected the ideological perspective of neoliberalism. Specifically, they focused on pushing "developing" countries into becoming fully integrated into the global economy by reorienting their domestic economies toward trade. The bankers, bureaucrats, and government officials who were making these decisions based on neoliberal assumptions insisted that the only way out of poverty for the "two-thirds" world was through integration into the global economy, and that meant export-oriented growth.[12] The structural adjustment programs that the IMF and the World Bank imposed on member countries went far in solidifying the growing role that corporations were beginning to play in the "two-thirds" world. Global integration of the "developing" world into the global economy was definitely the goal of the structural adjustment programs, and they accomplished this goal by requiring the removal of restrictions on foreign investments in local industry, banks, and other financial services; reducing wages or wage increases to make exports more "competitive"; cutting tariffs, quotas, and other restrictions of imports; devaluing the local currency to make exports more competitive; and privatizing state enterprises.[13] Not coincidentally, each one of these actions benefited the newly forming entities of multinational and transnational corporations that were able to take advantage both of the misfortunes of the countries' financial crises as well as the monies that were flowing into the countries in the form of direct foreign investment.

While the size and power of transnational corporations grew during the 1980s debt crisis, the end of the Cold War saw the next big push toward the realization of the dream of a global economy. By the 1990s the traditional communist trading bloc that had heretofore shunned capitalism and refused to participate in trade with the "free" world was ready to embrace the "free market" and eager to grow fat and wealthy like the United States. The loss of the Soviet Union as a trade partner accelerated Chinese leader Deng Xiopeng's interest in capitalist trade, although China has not yet fully moved toward embracing open economies, transparency, and free trade. Economic policy advisors flooded the former eastern states, as did corporations eager to profit from the privatization of formerly state-owned enterprises.[14] As the Cold War trading blocs disappeared, the 1990s saw the emergence of a new form of trading bloc manifested in regional trade agreements and alliances. The European Union, the North American Free Trade Agreement, and the Asia-Pacific Economic Cooperation organization (APEC) are all aimed at reducing barriers to trade in order to promote a more expanded role for regional trading.

This narrative overview traces the history of how trade liberalization has come about in recent decades as big business has responded to a variety of political, economic, and consumer circumstances. What it does not tell us is why trade liberalization has become one of the policy hallmarks of neoliberalism. This is a more difficult question to answer. Neoclassical economics has always been about approaching the market as if its theory were a certainty, a road map of how to build a prosperous future. These economists have believed, in effect, that there are "market rules" that can help to predict and explain the behavior of the market. At the same time, neoclassical economics is also oriented toward growth and profits. Throughout the 1970s and '80s and even into the '90s, big business discovered that it could indeed increase its profits through increased trade. The more trading partners there are, the better chance corporations have to make a better deal, to increase their profit margins. As big business led the way in promoting trade liberalization and proved that it was, in fact, able to grow and profit from "free trade," the neoliberal economists provided the theories to "explain" why trade liberalization was indeed the superior economic policy for a globalizing world. To put it crassly, the reason trade liberalization has been adopted by big business is because it makes money. In the current economic environment, it is acceptable to focus on money, profit, wealth, and growth. But as we will see in later chapters, resistance voices are challenging the acceptability of these foci and questioning the consequences and morality of trade liberalization.

The Role of Deregulation in Strengthening the Market

In many ways the activities of corporations, commercial banks, the multilateral lending institutions, the World Trade Organization, NAFTA, the European Union, and many other economic agents have been pushing toward the establishment of "open" economies as the goal of economic globalization. Open economies are the fulfillment of laissez-faire capitalism. They represent economies supposedly unfettered by governmental regulation that are "open" to the free movement of goods and services across borders. From the perspective of the corporation, the regulatory behavior of the government functions to interfere with the presumed "natural" behavior of the market. High tariffs, import quotas, controls on foreign exchange, and other restrictive measures characterize a "closed" economy and in turn impede its growth. Countries that open up their economies to increased trade allow domestic production to become competitive with the rest of the world, and this consequently increases efficiency.[15] The assumption underlying this belief is, once again, the principle of the "free market" discussed above. The present focus on deregulation that currently dominates economic policy is rooted in the belief that governmental involvement in the marketplace must be severely limited.

University of Chicago economist Milton Friedman articulated several reasons for limiting the role of government. First, he argued that the most important achievements in human history have all come from individual genius and initiative rather than from centralized government.[16] Friedman argued that government bureaucracy is inherently inefficient and stifling for innovation and entrepreneurship, qualities that he saw as necessary for growth and expansion in the business sector. Second, Friedman believed that competition is the essence of a thriving marketplace and that governmental intervention impedes the ability of businesses to compete in a free environment.[17] Third, perhaps his most deeply held ideological belief was that governmental interference in the marketplace results in the direct violation of individual freedom:

> A citizen of the United States who under the laws of various states is not free to follow the occupation of his own choosing unless he can get a license for it is likewise being deprived of an essential part of his freedom. So is the man who would like to exchange some of his goods with, say, a Swiss for a watch but is prevented from doing so by a quota. So also is the Californian who was thrown in jail for selling Alka Seltzer at a price below that set by the manufacturer under so-called "fair trade" laws. So also is the farmer who cannot grow the amount of wheat he wants. And so on. Clearly, economic freedom, in and of itself, is an extremely important part of total freedom.[18]

As we observed earlier, within neoclassical economic theory there has been a longstanding debate regarding the level of appropriate governmental involvement in the marketplace. The neoliberal perspective presumes that governmental regulations function to hamper free trade between nations by tampering with the level playing field of the market. The fact that the concept of a "level playing field" is a theoretical abstraction does not seem to affect the neoliberal belief that it actually exists, nor does the reality of the disparity of power between poor and rich nations when they supposedly engage one another on this "level playing field."

Governmental regulations that function to cushion a country's workforce or economic interests from outside forces also are seen as unnecessary interference and are referred to as "protectionism." From the perspective of neoliberalism, while regulations might be intended to promote a larger common good, they are inevitably going to be controlled and abused by special interest groups.[19]

Regulatory protections have traditionally been the strongest political tools for restraining raw capitalist economic power, as evidenced by such problems as corporate misbehavior, inhumane working conditions, and environmental degradation. These protections have evolved simultaneously alongside industrial development. Consequently, many of these regulatory laws are concentrated in the "first" world due to the longer period of time they have had to develop. These laws are intended to buffer the jobs of workers, to protect the environment and the health of citizens, and to establish minimum work and safety conditions for employees. Governmental regulations are intended to provide better working conditions and to promote a minimum standard of care for people and the environment. Small businesses and "developing" countries argue that these regulatory laws often have a discriminatory effect on countries whose industrial sectors have not matured and on businesses that do not possess the resources to compete on an equivalent plane with the deep pockets of big business.

The first class of regulations are known as "tariffs." Tariffs are taxes that are imposed on imported or exported goods and are often used to ensure that there will be a market for domestic products. In March 1999, the U.S. House of Representatives overwhelmingly passed the Steel Quota bill, which aimed at limiting steel imports from other nations by any means necessary. Financial crises in Russia and Asia had resulted in an excess of steel that was being "dumped," or sold below cost, on the U.S. markets. The Steel Quota bill, was passed in response to the complaint of the United Steelworkers of America (USWA) that this low-cost dumping was undermining the U.S. steel industry and jeopardizing "American" industry. George Becker, USWA president, summed up the sentiment of those who support some level of regulatory protection for U.S. workers and their jobs: "Steelworkers and steel communities hold dear the notion that America's trade policies should benefit Americans first."[20] The Clinton administration, big supporters of free trade and deregulation, quickly organized after the House's action and managed to derail the legislation on a technicality.[21] Ultimately, whether the Senate would have agreed or disagreed with Becker regarding U.S. trade policies was irrelevant as the neoliberal forces rallied to enforce the deregulation agenda that has dominated U.S. economic policy since the 1980s.

The second class of regulations are referred to as "non-tariff barriers." These regulations include safety standards, import quotas, and environmental regulations. The World Trade Organization (WTO), which was created through the Uruguay round of the General Agreement on Tariffs and Trade (GATT) in 1995, functions to facilitate the transfer of goods and services across national borders through the market mechanism of trade. One of the WTO's major tasks is to introduce international trade standards that will govern member nations' trade practices. These standards, which supersede the laws of individual member countries, allow for governments to challenge any law of another member government that they feel unfairly impedes trade. Under one of the GATT regulations that countries cannot "discriminate between like products on the basis of the method of production," the U.S. Marine Mammal Protection Act was declared in violation of international trade rules.[22] This act established rules prohibiting tuna fishers from engaging in practices that indiscriminately kill dolphins in their nets. A GATT Council decided that this provision constituted an artificial trade barrier and functioned as a form of protectionism for U.S. tuna fishers. This means that even if the United States continues to force its own fishing industry to use "dolphin-safe" nets, it cannot require imported tuna to fulfill these requirements. In a similar fashion, the United States pressured British Columbia to stop a publicly funded tree-planting program on the grounds that it was an "unfair subsidy" to the Canadian timber industry.[23]

Capitalists, however, are not anarchists. They do believe in some role for the government.[24] Simply stated, the role of government is to provide those conditions and services that the market is not capable of providing. This boils down to the maintenance of law and order, to prevent coercion and violence among individuals; the enforcement of contracts; the defining of property rights and arbitration of discrepancies related to property disputes; and finally, the provision and maintenance of a monetary system. The world has changed considerably since Friedman articulated these roles for government in 1962. In the early twenty-first century, law and order are sometimes hired out by corporations to protect their interests, and the stabilization of monetary systems is orchestrated as often by the IMF and international banking institutions as by governments. In fact, with an increase in the power and influence of corporations has come a corresponding decrease in the role and function of government in general.

Privatization as a More "Efficient" Form of Market Organization

Even prior to the multinationalization of corporations, businesses functioned in many ways as informal and formal agents of the government. Corporations were chartered by governments to perform necessary economic and productive tasks that were impractical for the government to pursue—building railroads, smelting iron ore, processing food, to name a few. A political consensus that predated neoliberalism had determined that governments ought to be responsible for enterprises that were necessary to ensure a stable society, such as law enforcement, national defense, the legal system, and the prison system. Governments also managed those enterprises that contributed to the common good or the improvement of civil society, such as education, park systems, the postal service, and road construction and maintenance. Traditionally there has been a clear division between acceptable arenas for profit-making and those areas considered to be the responsibilities of government. Proponents of neoliberalism argue that the market is a more efficient mechanism for administrating almost all activities, including those such as education, prisons, and parks, which have historically been run by the government. The argument is once again articulated by Milton Friedman in his excoriation of government's ability to administer anything as efficiently and productively as the private sector.[25] Clearly, the movement toward privatization is part and parcel of the same ideological assumption that motivates deregulation; namely, that government should stay out of business affairs.

To gain a deeper understanding of the wave of privatization that has washed across the globe in the past twenty years, we need to fill in the broad historical brushstrokes that preceded the recent surge of privatization. Once again, the story begins with the economic recovery programs that emerged following World War II. In addition to the material devastation of the war-torn countries that was mentioned earlier, there also remained the historical memory of the Great Depression after World War I and the crippling unemployment that had accompanied it. Daniel Yergin and Joseph Stanislaw, in their book *The Commanding Heights*, argue that the postwar mentality that generated a new form of "mixed economies" cannot be clearly understood without grasping that unemployment was the central fear in the postwar years.[26] They go on to detail the disreputable position that capitalism held in Europe at the end of the war: "Capitalism was considered morally objectionable; it appealed to greed instead of idealism, it promoted inequality, it had failed the people, and—to many—it had been responsible for the war."[27]

Added to this mistrust of capitalism was the strong position that the Soviet Union held at the time. Its economic model of "command-and-control" offered the promise of full employment and industrial development, two things Europe desperately needed. Even if Europe had wanted to adopt a capitalist model, there were no investors, no capital funds, no private sector to help rebuild. Something had to be done, and quickly, and so it fell to the governments to step in, take charge, and organize European recovery.

The mixed economies that resulted were seen as a middle way between capitalism and command economies. Theoretically they were based on John

Maynard Keynes's influential book, *General Theory of Employment, Interest and Money*, which argued, among other things, for combining a market economy with "active management of aggregate demand, through fiscal and monetary policy, to ensure full employment."[28] There had been some history of state-owned enterprises before the war, but the governments of Britain, France, Italy, and Germany each played an essential role in the postwar years of stabilizing the economic environment through a process of nationalizing a variety of essential industries (coal, steel, railroads, utilities, telecommunications, etc.) The premise of nationalization in the 1940s rested on the assumptions that these industries were inefficient, underinvested, and lacked scale.[29] As Yergin and Stanislaw explain it: "As nationalized firms, they would mobilize resources and adapt new technologies, they would be far more efficient, and they would ensure the achievement of the national objectives of economic development and growth, full employment, and justice and equality."[30]

These mixed economies, particularly Britain, became known as "welfare states" because the governments also created programs that provided for the basic welfare needs of their citizens through free health care, pension plans, government-supported housing, and education. Unlike the planned economies in the Soviet empire, however, government did not control the market and free enterprise grew up around the edges as Europe began to recover from the war. Indeed, in the first decade after World War II, European recovery was unprecedented. Yergin and Stanislaw point out that by 1955 "all the Western European countries had exceeded their prewar levels of production."[31] From 1948 to 1973 the world real GDP rose at an average of close to 5 percent per year.[32]

The neoliberal position argues that, while mixed economies worked well for a while, government mismanagement and bureaucratic inertia slowly overtook the state-owned enterprises throughout Europe. Neoliberalism views the state-owned companies' ability to function as monopolies as a barrier to innovation and competition within the industries. It holds that changes of some sort were needed to keep the European industries competitive in the increasingly globalizing marketplace of the 1980s. The solution that took hold was a movement toward privatization that began in Britain under the aegis of Prime Minister Margaret Thatcher. Indeed, as her government was beginning to develop a plan for addressing the problems that faced the state-owned companies, the privatization approach was so new that the young politician charged with developing the plan had to search for a new name to describe just what it was the British government was proposing.[33] "Privatization" came from economic and social theorist Peter Drucker's work and accurately captured Thatcher's vision[34]—a vision that spread throughout Europe and around the world in the 1980s and became a major part of the 1990s transformation of the former socialist states. Roughly speaking, the state-owned enterprises were simply put on the market and returned to the private sector. Since most of the nationalized enterprises were understood to be, at least to some degree, held in common by the state for the interests of the populace, many of these privatization programs included the issuing of vouchers to citizens for their portion of the companies. But for the most part, privatization was a way for debt-ridden governments to slough off major economic drains from their fiscal budgets while also turning a tidy profit. Yergin and Stanislaw estimate that after turning over some two-thirds of state-owned industries in 1992, Britain made well over $30 billion.[35]

Understanding Economic Globalization as Benevolent

Now that we have taken a closer look at aspects of the theory, history, and ideology of neoliberalism, we will turn our attention more explicitly to the ways in which this position experiences, understands, and interprets globalization. I say "explicitly" because we actually have been watching the unfolding of the neoliberal paradigm of globalization throughout this chapter. One of the remarkable things about the phenomenon of globalization is that people are often talking about it, even when they fail to use the term "globalization." For big business, the blueprint of what globalization looks like has already been implicitly defined by the assumptions outlined above. We will now take an explicit look at what big business has to say about globalization by examining neoliberal interpretations of globalization as seen in documents, reports, and media outlets that purport to support the agenda thus far described.

In sum, for neoliberalism, "globalization" refers to an integrated global economy that revolves around export-oriented trade, which is best facilitated by a low-barrier market (deregulation) and a highly competitive private sector (no government-owned corporations).[36] For proponents of big business, these factors represent what they believe to be a fairly straightforward policy agenda of globalization that promotes economic growth, increased trade, and integration into the global economy. From this perspective, globalization is viewed as unequivocally benevolent and corporations are seen to be leading the way in spreading the benefits of globalization around the world. As an editorial in *The Economist* concluded recently, corporations "should be seen as a powerful force for good. They spread wealth, work, technologies that raise living standards, and better ways of doing business."[37] Indeed, this is exactly how transnational corporations do see themselves, as free-market agents spreading the gospel of globalization to the farthest reaches of the planet. Globalization is described as "today's reality, like it or not."[38]

As for the market itself, the open economies that are the hallmark of the neoliberal model of globalization are built on the premise that an "opening up" of the marketplace is a healthy and stable progression for capitalism.[39] The argument is that the increased competition encouraged by an open economy leads to more innovation, more efficiency, and ultimately more growth. These benefits of increased competition are accomplished through the principle of comparative advantage.[40] This principle argues that countries should produce those goods that they are able to produce most efficiently (i.e., cheaply) and should then use these goods to trade for other necessities. In this way a country is able, as the Organisation for Economic Co-operation and Development (OECD) puts it, to "devote its natural, human, industrial and financial resources to their highest and best uses."[41] What supporters often fail to acknowledge is that the model of an open economy requires following neoliberal policy prescriptions that will generate an unfettered market over against implementing economic policies that will address domestic problems and priorities. In fact, because the neoliberal agenda has emerged primarily from the business community, its supporters are primarily concerned about domestic problems only to the extent that they might interfere with business production and trade.

In addition to the fact that globalization is good for market exchange, for businesses, and for those who have a propertied stake in the economy, proponents of this position also argue that it is good for consumers. The increased efficiency that globalization engenders does increase consumers' options and at times reduces the price of some goods and services. This in turn means that the average consumer has more spending power and thus access to more or better consumer products. The increased trade and competition fostered by globalization then provide greater availability and variety of consumer goods to those with purchasing power. Not long ago most people ate their foods with the seasons—strawberries and blueberries in the spring, tomatoes in the summer, corn and squash in the fall, with only the occasional mango or avocado as a treat. Today, grocery stores in the United States are ripe with all varieties of fruits and vegetables year-round, as globalization provides consumers with access to perpetual growing seasons. Of course, all of these purported "benefits" accrue only to those who have disposable income. The increased availability of expensive out-of-season produce is hardly relevant for people struggling to get by below the poverty level in any country.

Confronted with claims that unrestrained markets escalate environmental degradation, neoliberal supporters reply that, in fact, globalization provides promising new ways forward for protecting the environment that heretofore have been ignored. Their thesis is that increased trade drives economic growth and economic growth makes more people wealthy. As an editorial in *The Economist* put it, "As people get richer, they want a cleaner environment—and they acquire the means to pay for it."[42] Tom Bethell argues that the principle of private property is one of the most practical and efficient ways to promote environmental management and protection.[43] His theory is that private owners of land, wildlife, and natural resources are more likely to protect their land and provide careful stewardship than government bureaucrats following public policy. This is particularly true given the tendency of environmental policy to follow the prevailing "fads" of the times.[44] Bethell believes that rather than trusting the care of the environment to government policy, "the more sensible approach is to let myriad independent owners make their own decisions. Their different experiments and outcomes will point to the wisest course."[45]

Selling and trading emissions rights is another market-oriented policy solution that big business believes will help to green the environment. In this proposal companies that are able to reduce their emissions below federal safety standards are then allowed to sell the remainder of their emissions rights to companies that have not yet retrofitted their production facilities to comply with the allowable emissions levels. The most rigorous implementation of this type of policy has been in controlling sulfur emissions from power plants that contribute to acid rain. According to Richard Sandor, vice chairman of the Chicago Board of Trade, "Emissions have been reduced at a cost far lower than the most optimistic forecasts."[46] In fact, these days big business is laying its environmental eggs in the market-solution basket more often than not. There exists a strong sentiment among neoliberals that the ingenuity, creativity, and innovation that have always driven market competition will function to provide market solutions to the environmental problems that threaten our planet.

In the face of continuing skepticism about the blessings of neoliberal globalization, proponents of this position are accustomed to relaying the "facts" in order to prove that globalization is good. In a recent editorial defending open economies, Martin Wolf cited the following information:

> Over the century, world population has quadrupled, while world real incomes per head have risen four-fold. . . . In the U.S., life expectancy has risen by 30 years . . . and real incomes per head have risen more than seven-fold. . . . In the developed world, a man of today is, in many respects, richer than Cornelius Vanderbilt, and a woman need have no fear of the fate of Anne, queen of England from 1702 to 1714, who had 18 pregnancies and five live births, but not one child who survived into adulthood. . . . Even in the poorest countries, male life expectancy at birth, now 62, is higher than it was in today's high-income countries in 1900. In India, far from the most successful of developing countries, real incomes per head have risen more than 150 per cent since independence.[47]

Simply put, the neoliberals argue that the world is a much better place than it used to be, in large part because of the advances that globalization has allowed. World exports multiplied eighteenfold from 1950 to 1998, and production multiplied six and a half times. Wolf points out that "the dynamic growth in trade has been the engine of the longest and strongest period of sustained economic growth in human history."[48] For Wolf and other neoliberals, it is this growth that is responsible for long-term economic benefits that have strengthened our economies, reduced and eliminated disease, lengthened our life spans, and generally provided for a better standard of living for most of the world's people. As President Bill Clinton said to the World Economic Forum in Davos, "I think we have to reaffirm unambiguously that open markets and rules-based trade are the best engine we know of to lift living standards, reduce environmental destruction, and build shared prosperity."[49]

Proponents of this position believe that the promises and rewards of globalization extend beyond the corporation. They are convinced that the humanitarian and economic advances that globalization offers can be shared with the whole human race. Those who adhere to this position firmly believe that the economic development that globalization brings will raise the poor out of their misery. The neoliberal policy agenda is accepted as the road to success for all so-called "developing" countries. In fact, the main finding of a recent WTO study is that "in a world economy marked by increasing income gaps between poor and rich countries trade can be a factor in bringing about convergence in incomes between countries."[50] As Lawrence Summers, former U.S. treasury secretary, put it, "Quite simply, rapid, market-led growth is the most potent weapon against poverty that mankind has ever known."[51] Proponents argue that globalization fights poverty in a number of ways, including foreign direct investment, job creation, technology transfer, and deepening economic interdependence among countries.

Foreign direct investment means that transnational corporations are investing money in the local economies of their partner countries. Factories and offices are being built in locations that were previously void of industrial development. Money enters the economy through the purchase of land, materials, and labor to construct these new projects, but there is also a longer-term investment. By placing these industries in the global South, corporations are creating jobs in countries where the only other alternatives for survival are subsistence farming or migration to the cities to look for work. Research from OECD shows that foreign firms pay better than domestic ones and create new jobs faster.[52] In Turkey, "wages paid by foreign firms are 124% above average and their work forces have been expanding by 11.5% a year, compared with .6% in local firms."[53] The idea is that even if foreign companies reduce their labor costs by moving from a "first" world country to a "two-thirds" world country, they will still be paying higher proportional wages in their new locations. These higher wages will begin to push all wages upward. As Robert Reich, former U.S. secretary of labor, put it: "It's unrealistic to expect that workers in poorer nations will receive American-style wages and working standards. But we can and should insist that as these nations become steadily wealthier, their bottom-rung workers do better. The benefits of trade and growth should be widely shared."[54] Proponents argue that all of these factors work together to create a higher standard of living in all parts of the world.

In addition to the jobs that are created, another important aspect of foreign direct investment and globalization is the transfer of technology and the skills training that corporations provide for their employees. "Big foreign firms are . . . the principal conduit for new technologies, as is clear from the fact that 70% of all international royalties on technology involve payments between parent firms and their foreign affiliates."[55] The idea is that when foreign subsidiaries invest in "developing" countries, they are investing ideas, on-the-job training, and management skills as well as capital. While these subsidiaries are most likely producing for an export market, their investment in the country's intellectual and human capital can, over time, raise the industrial experience of the population and create an atmosphere in which local entrepreneurship flourishes.[56]

Another way that proponents of this model claim that globalization benefits the "developing" world is through encouraging and facilitating the deepening of the economic interdependence of nations. The idea behind this is that economic interdependence promotes a higher degree of peace and stability because war and armed conflict interfere with market trading. "Developing" countries that have integrated into the global market now have a vested interest in maintaining peace and stability in their domestic situations as well as their international relationships given their need to maintain trading partnerships. "Developed" countries also now have a stronger desire to aid countries in settling their differences peacefully, since a major armed conflict holds the potential to disrupt market confidence.

In sum, proponents of the big business perspective on globalization believe that the neoliberal ideology of trade liberalization, privatization, and deregulation benefits everyone—workers, the environment, consumers, the so-called "developing" countries, and of course, stockholders. Big business argues that the success of growth and trade policies in the West means that globalization offers the same promise of hope to the global South. The neoliberal ideology proclaims the market's ability to govern itself and to provide answers to the most pressing problems of our time, including poverty, the environment, and armed conflict. Its adherents firmly believe that all of these dilemmas have market solutions. In their opinion, we have only to be patient until innovation catches up with reality and offers us concrete solutions to pressing world problems.

A Neoliberal Vision of the Good Life

We have looked at the historical and theoretical roots of neoliberalism in the laissez-faire tradition of neoclassical economics and identified the policy hallmarks that guide this position's engagement in the globalization discussions. We also have outlined how this corporate model interprets the value of globalization to the rest of the world. Embedded within the description of neoliberalism that we have just encountered lies a moral vision that is particular to this position, a vision of what constitutes "the good life."

Our values exist in a dialectical relationship with our actions, such that the moral vision that is embedded within neoliberalism both shapes and is shaped by the acts and actions of people who support this position. That is to say, what we value certainly shapes our understanding of what constitutes the good life and influences our actions and behaviors accordingly. At the same time, our experience of the world and of the "good life" we have envisioned also functions either to reinforce or contradict our formative values. When our experience of the world reinforces our original values and convictions, we generally continue along the same moral path. But when contradictions challenge those values and moral convictions, we often are forced to interrogate the assumptions and consequences of our moral system more carefully. In this way our morality and our life experience are constantly spiraling around one another, testing the validity of our moral claims and challenging us to pay attention to the material consequences of our values and behavior.

Now that we have examined the neoliberal paradigm, we must ask: What is the moral vision of this position, and how does that play into an understanding of what constitutes the good life?[57] The big business position envisions the good life as a combination of hard work, a devoted and adoring family, and the reward of success and happiness. Supporters of this position believe that the good life is accessible to everyone if only people will accept the responsibility of maintaining such a life—responsibility for taking care of oneself and one's family. They believe that work is always available and diligence and efficiency in the marketplace are rewarded with wages and the potential for upward mobility. In a sense, one of this position's unofficial goals is to globalize the "American Dream," the Horatio Alger sense of rising above one's circumstances, so that people around the world are able to see that efficiency and responsibility are rewarded with growth (for industry and state) and success (for the individual). Let us turn now to a deeper examination of the three key underlying values that constitute a moral vision of the good life within the neoliberal paradigm—individualism, prosperity, and freedom.

Individualism as the Context for Moral Agency

In the neoliberal model, moral agency is equated with an individualism that is focused on providing for self-interest. In fact, self-interested human nature is what ultimately drives big business. While one might think that this would lead to chaos, proponents argue that what is best for the individual is, ultimately, best for the whole society. This phenomenon is referred to as the "invisible hand of the market" that is believed to coordinate individual self-interest with the functions of the market. Proponents argue that while the distribution of wealth in this system may be uneven, this does not necessarily mean the system is unjust or unfair.[58] Andrew Carnegie provided the following justification for wealth in his famous treatise *The Gospel of Wealth*:

> There remains, then, only one mode of using great fortunes; but in this we have the true antidote for the temporary unequal distribution of wealth, the reconciliation of the rich and the poor. . . . It is founded upon the present most intense Individualism, and the race is prepared to put it in practice by degrees whenever it pleases. Under its sway we shall have an ideal State, in which the surplus wealth of the few will become in the best sense, the property of the many, because administered for the common good; and this wealth passing through the hands of the few, can be made a much more potent force for the elevation of our race than is distributed in small sums to the people themselves.[59]

The roots of neoliberal individualism grow from deep within the liberal tradition. Philosophers from Descartes to Smith to Mill have built the foundations of their theories on the individual identity, economic capability, and independent nature of *Homo economicus*. For Descartes, individuals capable of reasoning and rationalization provided a respectable intellectual break with the traditionalism of the Middle Ages.[60] Theologian Carol Johnston describes the significance of the concept of individualism in the minds of Enlightenment philosophers:

> Enlightenment individualism was based on Newtonian physics, which assumed that the world is composed of discrete, independently existing individual entities. In this atomistic individualism, relations between entities are strictly external—they exist as they are whether they have any relationships or not. It is important to understand that Enlightenment thinkers, as they considered the meaning of Newtonian physics for their understanding of the world, believed that the individualism they were promoting in social relations was not a matter of social choice but rather simply a matter of getting in tune with the way the world actually is.[61]

Thus for a moral philosopher, such as Adam Smith, the elevation of individualism in his own theoretical work was an attempt to respond to the insights provided by science in understanding human nature.

The concept of individualism, which celebrates the autonomous independent person, has far outlasted Newton, Smith, and other early modern thinkers. Individualism remains a core value for people who follow the big business model of globalization because it affirms and reinforces their vision of how capitalism works. Indeed, economist Friedrich von Hayek singles out individualism as both one of the most confused and ambiguous political terms in his day and one of the most important for understanding the political economy of capitalism.[62] For Hayek, individualism is primarily a theoretical understanding of society.[63] In this theory, society is made up of a collection of individuals and it is their participation in that larger social grouping that determines their nature and character. The most interesting and unique aspect of this interpretation of individualism, however, is its argument for the collective social benefits of individual self-interested behavior. Without pretending to understand or explain why, Hayek (and the neoliberals with him) believes that the combined effects of individual actions work together for the larger benefit of humanity. As Hayek puts it, "The spontaneous collaboration of free men often creates things which are greater than their individual minds can ever fully comprehend."[64] Respect and appreciation for individual freedom are viewed as the most efficient ways to organize markets and provide for the needs of the less fortunate.

As a foundational value of neoclassical economics, individualism supports the neoliberal understanding of human nature and activity. But there are many values that arguably could be embraced by neoclassical economics. The question remains, then, why has this value been elevated to such a prominent position? I believe the answer lies in the neoliberal vision of the good life.

One hundred years ago when Max Weber was assessing the connections between capitalism and Protestantism, he presented a vision of the good life in early America.[65] Its ethical principles mandated that all people approach their life's work with a sense of duty, responsibility, and blessedness—no matter what the task. This sense of call endowed all forms of work—cooking and raising children as well as farming and business—with a sense of importance and honor. All work was respected as a necessary part of society and workers were respected for doing their part. At the same time, there was an ethic of personal moderation and responsibility toward others that changed the way people lived. The Protestant ethic discouraged indulging oneself with gifts and possessions that went beyond meeting one's basic needs. It also encouraged taking one's extra wealth and using it to care for the less fortunate in society.

Indeed, it was this sort of spirit of capitalism out of which the neoliberal position arose with all of its emphasis on individual responsibility. Over the years, however, the moral framework of society has shifted, and visions of the good life have shifted as well. As belief in stewardship has weakened, individual and communal responsibility to care for others and the ethic of philanthropy also have dwindled. This has led to an increase in and a desire for personal wealth. Today people strive to get ahead in big business, to get the promotion, to provide for their families, to be able to buy the things they want, to take European vacations and spend summers at the beach; and all of these desires require that a person work very hard. The good news for people who buy into this vision is that it is universally attainable. In a free society, all individuals possess the potential to attain "the good life," to become millionaires, if you will. The good life, in many ways, has become equated with material possessions, wealth, and the ability to buy things that will make one happy. Life is seen as a pyramid with everyone able to reach the top, but everyone also knows that only so many people will "make it." The farther one is able to climb, the better life will be. Individuals are rewarded for their behavior and possess the ability to better their circumstances.

Capitalism relies on the value of individualism as much as on the concept of "economic man." Not only is the individual actor, as consumer, the engine that keeps the market going, but the creativity, genius, and hard work of individual entrepreneurs are what continue to allow for competition, growth, and progress in our contemporary world. The freedom of individual thinking is also the foundation of the advances that have been made on behalf of women, minorities, and other oppressed groups.

Prosperity as Humanity's Telos

When considering an answer to the teleological question of humanity's purpose or chief end, the value of prosperity emerges foremost from the neoliberal perspective. Prosperity represents the rewards of working hard and leading the good life. Prosperity is that value that signifies success, achievement, or purpose, if you will. In late industrial capitalism, prosperity and success have come to be equated with wealth, which is represented by property, material possessions, and financial assets. Tom Bethell argues that property is one of the fundamental keys to securing prosperity. For Bethell, if private property is the foundation of exchange and thus the free market system, then likewise, it is essential to ensuring prosperity. As he puts it, "Prosperity and property are intimately connected. Exchange is the basic market activity, and when goods are not individually owned, they cannot easily be exchanged. Free-market economies, therefore, can only be built on a private property base."[66]

This predilection toward interpreting prosperity and the good life as the maximization of wealth is related to the classical economic notion of *Homo economicus* ("economic man") attributed to John Stuart Mill. Mill viewed humanity's sole purpose as the desire to possess wealth. Wealth maximization gradually became the modus operandi of capitalist players in the Western world.[67] In fact, this idea was supported through a theological anthropology that interpreted the Genesis creation story to show that humanity had been created by God with the express intention of using the physical world for our own resources and pleasure. Brian Griffiths went so far as to claim, "If we accept therefore that man is created with a desire to work, subject to a charge to control and harness the earth, it follows that the process of wealth creation is something intrinsic to a Christian view of the world."[68] Proponents of the neoliberal position do, in fact, believe that Christianity provides humanity with a positive mandate to create wealth, that it is God's intention for us to use our talents and gifts in the service of managing and exercising dominion over the world. Michael Novak, for instance, has pointed out:

> The earth has long been rich in oil, copper, iron ore, rubber, and countless other resources. But for millennia, many of these resources went unknown, neglected, or unused. The imagination and enterprise unleashed by democratic capitalism brought recognition of the actual wealth lying fallow in the bosom of nature; invented new uses for these resources; and conferred wealth on many regions of the world that the inhabitants of those regions did not know they possessed.[69]

Novak has also pointed out the important role that this shift in consciousness played in the early eighteenth century.[70] Life in premodern Europe was rural and agrarian and deeply marked by poverty and social caste. The possibility for self-improvement and rising beyond one's origins was virtually nonexistent. Moral philosophers such as David Hume and Adam Smith saw new possibilities for improving the human condition through commerce and industry and the values of freedom and prosperity that they offered to all those who desired to work hard and to advance their individual circumstances. Prosperity and a better way of life achieved through the market were held out as an inspiration to people who had never thought about the possibility of changing their circumstances. Novak argues that Hume and Smith were attempting to establish a new ethos for the Western world that would continue to yield "abundance and material comfort" for the aristocracy while also raising the standards of living for everyone and creating an atmosphere of peace and respect for the law.[71] Prosperity, the idea of the good life as consisting of success, comfort, and abundance, has indeed proven to be a powerful incentive for promoting neoliberalism. As Novak says:

> Every man and woman has a fundamental right to engage in personal economic enterprise. . . . Humans were not created to be receivers only, or clients only, but also creators. God gave them minds and imaginations, as well as courage and a zest for trial and error. He implanted in them a desire to better their condition, for their families and for the whole of human society. The creation of wealth is a social task and the supportive efforts of all are necessary to its accomplishment.[72]

Freedom as What Constitutes Human Flourishing

In response to the final question, neoliberalism and big business answer resoundingly that the value of freedom must be upheld above all others as the marker of true human flourishing. Indeed, Milton Friedman details his economic philosophy in his book, *Capitalism and Freedom*. But it is not enough merely to acknowledge that neoliberalism is rooted in the value of freedom; we also must ask exactly how freedom is understood in this context. Once again, the answer is clear in Friedman's own work. Freedom does not merely refer to the democratic value that all persons have the right to be free persons, to govern themselves, and to make their own decisions under the rule of law. Rather, the neoliberal interpretation of freedom goes one step further and is more closely aligned with the notion of liberty, which is concerned with individual freedom to act as one chooses. In the neoliberal model, freedom is interpreted as individual freedom from constraint and control; and power concentrated in the hands of the government is viewed as the most serious threat to individual freedom.

Another way to examine what freedom means to Friedman is to examine what he is against. In his book he lists fourteen government activities that he believes violate freedom.[73] Among the programs that Friedman would eliminate is social security. His basis for this position is that citizens are forced to contribute to a fund that is administered entirely outside of their control. For Friedman, social security epitomizes an infringement on individuals' personal liberty and freedom to control their own affairs. He also opposes price supports for agriculture, minimum wage laws, national parks, and public housing, among other things. Friedman does believe that there are some areas in which government oversight is necessary, and not surprisingly, each of these areas relates to establishing a safe environment in which people can function as capitalists. He supports national defense, the maintenance of law and order, enforcement of contracts and property rights, and a monetary system regulated by the government.

Milton Friedman's ideas, while discredited and ignored for twenty years, have taken hold in a powerful way in recent years. We can see very clearly that the value of freedom from constraint undergirds a number of neoliberal policy goals, most prominently privatization, as noted earlier. From this perspective, it is critical that the role of the government is carefully circumscribed so that it does not constrain individual freedom or interfere with the activities of the market. It is important to reiterate that the government is not eliminated from the market process; rather, the value of freedom as non-constraint requires that the government play a very particular kind of role, a role that protects and reinforces the space for individual actors to pursue economic goals freely.

Conclusion

While it is true that proponents of big business frequently claim to share some of the values to be presented later as constitutive of other positions, the values of individualism, prosperity, and freedom presented here are most distinctive and fundamental to the theory of globalization as benevolent. Clearly these three values work together to support and reinforce each other. It is not coincidental that proponents of this position specify freedom as individual freedom or that their understanding of humanity's capability of flourishing is thought to be most achievable under conditions of freedom as unrestrained economic activity. Unfettered individualism in the sense meant here is really unfettered freedom to seek personal and private goals valued by the "economic man" of neoliberalism. How sharply other positions' moral visions of fulfillment clash with this one will become clearer in chapters 5 and 6.

Notes

1. The principle role of the IMF was to regulate the economies of countries facing fiscal deficits. The principle role of the World Bank was to promote development in "underdeveloped" areas.
2. Ray Kiely and Phil Marfleet, *Globalisation and the Third World* (London: Routledge, 1998), 25–27.
3. Catherine Caufield, *Masters of Illusion: The World Bank and the Poverty of Nations* (New York: Henry Holt & Co., 1996), 53.
4. Daniel Yergin and Joseph Stanislaw, *The Commanding Heights: The Battle between Government and the Marketplace That Is Remaking the Modern World* (New York: Simon & Schuster, 1998), 65.
5. Giovanni Arrighi, in his book *The Long Twentieth Century: Money, Power, and the Origin of Our Times* (London: Verso, 1994), identifies four historical cycles of accumulation and economic hegemony, which he denotes as Genoese, Dutch, British, and American. Interestingly, he identifies a period of high finance at the end of each of these cycles of accumulation.
6. Stagflation occurs when a sluggish economy coincides with a period of high inflation.
7. McNamara's first five-year plan projected lending $11.6 billion, more money than had been lent in the first twenty years of the Bank's existence. McNamara believed that more money dispersed more broadly would ease the burden of poverty more quickly. For more details see Caufield, *Masters of Illusion*, chap. 6.
8. Arrighi, *Long Twentieth Century*, 304.
9. While the majority of the people in these countries were desperately poor, even if the elite constituted only the top 1 percent to 5 percent of the population, this still represented a largely underdeveloped consumer base.
10. David C. Korten, *When Corporations Rule the World* (West Hartford, CT: Kumarian Press, 1995), 125.
11. While it is true that it is governments who borrow these high-interest "development" loans, the money most often ends up in the hands of the industrialists who bid on the development projects and the pockets of government officials who skim their share off the top.
12. While it would be reactionary to suggest that there was some sort of conspiracy afoot involving the IMF, the World Bank, and the transnational corporations, clearly the leaders of these various institutions were on the same page regarding a new economic paradigm that revolved around a global economy. As we will see

later, many of their top executives were also involved in informal dialogues aimed at shaping this new model.

13. Walden Bello, "Structural Adjustment Programs: 'Success' for Whom?" in *The Case Against the Global Economy*, ed. Jerry Mander and Edward Goldsmith (San Francisco: Sierra Club Books, 1996), 286.

14. Azerbaijan is one example. Nestled between Russia and Iran, just about the only thing Azerbaijan has going for it economically is oil, and lots of it. Sitting atop twenty billion barrels of oil, its reserves are just a little smaller than Kuwait's. Prior to 1991 the state owned the entire oil industry. Now, with independence, the government is looking for partners to modernize its antiquated, dangerous, and environmentally unsound oil operations and there is no dearth of offers. Multinationals from the United States, Britain, France, Germany, Norway, Japan, Italy, and even Russia are all angling to get in on the action. Information on Azerbaijan's oil industry is taken from Jeffrey Goldberg, "The Crude Face of Global Capitalism," *The New York Times Magazine*, October 4, 1998, 50ff.

15. For step-by-step instructions of how to achieve this, see Rudiger Dornbusch and F. Leslie Ch. Helmers, eds., *The Open Economy: Tools for Policymakers in Developing Countries* (New York: Oxford University Press for The World Bank, 1988).

16. Milton Friedman, *Capitalism and Freedom* (Chicago: University of Chicago Press, 1962), 3–4.

17. Ibid., 4.

18. Ibid., 9.

19. Yergin and Stanislaw, *Commanding Heights*, 148.

20. David E. Sanger, "Dangerous Selectivity about Rules of Global Trade," *New York Times*, March 21, 1999, Business section, p. 4.

21. Information from a personal phone conversation with Gary Hubbard, public affairs director of United Steelworkers of America, August 30, 2000.

22. Paul Hawken, *The Ecology of Commerce: A Declaration of Sustainability* (New York: HarperCollins, 1993), 97.

23. Richard J. Barnet and John Cavanagh, *Global Dreams: Imperial Corporations and the New World Order* (New York: Simon & Schuster, 1994), 351.

24. For a more detailed explanation of M. Friedman's position, see *Capitalism and Freedom*, chap. 2.

25. M. Friedman, *Capitalism and Freedom*, esp. chap. 2.

26. Yergin and Stanislaw, *Commanding Heights*, 22.

27. Ibid., 22.

28. Martin Wolf, "Painful Lessons from a Turbulent Century," *The Financial Times* (London), December 6, 1999.

29. Yergin and Stanislaw, *Commanding Heights*, 25.

30. Ibid., 25.

31. Ibid., 45.

32. Wolf, "Painful Lessons," 15.

33. Yergin and Stanislaw, *Commanding Heights*, 114.

34. Ibid., 114.

35. Ibid., 123.

36. The neoliberal globalization dialogue has shifted somewhat since the anti-globalization protests held in conjunction with the WTO meeting in Seattle and the IMF/World Bank meetings in Washington. The widespread publicity that these activities generated has forced neoliberal proponents of globalization into a defensive posture that is apparent in speeches by the director general of the WTO, Mike Moore, and the secretary general of the International Chamber of Commerce, Maria Livanos Cattaui.

Recent reports released by some of the institutions of big business are also focused on justifying the neoliberal model as beneficent toward the poor: Dan Ben-David, Hakan Nordstrom, and L. Alan Winters, *Trade, Income Disparity, and Poverty*, World Trade Organization Special Studies 5 (Geneva: World Trade Organization, 1999); and International Monetary Fund, "Globalization: Threat or Opportunity?" (Washington: IMF, 2000).

While the neoliberal globalization rhetoric has expanded to incorporate "poverty" as a growing concern, this concern has yet to alter the position's basic view of globalization or the position's policy agenda. If anything, neoliberal concern for poverty reduction is being used as a further buttress for the argument that more rapid and widespread globalization is in order as the only viable, long-term remedy for poverty.

37. "The World's View of Multinationals," *The Economist* 354, no. 8155 (January 29, 2000): 21–22.

38. Maria Livanos Cattaui, "The Case for the Global Economy," International Chamber of Commerce (September 21, 1999). Online: http://www.iccwbo.org/home/news_archives/1999/case_for_the_global_economy.asp.

39. For a more detailed presentation of this position, see Organisation for Economic Co-operation and Development (OECD), *Open Markets Matter: The Benefits of Trade and Investment Liberalization* (Paris: Organisation for Economic Co-operation and Development, 1998).

40. David Ricardo developed the theory of comparative advantage in the early nineteenth century. See Carol Johnston, *The Wealth or Health of Nations: Transforming Capitalism from Within* (Cleveland, OH: Pilgrim Press, 1998), chap. 2, for a more detailed look at Ricardo's theory from a theological point of view.

41. OECD, *Open Markets Matter*, 10.

42. "Why Greens Should Love Trade," *The Economist* (U.S. edition) 353, no. 8140 (October 9, 1999): 17–18.

43. Tom Bethell, *The Noblest Triumph: Property and Prosperity through the Ages* (New York: St. Martin's Press, 1998), esp. chap. 18.

44. Environmentalist Alston Chase wrote, "At the turn of the century, saving big game animals was the rage. Officials fed elk, bred bison and bashed wolves. Today they do the opposite—batter bison, breed wolves and encourage hunters to shoot elk. A generation ago, old-growth forests were called 'biological deserts.' Now they are revered for 'biodiversity.' Over the years, the field known as 'restoration ecology' went into, then out of, then back into popularity, without once having been tried. Wildfires were first thought good, then bad, then good and seem to be

on their way out again. Ditto the mysterious doctrine called 'sustainable development.'" As quoted in ibid., 273–74.

45. Ibid., 274.

46. Peter Passell, "Trading on the Pollution Exchange: Global Warming Plan Would Make Emissions a Commodity," *New York Times*, October 24, 1997, Business section, p. 4.

47. Martin Wolf, "Ascent towards an Open Future," *The Financial Times* (London), December 22, 1999, Comment and Analysis section.

48. Martin Wolf, "Trade Expansion Remains the Engine of Growth," *The Financial Times* (London), February 9, 2000, Survey-World Trade section.

49. Martin Wolf, "The Big Lie of Global Inequality," *The Financial Times* (London), February 9, 2000, Comment and Analysis section.

50. Ben-David et al., *Trade*, 1.

51. Martin Wolf, "Kicking Down Growth's Ladder," *The Financial Times* (London), April 12, 2000, Comment and Analysis section.

52. "World's View of Multinationals," 21–22.

53. Ibid.

54. Robert B. Reich, "Trade Accords That Spread the Wealth," *New York Times*, September 2, 1997, op-ed section.

55. Ibid.

56. For a detailed account of how this occurred in the informatics industry in Brazil, India, and Korea, see Peter Evans, *Embedded Autonomy: States and Industrial Transformation* (Princeton, NJ: Princeton University Press, 1995), esp. chap. 7.

57. Of necessity the descriptions of "the good life" in each chapter will be ideal visions and thus more utopian than practical. Nevertheless, these utopian ideals play an important role in both grounding the moral vision and motivating the behavior of individuals.

58. Theologically this position is supported by an ontological belief in the rational and improvable nature of humanity. The assumption is that God created humanity thus so that they would constantly seek to improve their situation in life. John Bird Sumner describes how this principle "[fills] the world with competitors for support, enforces labour and encourages industry, by the advantages it gives to the industrious and laborious at the expense of the indolent and extravagant" (341). For a fuller exposition of this theological position, see John Bird Sumner, "Reconciling Inequality and God's Purposes in the Free Market," in *Christian Social Ethics: A Reader*, ed. John Atherton (Cleveland, OH: Pilgrim Press, 1994).

59. Andrew Carnegie, "The Problem of the Administration of Wealth," in *The Gospel of Wealth and Other Timely Essays* (New York: Century, 1900); chapter reprinted in *On Moral Business: Classical and Contemporary Resources for Ethics in Economic Life*, ed. Max L. Stackhouse et al. (Grand Rapids: Eerdmans, 1995), 295.

60. Christopher Shannon, *Conspicuous Criticism: Tradition, the Individual, and Culture in American Social Thought, from Veblen to Mills* (Baltimore: Johns Hopkins University Press, 1996), xi–xii.

61. Johnston, *Wealth or Health of Nations*, 24.

62. Friedrich von Hayek, "Individualism: True and False," in *The Essence of Hayek*, ed. Chiaki Nishiyama and Kurt R. Leube (1946; repr., Stanford, CA: Hoover Institution Press, 1984). In this essay Hayek is interested in differentiating between two different interpretations of individualism. His own position, relayed above in the main text, is regarded as "true individualism" and is descended from the thought of John Locke, Bernard Mandeville, David Hume, Josiah Tucker, Adam Smith, Alexis de Tocqueville, and Edmund Burke and is referred to as "the English position." This position is juxtaposed against a different strand of individualism that is represented mainly by French and other Continental writers and is descended from Descartes and rationalism. This second position of individualism is characterized by Hayek as "rationalistic individualism [that] always tends to develop into the opposite of individualism, namely, socialism or collectivism."

63. Hayek's description of individualism, though penned in the late 1940s, has had a lasting effect on the development of neoliberal values and ideology. In fact, Hayek has been referred to as "the 'pope' of neoliberalism." For a more detailed description of Hayek's influence in the development of neoliberalism, see Jung Mo Sung, "Evil in the Free Market Mentality," in *The Return of the Plague* (London: SCM Press, 1997).

64. Hayek, "Individualism," 135.

65. Max Weber, *The Protestant Ethic and the Spirit of Capitalism*, trans. Talcott Parsons (1930; repr., London: Routledge, 1992).

66. Bethell, *Noblest Triumph*, 11.

67. For a more detailed account of how this happened, see Johnston, *Wealth or Health of Nations*, chap. 3.

68. Brian Griffiths, "Christianizing the Market," in *Christian Social Ethics: A Reader*, ed. John Atherton (Cleveland, OH: Pilgrim Press, 1994), 363.

69. Michael Novak, "Text 19: The Spirit of Democratic Capitalism," in *Christian Social Ethics: A Reader*, ed. John Atherton (Cleveland, OH: Pilgrim Press, 1994), 375–76. Excerpt from original first published as Michael Novak, *The Spirit of Democratic Capitalism* (New York: American Enterprise Institute/Simon & Schuster, 1982).

70. For a more detailed description of this historic shift, see Michael Novak, "Wealth and Virtue: The Development of Christian Economic Teaching," chap. 3 in *The Capitalist Spirit: Toward a Religious Ethic of Wealth Creation* (San Francisco: Institute for Contemporary Studies Press, 1990).

71. Ibid., 70–71.

72. Ibid., 79.

73. M. Friedman, *Capitalism and Freedom*, 35–36.

4

Globalization as Social Development

Reformation Attempts of Social Equity Liberalism

Despite the ascendancy of the neoliberal model of globalization to a position of political and economic hegemony, it has not received unqualified support. Not even all proponents of capitalist globalization share the ardent neoliberal confidence in the market's invisible hand. Proponents of the second theory of globalization, the development perspective, share confidence in the neoclassical principles outlined earlier, but also recognize a certain responsibility on the part of governments to protect and care for the most marginalized members of society. This recognition leads to a different understanding of the kind of public policy measures needed to shape the globalization process, an understanding rooted in the traditions of social equity liberalism that have heavily informed European public policy as well as certain periods of postwar U.S. politics. The hallmarks of this position, which are democracy and a strong state, are still prominent in certain political venues such as the social democracy parties of Europe and within elements of the U.S. Democratic party. The present triumph of neoliberalism is much more about the political power of big business to achieve its will than it is about any genuine consensus among political economists.

To identify this second position, I will draw on a subset of the development community who have come to value social development as a way to identify aspects of globalization and development theory that should be front and center in theory and practice. The people who share this perspective largely work in agencies, institutions, and nongovernmental organizations that hold a certain common assumption of how the development of the "two-thirds" world should take place. While some perspectives on how development should occur arise from neoliberal economic growth models,[1] the position that is identified here as social development is rooted in Nobel prize-winning economist Amartya Sen's "capability" approach.[2] This approach argues that the "development" of people in the global South must move beyond a strictly economic analysis of the problem of poverty to address requisite social, cultural, educational, and health needs as part of a holistic approach known as social development. This position is strongly associated with the United Nations Development Programme as evidenced in this excerpt from its *Human Development Report 1999*:

> Human development is the process of enlarging people's choices—not just choices among different detergents, television channels or car models but the choices that are created by expanding human capabilities and functionings—what people do and can do in their lives. At all levels of development a few capabilities are essential for human development, without which many choices in life would not be available. These capabilities are to lead long and healthy lives, to be knowledgeable and to have access to the resources needed for a decent standard of living—and these are reflected in the human development index. But many additional choices are valued by people. These include political, social, economic and cultural freedom, a sense of community, opportunities for being creative and productive, and self-respect and human rights. Yet human development is more than just achieving these capabilities; it is also the process of pursuing them in a way that is equitable, participatory, productive and sustainable.[3]

While the perspective identified in this second theoretical position on globalization does not represent all perspectives within the development community, in order to distinguish it from the other three perspectives in this study, it will be referred to as the "development perspective." Because a persuasive defense of social development is now being offered through the World Bank and the United Nations Development Programme (UNDP), their literature will provide specific textual sources for the characterizations presented here.

With regard to members of the development community, the voices represented in this study are mainly the voices of those who are in the position of giving aid (rather than receiving aid). This is significant because a level of unexamined power and authority accompanies this position that must be acknowledged as part of its social location. People who work for the World Bank or the United Nations Development Programme, even if they come from "two-thirds" world countries, are in a qualitatively different social location than the people who are on the receiving end of development aid. The power and authority associated with the positions of development workers afford them an epistemological vantage point different from that of the people with whom they work.[4] People who promote the model of development highlighted in this study are primarily either Western or "Western indigenous elites."[5] As in the neoliberal position, access to education (often advanced higher education) is an important aspect of the social location of people in the development community.

Like the neoliberal ideology we examined in chapter 3, social equity liberalism is a variant ideology within neoclassical economics. Broadly speaking, the public policy priorities of social equity liberalism include state-centered efforts to stimulate the economy and provide a social safety net for failures of the market to address politically desirable goals. The theoretical roots of social equity liberalism trace back to John Maynard Keynes, the twentieth-century British economist.

This theoretical model of globalization supported by members of the development community is held more widely in international circles than in the United States. Examining the modern history of development theory, that is, the intentional development of the "two-thirds" world as it has progressed since the Second World War, helps to show why this position is aligned more closely with international voices than with the U.S. business or governmental communities. While the basic assumptions of neoclassical economics are still operative, here we will look specifically at the ideology of social equity liberalism with an eye toward how this worldview differs from neoliberalism. We also will point out the important similarities that exist between the two positions. As we will see, the values of responsibility, progress, and equity mark the development community's vision of globalization and offer a different perspective on the nature of the good life.

Contextualizing Twentieth-Century Development Theory

"Development" was the regnant doctrine that replaced colonialism as the former colonies achieved their independence in the 1940s and '50s.[6] This "era of development" was launched by President Harry Truman's 1949 inaugural address.[7] In one of the most defining moments in history, Truman constructed evaluative categories of difference that have served to separate and judge the lifestyles, choices, and cultural patterns of people in the global South for the past half-century.[8] In his speech, Truman articulated the two most dominant convictions behind development theory. The first, humanity's moral obligation to help the less fortunate, provided the impetus. The second, the market's ability to provide greater wealth and prosperity, provided the means:

> More than half the people of the world are living in conditions approaching misery. Their food is inadequate, they are victims of disease. Their economic life is primitive and stagnant. Their poverty is a handicap and a threat both to

> them and to more prosperous areas. For the first time in history humanity possesses the knowledge and the skill to relieve the suffering of these people . . . I believe that we should make available to peace-loving peoples the benefits of our store of technical knowledge in order to help them realize their aspirations for a better life. . . . What we envisage is a program of development based on the concepts of democratic fair dealing. . . . Greater production is the key to prosperity and peace. And the key to greater production is a wider and more vigorous application of modern scientific and technical knowledge.[9]

Confidence in the market's ability to promote and achieve development in the "two-thirds" world betrays the neoclassical underpinnings of the development position. The economic theory that underlies development policy is the same neoclassical theory that promotes growth and trade as the primary engines of wealth creation. Remember that for the neoclassicists, wealth creation is the foundation of economic stability. The assumption is that economic stability (and all that "new" wealth) consequently promotes humanitarian well-being and that the "two-thirds" world will benefit from achieving parity with the economic status of the "first" world.

Like all who place the neoclassical economic paradigm foremost, development theorists in the immediate postwar period defined development in very narrow terms. In the 1950s and '60s, it was defined almost exclusively in economic terms. The major means toward achieving economic development was known as "import-substitution industrialization." In simple terms, this theory promoted the development of a domestic industrial sector that would supply the needs of the domestic market while simultaneously building a strong domestic base. The longer-term goal was aimed toward expanding the industrial sector to the point of generating surplus goods to trade on the lucrative export markets.[10] This movement eventually extended beyond the industrial sector to the agricultural markets, where the aim to increase crop yields through chemical fertilization, modern irrigation, and new high-yielding varieties of seeds sparked the "Green Revolution."[11] The motivating economic idea behind this stage of development theory was growth. The argument was that increasing the industrial and agricultural output of "developing" countries would allow them to become more self-sufficient as well as infuse their economies with cash as their excess goods were traded on the world market.

By the 1970s, however, it was clear that poverty was not being eliminated in the "developing" world, despite rising GNP figures. For the first time, skepticism arose regarding the efficacy of the official measures of development that focused exclusively on the aggregate national output without consideration of distributional equity of goods and resources. This skepticism gave rise to a new mode of development theory that focused on "redistribution with growth" and "basic needs."[12] According to authors Ray Kiely and Phil Marfleet, "These strategies argued that growth should remain a priority of development strategies, but that this should be combined with increased attention to those (basically the poor) who had been marginalised."[13] New development strategies emphasized rural development and agricultural growth as well as "developing labour-intensive technologies, which would both enhance labour productivity and ensure some 'trickle down' of wealth as more people were employed."[14] These strategies were, unfortunately, more well-intentioned than effective, and the massive debt crisis of the 1980s brought the most radical shift yet in development theory.

In the face of the potential default of numerous countries that were unable to meet their balance of payments in the early 1980s, confusion erupted around the world as economists, politicians, and businesspeople argued about solutions. Ultimately the neoliberals won the day by arguing that social equity liberalism and its reliance on government regulations (imports, tariffs, licensure) and control (i.e., not enough competition) had overburdened and stagnated the economy. New loans were offered to troubled countries that would allow them to meet their balance of payments. These loans, however, were contingent upon the acceptance of macroeconomic measures aimed at currency stabilization and public-spending cuts.[15]

Within the development community, this neoliberal "solution" to the debt crisis was not seen as a solution at all. Kiely and Marfleet argue the development case against neoliberalism well:

> Neo-liberalism is characterised by an excessive optimism concerning the role of market forces in promoting development. It assumes that nation-states can relatively easily break into export markets on the basis of their 'comparative advantage', but the reality is somewhat different. Producers in the Third World in particular face non-tariff protectionist barriers in First World markets, and even in a situation of free trade, competition often remains unequal. First World producers monopolise the most advanced technology, research and development, marketing practices and so on.[16]

Indeed, the neoliberal "reforms" of the 1980s only managed to increase the indebtedness of most "developing" countries, while their citizens bore the brunt of the structural adjustment policies that eroded what little public support had been established for education, health care, unemployment, and other social programs.[17] Furthermore, while the intentional devaluation of currencies may have helped in the process of economic stabilization, the human toll it wrought raises serious ethical questions about the moral acceptability of such economic tools. In most cases, poor people only became poorer when their currency bought less. While the middle and upper classes might have been squirming uncomfortably as they tightened their proverbial belts, the crushing poverty of the lower classes sent tens of thousands of rural workers into the cities looking for work. The subsequent overcrowding in major metropolitan areas reached unprecedented proportions in the 1980s and '90s, bringing with it a host of problems, including waste disposal, homelessness, and inadequate sewage, not to mention rending the fabric of families as husbands and wives were often forced to work in different communities as they sought enough income to care for their families.

The failure of neoliberalism to end poverty, and even to make life much better in many countries, brought with it an increased skepticism during the 1990s about the efficacy of this model of development. The development lexicon grew considerably as growing numbers of grassroots groups around the world pushed for sustainable development and called for debt forgiveness and an end to the multilateral organizations that control global finances (the World Trade Organization, International Monetary Fund, and World Bank). Even within mainstream development agencies such as the United Nations Development Programme and the World Bank, serious questions have been raised about accepted development strategies.[18]

Ideological Origins of Social Development

A brief exploration of modern political economy yields a number of insights that are helpful in our examination of globalization theories. First, while there have always been a heterogeneity of positions and theories regarding political economy, the neoclassical model spelled out at the beginning of part 2 has historically predominated in the Western world.[19] Second, within neoclassical economics there has been a century-long divide between two ideologically distinct models of political economy—laissez-faire and social equity liberalism. Third, economics as a discipline has been better at explaining the market than predicting it. Consequently, the rise and fall of various schools of thought within neoclassical economics reflects a predilection toward those theorists whose ideas best explain a given set of financial circumstances.

As noted earlier, the theorist who pioneered the development of social equity liberalism was John Maynard Keynes. His economic theory resonated with governmental officials who were desperate to address the social inequality and poverty generated by the Great Depression. He provided an economic model that seemed to explain why the Depression occurred and promised a way out of unemployment and a road to stimulation for economic growth. These ideas were seized upon at the end of the Second World War as the fear of another postwar depression loomed large.

Born in Britain in 1883, Keynes was the son of a well-known economist, John Neville Keynes. He enjoyed the privileges of the bourgeoisie and the honors that accompany brilliance. He attended Eton and then King's College at Cambridge. A brief stint in India in the civil service followed his undergraduate work before he returned to Cambridge and the beginning of his career as an economist. Over his lifetime Keynes served in the Treasury, edited the esteemed *Economic Journal* for thirty-three years, represented Britain on numerous economic and peace delegations, wrote economic treatises, and taught economics at Cambridge, all the while managing to make himself rich by speculating on the international markets.

Keynes was indeed an original and independent thinker. As he was working on his pivotal work, *The General Theory of Employment, Interest and Money*, he wrote to George Bernard Shaw, who had suggested he reread Marx and Engels:

> To understand my state of mind, you have to know that I believe myself to be writing a book on economic theory which will largely revolutionize—not, I suppose at once, but in the course of the next ten years—the way the world thinks about economic problems. . . . I can't expect you or anyone else to believe this at the present stage. But for myself I don't merely hope what I say—in my own mind, I'm quite sure.[20]

Indeed, Keynes is widely regarded to have done just that. Economist Robert Heilbroner does regard *The General Theory* as "revolutionary," claiming that it "stood economics on its head, very much as *The Wealth of Nations* and *Capital* had done."[21]

This was possible because the models of economic theory then current not only failed to explain why the world was in the middle of a phenomenal depression, but also failed to offer any way out. Keynes's brilliance lay in his ability to see beyond the limitations of the classical economic theory in which he had been trained. He was able to envision an alternative economic theory that not only explained what was happening to the world economy, but also offered practical policy recommendations for jump-starting a stagnating economy.

The State's Role in Stimulating the Economy

Traditional economic wisdom held that booms and busts were part of the "natural" flow of economic activity. More simply put, money flows through our economy in the forms of wages coming in and purchases going out. Any excess money that is not used for consumer goods (food, shelter, leisure) still reenters the larger economy either through investment or savings (used by banks for loans). Depressions happen when businesses do not use the money available in savings so that it sits idly in a bank—the "flow" is interrupted. The natural cycles of boom and bust have been described as a "seesaw" of savings and investment. As economist Robert Heilbroner describes it:

> The seesaw theory seemed to promise that there would be an automatic safety switch built right into the business cycle itself; that when savings became too

abundant, they would become cheaper to borrow, and that thereby business would be encouraged to invest. The economy might contract, said the theory, but it seemed certain to rebound.[22]

Unfortunately, during the Great Depression the rebound failed to materialize. Interest rates fell, but investment remained stagnant. Keynes's insight into this economic conundrum was that there was no automatic safety mechanism. Rather than a seesaw always seeking to balance itself, the economy was more like an elevator going up and down, or just standing still. That is exactly what the economy in the 1930s was doing—just standing still. Keynes argued that if private enterprise was unwilling or unable to initiate investment in the economy, then someone else needed to fulfill that essential economic role. Keynes proposed that government should become that someone.

Essentially Keynes argued that governmental investment in public-works projects was capable of playing a similar function that private investment traditionally played in a market economy. Namely, these public-works projects would provide employment for the large numbers of unemployed that would unclog the hole that had plugged up the economic flow. He even argued that mass public employment had proven successful in the past; we need only look at the role that pyramid-building played in ancient Egypt and cathedral-building played during the Middle Ages to see the positive effects of large-scale public-works projects.

The ravages of hyper-unemployment in the United States had already dictated work relief as a political necessity. So when *The General Theory* came out in 1936, it did not so much prescribe a cure as reinforce a course of action that was already being pursued. However, Keynes provided what the U.S. government had not yet developed: an explanation of the problem and a defense of its actions.[23] Keynes's theories were further justified after the start of World War II as governments became the major economic investors. Between clothing, housing, and feeding the troops and producing military hardware, the U.S. government's concerns shifted from unemployment to a labor shortage.[24] The war economy did more for ending the Depression than any peacetime measures that were attempted. This fact went a long way in supporting Keynes's theory that government investment was a necessary stabilizing force in the unpredictable natural flow of economic activity.

Make no mistake, Keynes's approach was still firmly rooted in neoclassical economic theory with its emphasis on growth, scientific analysis, individualism, and the free market. What he offered was a correction to the laissez-faire economists who argued that the markets worked best when governments left them alone. In broad terms, Keynes's justification of the necessity of governments sometimes to take an active role in directing and controlling markets was his most lasting contribution to economic theory.

The State's Responsibility to Provide a Social Safety Net

The Keynesian economic model has been labeled "social equity" liberalism because it exhibits concern for the devastating human effects that accompany unemployment and inflation, particularly among the poorer classes in society. Keynes encouraged economic relief for the poor because he argued that a higher percentage of the money that entered the economy at lower levels (i.e., the poor and lower-middle classes) reentered the economy through consumption. This disparity is due to the fact that the poor and lower-middle classes spend a higher proportion of their income on necessities, leaving a smaller margin for savings, while the expenses of the rich are not so variable.[25] In other words, if more money is made available to the poor and working classes, it is more likely to enter the economy and stimulate needed growth. Consequently, public policy measures that follow a "Keynesian" model promote government spending that encourages "employment of people at the low end of income distribution. Getting the most for the money is accomplished by providing income to those whose marginal propensity to consume is much higher than it is with the wealthy, which would be more effective in generating full employment."[26]

We have already seen that proponents of development theory have pursued a number of different public policy approaches over the years. The unifying factor has been the shared neoclassical confidence that growth and trade will bring development to the "two-thirds" world. The two primary public policy concerns of social equity liberalism elaborated here—recognition of the positive role that governments can play in stabilizing market economies and concern for the general welfare of people—are what set the development perspective highlighted in this study apart from neoliberal models of development.

Viewing Globalization from a Development Perspective

The particular strand of development theory on which we will focus in mapping the globalization debates is the strand based on a Keynesian or social equity model of economics. As we have already seen, both the neoliberal and the social equity model follow neoclassical economic theory—the differences between these two positions are not economic. Where these two ideologies differ is in their public policy assessments about the role that government or nation-states should play in the market arena. In essence, their differences are political rather than economic. These political differences shape the theory of globalization that emerges from each of these positions in distinctly different ways.

The social equity development model that we are examining here is well reflected in the work of the United Nations Development Programme and its annual *Human Development Report* (*HDR*). It is a particular branch of development theory associated with "human-centered" development.[27] This report is remarkable because it utilizes an alternative indicator of "success." Rather than focusing on the traditional, but flawed, Gross National Product (GNP), which is the most commonly accepted indicator of economic health,[28] the *HDR* has adopted the controversial Human Development Index (HDI). The HDI was developed as an alternative measure of development and is based on three components—indicators of longevity, education, and income per head. In this way the HDI expands, somewhat, beyond the narrow economic parameters of the GNP. Economist Amartya Sen comments that the best thing about the HDI is that it has stimulated people's interest in reading the *Human Development Report*, which is a much more complex representation and critical analysis of the process of development around the world.[29]

The publication of the *Human Development Report* began in 1990 as a response to the development theory of recent decades that focused exclusively on economic development almost to the detriment of human development. The intention of the *HDR* was to broaden the public's understanding and the public discussion of just what constituted "development." There was a definite sense that the driving focus of development work must shift from economics and economic well-being to a broader and more culturally informed understanding of humanity and human well-being.

From the development position's ideological perspective, globalization is a knitting together of the seams that separate people. It is the opportunity to improve the lives of the world's poor by offering them new opportunities for growth and development. Globalization is about sharing the privileges and lifestyles that have traditionally been limited to the "first" world with all people of the world; it is about improving the standard of living for everyone. Proponents of this position believe that globalization is the way in which we will be able to improve education, health care, and other social services—by allowing the efficiency of the market to improve these sectors. Globalization is the power of the Internet to connect people around the world, for research, educational and training purposes, advocacy, public policy formation and information sharing, as well as social and entertainment purposes. Globalization is about our ability to transcend the borders that separate people in order to be able to improve lives. In many ways, we can see that the development community understands the globalization agenda as very similar to its own development agenda.

When development is understood, as it is by the World Bank, as a comprehensive process of transforming society and moving away from "traditional" ways of being and doing to more "modern" ways, then development becomes synonymous with globalization.[30] Helping others help themselves and achieve a "better" life, a life that is marked by better health, jobs, water, and food is the goal of development; proponents of this position also understand this to be the task of globalization. In a sense, development theorists have elided the separate tasks of development and globalization in such a way that they see development as a globalization process and the appropriate task of globalization as social development. This fusion of the responsibilities of development with the process of globalization can be seen in the mandate to eliminate poverty. While this used to be understood as one of the primary goals of development, it is now a task that is also associated with globalization. In the words of the *Human Development Report 1999*:

> This era of globalization is opening many opportunities for millions of people around the world. Increased trade, new technologies, foreign investments, expanding media and Internet connections are fuelling economic growth and human advance. All this offers enormous potential to eradicate poverty in the 21st century—to continue the unprecedented progress in the 20th century. We have more wealth and technology—and more commitment to global community—than ever before.[31]

It is not that either development or globalization ought to be working toward eradicating poverty; rather, there is a sense in which the opportunities that define globalization are the very requirements development theorists believe will enable social development. Likewise, development is seen as an aspect of globalization as the world continues "to shrink from a size medium to a size small."[32] As James Wolfensohn, president of the World Bank, has said, "Globalization can be more than the unleashed forces of the global market. It can also be the unleashing of our combined effort and expertise to reach global solutions."[33] Global cooperation and global governance is one way the World Bank envisions globalization as aiding it in addressing its mandate to reduce poverty. In recent years the Bank staff have become more aware of the necessity of a model of development that focuses on the institutional, structural, and social dimensions of development. Joseph Stiglitz, former chief economist at the World Bank, has indicated four main focal areas through which development can bring about the transformation of society: raising living standards (as evidenced by GDP, health, and literacy); reducing poverty; strengthening the environment through development models and policies that are sustainable; and establishing durable, deep-rooted policies undergirding all societal transformations so that they will withstand "the vicissitudes sometimes accompanying democratic processes."[34]

The Development Position's Assessment of the Dangers of Globalization

Those who espouse the development position also recognize that the current neoliberal model of globalization differs from their view of globalization as social development. With this recognition comes a critique of the downsides of globalization in its current incarnation. The *Human Development Report 1999* is careful to present an even-handed assessment of the reigning model of globalization, promoting its more productive and useful aspects while questioning and challenging some of its dangers. People who work in the field of development are brought into daily contact with the vagaries of the prevailing neoliberal model of globalization presented in chapter 3. The social location of big business may allow its proponents to exist more than once-removed from poverty and the downsides of economic policy, but the social location of development workers usually does not. While members of the development community are mostly from privileged backgrounds, they often live and work in close proximity with the poorest of the poor. Even when development workers are one step removed from the poverty, they are still privy to the stories and experiences of various communities who have experienced the harsher effects of neoliberal globalization and the inequality it generates. The *HDR 1999* focuses on three main aspects of the current form of globalization that threaten successful human development—rising inequality, the marginalization of caring labor, and growing insecurity.

Rising Inequality as Evidence of Injustice

Proponents of the development perspective argue that one of the most significant dangers of the current model of neoliberal globalization is that the benefits of economic growth, particularly in "developing" countries, are far from distributed equally.[35] In fact,

> [m]ore than 80 countries still have per capita incomes lower than they were a decade or more ago. While 40 countries have sustained average per capita income growth of more than 3% a year since 1990, 55 countries, mostly in Sub-Saharan Africa and Eastern Europe and the Commonwealth of Independent States (CIS), have had declining per capita incomes. . . . Inequality between countries has also increased. The income gap between the fifth of the world's people living in the richest countries and the fifth in the poorest was 74 to 1 in 1997, up from 60 to 1 in 1990 and 30 to 1 in 1960.[36]

Indeed, a number of factors play into this pattern of unequal distribution, including graft, corruption, and thievery among some of the political and wealthy elite in "developing" countries, as well as the self-fulfilling prophecy of foreign investors' willingness to support countries that develop a track record of success. While the reasons that inequality is growing under globalization are certainly not unimportant, they do not change the moral assessment that globalization has been deepening injustice around the world.

Marginalization of Caring Labor as Evidence of Disregard for Social Well-Being

In addition to the growing inequalities within and between nations, the development perspective is deeply concerned about the growing neglect and indifference toward the tasks of care and nurturance in our societies.

Traditionally, in most cultures, caring labor has been the responsibility of women. As difficult financial situations are forcing women to increase the time they spend working in positions of paid labor, their unpaid and often unacknowledged caring labor is marginalized even further. The development perspective recognizes that care is "the invisible heart of human development."[37] Not only is advanced industrial capitalism threatening the ability of women to continue performing caring labor, but the neoliberal economic policies are forcing governments to cut back on state-supported care services.

Growing Insecurity as Evidence of Rising Social Disorder

Globalization has brought with it a particular set of growing insecurities, including economic, job-related, health-related, cultural, personal, environmental, and political insecurities. These insecurities affect multiple facets of human life and represent a rising social disorder that is increasingly characterizing the contemporary world.

Increased Economic Insecurity as a Destabilizing Social Factor. Economic insecurity is the direct result of the increasing volatility of the market that is apparent in the rapid growth and recent fall of financial markets.[38] More than $1.5 trillion is exchanged in the world's currency markets each day, up from $10 to $20 billion in the 1970s.[39] Such huge volumes of currency flowing in and out of countries' coffers make them more susceptible to the kinds of financial chaos that struck Indonesia, Thailand, and other east Asian "tigers." Journalist William Greider described how the vagaries of globalization and the market affected Thailand:

> Three decades of rapid growth lifted incomes generally, but also deepened the inequalities. The richest 20 percent now claimed an even greater share of national incomes—56 percent—while the bottom 40 percent had lost ground, from 17 to 12 percent. Labor unions were weak and fractured and severely restricted by law, but a working-class consciousness was slowly, haltingly developing among the former peasants who have become new industrial workers. Yet, as they found voice and pushed for improvement, better wages and working conditions, Thailand bumped up against the market realities—the easy flight of investment capital to cheaper locales.[40]

While the 1990s saw enormous investment increases in a number of these markets, with money freely flowing in and bolstering their economies, when the tides turned and the flow started outward in 1997, it seemed as if nothing could slow the hemorrhaging. Lawrence Summers, former U.S. treasury secretary, likened the flows to jet planes, observing that "jets bring enormous efficiencies and benefits to the world—but . . . the crashes are more spectacular than ever."[41] The enormous volatility of capital flows in recent years is based on the same impetus that caused short-term investing to explode in the 1990s. Namely, day traders, hedge fund managers, and speculators of all sorts are out to gain as much profit as they can in as short a time as possible. Emerging markets represent a very high rate of return, precisely because the potential for failure or crisis is high. Trading in foreign securities in the United States was 2 percent of the GNP in 1975; by 1997 it had risen to 213 percent.[42] Make no mistake, capital flows into "developing" countries have certainly contributed considerably to the economic growth of many countries; the danger comes when speculation overtakes sound investment and threatens the livelihood of millions of poor and working people who most often bear the brunt of collapsed economies and overinflated currencies. As the *HDR 1999* reports, "The human impacts are severe and are likely to persist long after economic recovery."[43]

Increased Job Insecurity as a Result of Global Competition. Job insecurity has been an increasing consequence of globalization. The policies of downsizing and the externalization of costs that took hold in the last decade have meant that many workers around the world have lost their jobs. In many ways what these policies represent is the newest form of corporate globalization, what Bennett Harrison has termed the "lean and mean" corporation.[44] What Harrison is referring to is an emerging paradigm of networked production that he calls "concentration without centralization."[45] In this new paradigm the concentration of power and authority is still vested in the transnational corporation itself, but the corporations are moving toward organizational decentralization. The two key factors of corporate transnational decentralization are downsizing and outsourcing.

Downsizing refers to the process of dividing permanent or "core" jobs from contingent or "peripheral" jobs. According to author David Korten: "The larger scheme is to trim the firm's in-house operations down to its "core competencies"—generally the finance, marketing, and proprietary technology functions that represent the firm's primary sources of economic power. The staffing of these functions is reduced to a bare minimum and consolidated within the corporate headquarters."[46]

Then the contingent work is subcontracted out to the lowest bidder, often in low-wage "two-thirds" world countries in a process known as outsourcing. Harrison makes note of this "dark side of flexible production" that produces a two-tiered labor system providing stable employment, an ample salary, and benefits for the few while adding to the problem of "working poverty" for a large number of former corporate employees.[47]

The precariousness of employment for many contemporary workers is representative of a new atmosphere or culture within which business and employment decisions are being made. This new business culture has been referred to as a "shared phenomenal world" that reflects a new consciousness rooted in the shared knowledge that factories and jobs are no longer bound by physical or national ties to particular locales.[48] This new phenomenal world is considered by some to be one of the markers of globalization as the technological advances that draw people closer together also function to compress the traditional distance that formerly separated time and space.[49] In other words, our world is now experiencing a "time/space distantiation" in which space is being overcome by the technological advances that now connect people across traditional "space."[50] Political economist Ankie Hoogvelt argues that this shared phenomenal world is facilitating the emergence of a global market discipline that goes beyond the traditional global marketplace.[51]

Awareness of global competition also contributes to this new global market discipline, which is driving the incredible growth of power experienced by transnational corporations in recent decades. This knowledge has been internalized by workers, managers, and governments as a particular kind of discipline that guides behavior and attitudes. Global market discipline encourages governments to offer tax breaks to transnational corporations and to waive environmental and labor regulations in order to attract business. It discourages workers from labor organizing or otherwise causing any waves with management in fear that the corporation will simply relocate.

Rising Health Insecurity as a Neglected Consequence of Increased Mobility. With the increased travel and migration that have accompanied globalization, the spread of diseases around the world has generated growing concern for the security of humanity's physical health. While HIV/AIDS is being treated rather effectively in "first" world countries, the prohibitive expense of the drugs has turned it into a poor person's disease. Ninety-five percent of the 16,000 people infected each day live in "developing" countries.[52] The rapid spread of the SARS virus as well as avian influenza also has raised deep concerns within the medical community about its ability to continue to contain outbreaks of new virulent and deadly viruses.

Cultural Insecurity as a Result of an Expanding Consumer Culture. Cultural insecurity has been growing as "first"-world media outlets aggressively seek to build their markets in the "developing" world. The popularity of MTV and American television and movies around the world has increased the access that advertisers have to local communities in remote areas. The global entertainment and advertising industries are each working in different ways toward the same purposes—the most obvious being increased profit for their parent companies through the sale of their products, whether CDs, videos, soda, or antiperspirant. The subtler goal toward which these media enterprises strive is the creation of the global citizen, the global consumer, and the homogenization of culture.

In the 1980s advertisers argued that there was really no need to pay attention to the differences of culture and taste that separate consumers. They argued for the creation of the global ad campaign because, after all, a headache is a headache and an aspirin, an aspirin.[53] Theodore Levitt, professor at Harvard Business School, argued that "the products and methods of the industrialized world play a single tune for all the world and all the world eagerly dances to it" and that corporations should think of themselves as global rather than multinational.[54] While the multinational corporation adapts itself to its local environment, the global corporation "sells the same things in the same way everywhere."[55] Although this marketing philosophy was later recognized as simplistic and inadequate, it has certainly made inroads in the field as advertisements for de Beers, Levi's, Bennetton, and other transnational corporations illustrate. This is just one more example of the way in which the media culture continues to move toward an annihilation of particularity in this era of globalization. Advertising and public relations campaigns continue to become more aggressive as they seek out new and unexploited venues of access to consumers and potential consumers.

Personal Insecurity as Indicative of Economic Marginalization. The *Human Development Report 1999* also notes that criminals are reaping the benefits of globalization as increased mobilization and communication also have helped increase illicit trade in the form of drugs, women, weapons, and laundered money.[56] *The Economist* recently reported on the trafficking of women by organized crime in Eastern Europe: "Conservative estimates put the number of women smuggled each year into the European Union and the more prosperous Central European countries at 300,000, though not all end up in the sex trade. But the figure could well be double that."[57]

The sex-trade industry is estimated to be worth $9 billion a year in Europe alone.[58] In 1995 illegal drugs were estimated to make up 8 percent of world trade, surpassing the motor vehicle, iron, and steel industries.[59] Rising crime rates and weapons trading also have accompanied the sexual slavery of women and the drugs trade, all of which are contributing to growing feelings of personal insecurity in many parts of the world.

Environmental Insecurity as a Threat to Survival. Environmental degradation, perpetrated by almost all human inhabitants of the earth, has finally led to an uncertain and insecure future for our planet. While the industrial revolution certainly wrought the most considerable damage to our air, our water, and the land itself, we cannot merely point our fingers and walk away from the problem as if it were someone else's mess to clean up. All people in the "first" world are voracious consumers. In the United States alone, each person "consumes about 136 pounds of resources a week, while 2,000 pounds of waste are discarded to support that consumption. This waste consists of everything from paper to CO_2, from agricultural wastes to effluents, from packaging material to nitrous oxides."[60] Our fast food, packaged food, disposable diapers, soft drinks, and other garbage that we generate are filling up landfills so quickly that some large cities are having to pay other people to take their garbage. But it is not just our insatiable daily consumer habits that threaten the environment—it is also the structural problem of our industries not being required to assume responsibility for the long-term environmental impacts of their products.[61]

Of course, the "first" world is hardly solely responsible for the environmental problems facing the world today. The "two-thirds" world is currently going through stages of development through which the "first" world passed years ago. Environmental laws are considerably more lax in most "developing" countries. The inability of metropolitan areas to keep up with their own rate of growth have led to unmanageable smog and pollution in places such as Mexico City and Sao Paolo, Brazil, as well as open sewage and dangerous filth in cities such as Accra, Ghana. Additionally, with growing population rates, the traditional practice of collecting firewood by poor and indigenous peoples in many countries is beginning to put a strain on the resources in some areas.

Political Insecurity as a Result of Deepening Global Instability. The collective effect of many of these forms of rising insecurities around the world has led to "the rise of social tensions that threaten political stability and community cohesion."[62] Threats to cultural integrity and independence have led to violent civil strife in the Balkans, Rwanda, and Burundi. The continued rise of global inequalities is engendering larger and larger groups of people who are dissatisfied with the current model of globalization that is being promoted by big business. The development community has taken a strong stand regarding globalization and the growing insecurities that threaten the stability and livelihood of the whole earth community. Institutions such as the World Bank and the United Nations Development Programme have not only questioned the prevailing "wisdom" of the dominant form of globalization,[63] but also suggested new policy directions that proponents of the development position believe can help turn globalization onto a more humane path. In other words, proponents of the development position propose a theory of globalization that affirms growth and trade as essential elements of economic development, but they also hold that an adequate theory of globalization will address not only poverty, but also environmental degradation, insecurity, and the rising disregard for personal well-being.

Policy Prescriptions Offered by the Development Community

While the development community recognizes potential problems associated with the neoliberal model of globalization, it still firmly supports the economic agenda of growth and trade as the best antidote to poverty. From the development perspective, what is needed is more oversight and control of the process as a way of minimizing the negative outcomes that have been associated with the neoliberal model. There are three main policy directions that govern the development perspective's move toward a more human-centered form of globalization.

The Importance of Grounding Globalization in Social Transformation

The first policy shift was most notable in the "new development strategy" that Stiglitz proposed for the World Bank in 1998. This new strategy was a bold move for the Bank, as it had criticized the Washington Consensus model of development for some time.[64] Stiglitz argued that the neoliberal model of development focused too heavily on economics, consequently marginalizing other aspects of development that are essential for human thriving. While the new strategy maintained the Bank's historic fight against poverty, it addressed the task with a new and improved toolbox. Namely, it expanded the traditional focus on economics by asserting that development would be successful only if it generated society-wide changes. According to Stiglitz, moving toward social transformation begins with creating a vision of what society should look like and then figuring out how to get there. This emphasis on society-wide transformation is a good step toward narrowing the increasing income and knowledge gaps between the rich and the poor. This approach to development also highlights ownership and participation by local communities and citizens as key elements in successful social transformation.[65]

The Necessity of Stronger Forms of Governance

Issues of governance will undoubtedly play a central role in any new strategies of development promoted by the development position. As the *HDR 1999* points out, "Governance does not mean mere government. It means the framework of rules, institutions and established practices that set limits and give incentives for the behavior of individuals, organizations and firms."[66]

Understood in this way, increased and stronger measures of governance are the means by which the development community proposes to effect lasting change through the transformation of society. The narrow focus on economic development through most of the postwar period has led to the realization that economic wealth alone does not create stability or well-being, particularly when it is concentrated in the hands of a few rather than equitably shared throughout society. The development community believes that stronger governance policies, if adequately supported and followed, will establish stabler and more democratic governments, consequently reining in the corruption and graft that have plagued the former Eastern bloc countries and the "two-thirds" world. Stronger governance also can provide a check on the "casino capitalism" that currently allows any country's currency to become the pawn of speculators and traders whose only interest is in turning a profit.[67] The development community also hopes that stronger governance and increased stability will help to quell domestic and civil strife. In presenting the case for stronger governance, the *HDR 1999* illustrates the fundamental values that the development position promotes through the following set of commitments:

- to global ethics, justice and respect for the human rights of all people
- to human well-being as the end, with open markets and economic growth as means
- to respect for the diverse conditions and needs of each country
- to the accountability of all actors.[68]

Increased Accountability as a Way of Strengthening Democracy

The development position holds that stronger accountability policies are essential if we hope to tame the harsher and more dangerous aspects of globalization. While good governance can stabilize local communities and nation-states, in a globalized world those traditional boundaries are no longer adequate. Transnational corporations and multilateral institutions have created a world in which the traditional boundaries of the nation-state not only are transgressed, but no longer retain much meaning.

In chapter 3 we discussed the origins of corporations as entities originally chartered by the state to perform certain functions. Additionally, corporations provided jobs for a large number of workers and supplied the population with necessary goods and services. For centuries there was a mutually reinforcing interdependence between governments and the economic institutions that they chartered. Granted, these corporations were not social welfare organizations and were always motivated by profit. But it was this move toward multinationalization that marked the transformation of the corporation from the status of a partner of the state to an independent entity that sees itself as transcending the boundaries of traditional nation-states.

Multinational corporations have moved from understanding themselves as institutions embedded within their host country—with civic responsibilities such as paying taxes, following the laws of the countries in which they are located, and not harming people or the environment—to viewing themselves as transnational corporations, independent entities that transcend the nation-state and that are most successful when they have to answer to no one.[69] After all, taxes, environmental laws, tariffs, and health codes only eat into their profit margins. In this new world of the transnational corporation, instrumental rationality becomes not only the dominant philosophy, but the only one. Everything is viewed only in relation to how it can help maximize efficiency and increase profit margins.

Individual countries are not in a position to rein in transnational corporations or even to require that they abide by local environmental and labor regulations. The economic and employment opportunities offered by these corporations are simply too critical for nation-states to enforce their own constitutionally approved regulations. The development community argues that what is needed are "standards and norms that set limits and define responsibilities for all actors."[70] The World Trade Organization offers one model of how global accountability might be structured.

The World Trade Organization functions to facilitate the transfer of goods and services across national borders through the market mechanism of trade. One of the World Trade Organization's major tasks is to introduce international trade standards, because trade often is hampered by the laws and regulations of individual countries. Currently the WTO is set up so that those international trade standards supersede the laws of any individual member countries. While the development community admits there are some problems with the way the WTO is currently set up,[71] it generally supports the idea of a world trade organization and would like to see a number of other global accountability organizations, such as a global central bank, a world environment agency, a world investment trust, an international criminal court, and a broader United Nations system.[72] The development community believes that the only way truly to ensure accountability for trade, business, and corporations that transcend national borders is to create concomitant institutions of global governance that will establish and enforce commonly agreed-upon guidelines and rules that protect human and environmental rights while still promoting human development.

Ultimately what we can see in this position is a theory of globalization that understands its vision to be one of the social development of the world's people. This vision is rooted in an awareness and concern for the crushing poverty that dominates our globe and the death, disease, and misery that poverty engenders. This second theory of globalization holds firmly to the neoclassical principles of economic growth and trade as the most expedient and efficient way to alleviate poverty. At the same time, people who work in the development community are cognizant of and sensitive to the pitfalls and dangers that accompany widespread growth and change and they are committed to addressing these problems as they work toward implementing their vision of globalization.

A Development Vision of the Good Life

Two important aspects of the development position's theory of globalization need to be recalled as we turn toward an explication of the values of this position. First, the development position holds an extreme amount of confidence in markets and capitalism and, indeed, is convinced that the economic opportunities of capitalism will eventually support and sustain economic development around the world. This market confidence betrays the neoclassical economic foundations of the development perspective. At the same time, the second thing we need to recall are the ways in which this position is distinctly different from the neoliberalism we examined in chapter 3.

From an outside perspective, it is apparent that both of these positions are ultimately working toward the same goals—growth, opportunity, efficiency, increased wealth, production, and trade—goals that can be traced back to neoclassical economic theory. Yet each of these positions follows a different path for how those goals should be achieved; in fact, they even hold a different understanding of why these goals should be achieved. While the means toward achieving similar goals may not seem to make much difference from a utilitarian point of view, these differences are not insignificant from a moral point of view. We must remember that the economic statistics and indicators used by economists, businesspeople, and politicians to argue for different public policy approaches to markets represent people and their lives. These statistics are not mere numbers; they reflect the job losses, hunger, death, disease, and poverty of countless marginalized people across the globe. From this perspective the means toward how we achieve an agreed-upon set of goals matters immensely. Furthermore, from the perspective of someone who believes that humanity's continued thriving is intimately tied up in our relationship with the earth and all of creation, I would argue that our understanding of why we seek to achieve those same goals also is morally significant.

Of course, this position has grown over the last few decades beyond a narrow focus on economics as the sole indicator of development and well-being. The development community's sustained interaction with people and cultures in "developing" countries has taught it that global human development also incorporates other aspects of human well-being; namely, culture, education, literacy, health, and the environment. Attention to a broader array of development concerns has generated a vision of the "good life" from this perspective that upholds three primary values—responsibility, progress, and equity.

Responsibility as the Context for Moral Agency

Examination of moral agency in the development perspective yields strong faith in the position that people possess a certain amount of responsibility toward their fellow human beings and increasingly toward the environment. Broadly speaking, responsibility reflects a sense of "obligation and accountability for personal attitudes and actions."[73] However, attention to responsibility in this position is focused more on social and communal accountability than on individual actions. The specific collective nature of responsibility reflected in the development position hearkens back to Truman's inaugural speech of 1949 and his reminder to the American people of our moral obligation to help the world's poor.

The development attitudes that we have been examining in this study reflect the distinct perspective that there is an ethical responsibility or moral obligation on the part of wealthy people and nations toward people and countries in poverty. Over the years Americans have constructed a sense of moral obligation that goes with being the leading country of the "free world." When John F. Kennedy addressed Congress on the topic of development in the early 1960s, his words reflected both the supremacy of U.S. political power and our consequent moral obligation to aid the less fortunate: "Looking toward the ultimate day, when all nations can be self-reliant and when foreign aid will no longer be needed . . . [with the] eyes of the American people, who are fully aware of their obligations to the sick, the poor, and the hungry, wherever they may live . . . as leaders of the Free World."[74] While the respective success of different development approaches over the years is debatable, what is not debatable is that a certain amount of compassion (a very un-neoclassical emotion) has served as a significant motivator for the promotion of development.

One of the strongest advocates of this approach to development was World Bank president Robert McNamara. He was a man of deep compassion who approached the World Bank as a vehicle through which he hoped to make a positive difference in the world. He knew that suffering and poverty wracked the "two-thirds" world, and as a Presbyterian elder and a man of deep moral convictions, he was determined that the World Bank, under his leadership, would improve the lives of the poor. While McNamara's predecessor, George Woods, had promoted "social lending" for health, education, and sanitation, these projects were to become the legacy of the McNamara Bank as he pushed social lending ever forward on the Bank's agenda.

McNamara was the first president to bring to the World Bank an attention to the moral obligations that undergirded its work. While previous bank presidents had promoted the development work of the Bank as strategic economic investments or necessary for international stability, McNamara moved development into a new standing. In a speech to the Board of Governors of the Bank and the International Monetary Fund in Nairobi in 1973, he presented his opinion that although there are many justifications for development aid (expansion of trade, international security, reduction of social tensions, etc.),

> the fundamental case for development assistance is the moral one. The whole of human history has recognized the principle—at least in the abstract—that the rich and the powerful have a moral obligation to assist the poor and the weak. That is what the sense of community is all about—any community: the

community of the family, the community of the village, the community of the nation, the community of nations itself.[75]

McNamara's persistent attention to "assist the poor and the weak" unfortunately made more of an impact on the ideology of development than on its practice.[76]

This attitude reflects the ethic of responsibility promoted by theologians such as Dietrich Bonhoeffer and H. Richard Niebuhr in the mid-twentieth century. This ethic of responsibility was intended to correct a perversion of Christian tradition that some theologians recognized in the church's historic withdrawal from social concerns and public life.[77] Theologically Bonhoeffer and Niebuhr believed that God called humanity to live and work in the world and that it was humankind's responsibility to address the urgent social questions of their day. Surely the extreme poverty of the poorest one-fifth of humanity qualifies as one of the pressing social problems of our time. This same ethic of responsibility permeates the Hebrew Bible and the New Testament and is perhaps most well-known in the admonitions of the prophets to care for the people and in Jesus' charge to clothe the naked and feed the hungry.[78]

Progress as Humanity's Telos

One of the most prominent features of the development position's vision of the good life is rooted in an Enlightenment belief in the possibility of progress. With the notion of progress embodying a belief that life can get better, in many ways it is the foundational value of the development perspective. Certainly for the millions of people who live under $1 a day, the development community has a vision that their life can, should, and will get better. Like all of the values examined in this study, progress can be understood in a multitude of ways. The good life is here envisioned as a life free from want, suffering, and untimely death. While the aim is not for a kind of consumer progress that puts a TV in every home and a car in every driveway, this group does aim for a material progress that manifests itself in bettering the physical, emotional, and spiritual well-being of the poor.

In other words, the value of progress that marks the development perspective differs significantly from the value of prosperity upheld by big business. While the former is concerned with a broader social concern of the good life as representative of a life that has been improved in some way (through labor-saving devices, adequate or better food and shelter, or longer life expectancy), the latter is concerned with material possessions, status, and wealth. As the *HDR 1999* expresses it: "The real wealth of a nation is its people. And the purpose of development is to create an enabling environment for people to enjoy long, healthy and creative lives. This simple but powerful truth is too often forgotten in the pursuit of material and financial wealth."[79] Here we see the difference between the progress of the development perspective, identified by "long, healthy and creative lives," and the prosperity of the proponents of big business, which is represented by "material and financial wealth."

Another unique feature of the understanding of progress offered by the development position is reflected in the attitude that progress in the "two-thirds" world is exemplified by a closer approximation of Western standards of living. Lawrence Summers, former chief economist of the World Bank, describes this kind of progress in the following words: "The human condition has changed more in the last half-century than in any previous century in human history. A child born in the developing world today is half as likely to die before the age of 5, twice as likely to learn to read, and can expect more than twice the material standard of living of a child born just a generation ago."[80] The underlying assumption of such a notion of progress is that Western culture represents a "higher," or better, standard than the cultures found in "developing" countries.

Philosophically speaking, this idea of progress can be traced to evolutionary theory.[81] That is, alongside Darwin's theory of change and development in the physical world came a concurrent move to apply the principles of this theory to ethics. Of course, along with this notion of progress come very specific ideas about what constitutes a "primitive" society and what constitutes a "developed" one. In these value judgments lie one of the most controversial aspects of the development position.

Progress involves a belief that human will and reason can overcome and conquer adversity and strife; beliefs similar to this are what the development community desires to engender in grassroots people in the "two-thirds" world. Proponents of the development position have learned in very concrete ways that progress cannot be imposed by external authorities or powers. In recent years the World Bank and the UNDP have advocated an approach to development that acknowledges that progress is a value that the development community hopes to instill in others. Joseph Stiglitz has characterized development as the "transformation" of society. He described this process as "a movement from traditional relations, traditional ways of thinking, traditional ways of dealing with health and education, traditional methods of production, to more 'modern' ways."[82] What Stiglitz advocated as the World Bank's "new paradigm of development" entailed transforming what he called the "traditional" worldview of "developing" people to the "modern" worldview accepted in the West. This modern view of progress is based on a positivistic approach to development that holds that "science" and "scientific" ways of thinking (and developing) will provide us with a viable escape route from poverty.[83] As Stiglitz himself expressed it:

> A characteristic of traditional societies is the acceptance of the world as it is; the modern perspective recognizes change, it recognizes that we, as individuals

> and societies, can take actions, that, for instance, reduce infant mortality, extend lifespans, and increase productivity. Key to these changes is the movement to "scientific" ways of thinking, identifying critical variables that affect outcomes, attempting to make inferences based on available data, recognizing what we know and what we do not know.[84]

Proponents of the development perspective firmly believe that if progress can become a broadly shared social value, then the development community will be able to help provide the means toward achieving such a goal.

Equity as What Constitutes Human Flourishing

A great deal of the development agenda is focused on addressing issues of inequality. Development workers tirelessly repeat, with growing alarm, the disparities that separate the superrich from the superpoor in our increasingly integrated global economy. The *HDR 1999* notes:

> By the late 1990's the fifth of the world's people living in the highest-income countries had:
> - 86% of world GDP—the bottom fifth just 1%
> - 82% of world export markets—the bottom fifth just 1%
> - 68% of foreign direct investment—the bottom fifth just 1%
> - 74% of world telephone lines—the bottom fifth just 1.5%.[85]

Much of the *Human Development Report* is devoted to providing statistics that show the uneven and unequal growth produced by the hegemonic processes of globalization. The *HDR 1999* reports that "the assets of the three richest people were more than the combined GNP of the 48 least developed countries."[86] This data is used increasingly by both the UNDP and the World Bank to argue that changes need to be made in the process of development. As the development community ponders the question of what constitutes human flourishing it is repeatedly confronted by this rising inequality that has, thus far, accompanied the neoliberal model of globalization. As an alternative to the first model of globalization that promotes freedom as necessary for human flourishing, the development community insists instead that the value of equity must mark the globalization processes of the future. Globalization processes marked by equity would insist that fairness and justice predominate in the marketplace as well as in the courts and in human relationships.

The changes advocated by the development community to create a more equitable society are broadly aimed at addressing this issue of rising inequality by attempting to democratize the development process to include development recipients and communities and by increasing the focus on improving structures of governance worldwide. The development perspective represented in this study reflects these priorities, and it is this development perspective that envisions equity as the deepest symbol of human flourishing.

Commitment to the value of equity does not mean the development community wishes to forgo markets, neoclassical economics, or even capitalism for that matter. No, for the development community equity can best be achieved through improving the conditions of globalization, a view shared by the World Bank and the UNDP. Of course, there are a number of different proposals for shaping globalization in beneficent directions that will promote equity; some of these include establishing increased regulations and restrictions on trade,[87] reshaping the UNDP's HDI to incorporate distributional inequality,[88] increasing participation and ownership in the development process,[89] and strengthening global governance.[90] This diversity of opinion over just how to modify and control the hegemonic neoliberal form of globalization reflects the reality that the basic commitment to trade and markets is not, here, under dispute. Rather, the conversation in the development community revolves around the methodological considerations of how to make globalization and its concomitant social, cultural, and economic policies more reflective of its vision of globalization as social development. As James Wolfensohn has said, "For me, globalization . . . is not some glossy, exotic idea. For me, it is a practical methodology to empower people to improve their lives. And for me, that is the dream of this new age."[91] This vision of human flourishing, of the good life that thrives under conditions of equity, is a dream that the development community believes its model of globalization can help to realize.

Notes

1. For a Christian evangelical proposal of how to apply neoliberalism to the development of Latin America, see Amy L. Sherman, *Preferential Option: A Christian and Neoliberal Strategy for Latin America's Poor* (Grand Rapids: Eerdmans, 1992). For a neoliberal justification of how export-led growth is good for the development of the "two-thirds" world, see Paul Krugman, *The Return of Depression Economics* (New York: W. W. Norton, 1999), esp. chap. 1.

2. For an introduction to Sen's capability approach, see Amartya Sen, "Capability and Well-Being," in *The Quality of Life*, ed. Martha Nussbaum and Amartya Sen (Oxford: Clarendon Press, 1993), 30–53; and Amartya Sen, *Development as Freedom* (New York: Alfred A. Knopf, 1999).

3. United Nations Development Programme (UNDP), "Globalization with a Human Face," *Human Development Report 1999* (New York: Oxford University Press for the United Nations Development Programme, 1999), 16.

4. We will see a different interpretation of development aid in chapter 6 when we examine a postcolonial perspective on globalization.

5. Stephen A. Marglin, "Towards the Decolonization of the Mind," in *Dominating Knowledge: Development, Culture, and Resistance*, ed. Frederique Apffel Marglin and Stephen A. Marglin (Oxford: Clarendon Press, 1990), 17.

6. This brief overview of the past fifty years of development theory is necessarily attenuated. For critical treatments of the history of development theory, see Wolfgang Sachs, ed., *The Development Dictionary: A Guide to Knowledge as Power* (London: Zed Books, 1992); Ray Kiely and Phil Marfleet, *Globalisation and the Third World* (London: Routledge, 1998). For specific attention to the issue of inequality and development, see Douglas A. Hicks, *Inequality and Christian Ethics* (Cambridge: Cambridge University Press, 2000), esp. chap. 2.

7. Gustavo Esteva, "Development," in *Development Dictionary*, ed. Sachs, 6.

8. We will return to a more thorough examination of this topic in chapter 6.

9. Kiely and Marfleet, *Globalisation and the Third World*, 25.

10. Ibid., 28.

11. Ibid., 29.

12. Ibid.

13. Ibid.

14. Ibid., 30.

15. Ibid., 32.

16. Ibid., 33.

17. For two good assessments of the problems of structural adjustment as related to the World Bank, see Bruce Rich, *Mortgaging the Earth: The World Bank, Environmental Impoverishment, and the Crisis of Overdevelopment* (Boston: Beacon Press, 1994); and Catherine Caulfield, *Masters of Illusion: The World Bank and the Poverty of Nations* (New York: Henry Holt & Co., 1996).

18. Joseph Stiglitz, "Towards a New Paradigm for Development: Strategies, Policies, and Processes," address given at the 1998 Prebisch Lecture at UNCTAD, Geneva, October 19, 1998.

19. This is not to discount the important theoretical contributions of Marxism, socialism, communism, and other alternative economic theories, but rather to acknowledge that neoclassical economics continues to prevail in the Western world and, with the fall of the Soviet Union, has been declared universally superior to alternative economic models. For a good introduction to the heterogeneity of economic thought, see David L. Prychitko, ed., *Why Economists Disagree: An Introduction to the Alternative Schools of Thought* (Albany: State University of New York Press, 1998).

20. As quoted in Robert L. Heilbroner, *The Worldly Philosophers: The Lives, Times, and Ideas of the Great Economic Thinkers*, 6th ed. (New York: Simon & Schuster, 1992), 270.

21. Ibid., 271.

22. Ibid., 270.

23. Ibid., 276.

24. E. K. Hunt and Howard J. Sherman, *Economics: An Introduction to Traditional and Radical Views*, 5th ed. (New York: Harper & Row), 157–58.

25. "When our income increases our consumption increases also, but not by so much." Consequently, "the richer the community the wider will tend to be the gap between its actual and its potential production; and therefore the more obvious

and outrageous the defects of the economic system. For a poor community will be prone to consume by far the greater part of its output, so that a very modest measure of investment will be sufficient to provide full employment; whereas a wealthy community will have to discover much ampler opportunities for investment if the saving propensities of its wealthier members are to be compatible with the employment of its poorer members." John Maynard Keynes as quoted in Carol Johnston, *The Wealth or Health of Nations: Transforming Capitalism from Within* (Cleveland, OH: Pilgrim Press, 1998), 95.

26. Ibid.

27. This examination of globalization and development draws heavily from the UNDP *Human Development Report 1999* because it provides a benchmark assessment of the status of "development" within the United Nations and development circles and because the 1999 document is focused primarily on the relationship between globalization and development.

28. Critics of GNP point out that its exclusive focus on economic indicators (i.e., paid economy) results in two major weaknesses that undermine any beneficial qualities of GNP as an indicator of "well-being." First, because GNP lacks the ability to distinguish between healthy and harmful economic activity, natural disasters such as floods, earthquakes, and fires show up as positive contributions to GNP. Likewise, car accidents, domestic violence, and abuse end up "contributing" to our nation's welfare as presented by the GNP. Second, some of the most important human activity that occurs in a nation—childcare, cooking, parenting, elder care, teaching outside the classroom—is rendered unimportant to the welfare of a country. The reason is that these activities, the work of caring for life and for educating young people, are considered to contribute to the "economy" of the nation only when they are paid positions; only then do they show up in the GNP. Therefore, the GNP indicates that it is more beneficial if I pay someone to care for my children than if I care for my children myself. For a critique of traditional accounting measures that ignore women's unpaid work, see Marilyn Waring, *If Women Counted: A New Feminist Economics* (San Francisco: HarperCollins, 1988).

29. UNDP, *Human Development Report 1999*, 23.

30. Stiglitz, "Towards a New Paradigm."

31. UNDP, *Human Development Report 1999*, 1.

32. Thomas L. Friedman, *The Lexus and the Olive Tree: Understanding Globalization* (New York: Farrar, Straus, and Giroux, 1999), xvi.

33. James Wolfensohn, "Coalitions for Change," address given at the World Bank Annual Meeting, Washington, DC, September 28, 1999.

34. Stiglitz, "Towards a New Paradigm," 4.

35. A detailed representation of the criticisms and critiques of neoliberal globalization is beyond the scope of this work. For several good accounts see John Gray, *False Dawn: The Delusions of Global Capitalism* (New York: The New Press, 1998); William Greider, *One World, Ready or Not: The Manic Logic of Global Capitalism* (New York: Simon & Schuster, 1997); Jerry Mander and Edward Goldsmith, eds., *The Case against the Global Economy and a Turn Toward the Local* (San Francisco:

Sierra Club Books, 1996); David C. Korten, *When Corporations Rule the World* (West Hartford, CT: Kumarian Press, 1995); Jeremy Brecher and Tim Costello, *Global Village or Global Pillage: Economic Reconstruction from the Bottom Up* (Boston: South End Press, 1994); Kevin Danaher, *Fifty Years Is Enough: The Case against the World Bank and the International Monetary Fund* (Boston: South End Press, 1994); Pamela Sparr, *Mortgaging Women's Lives: Feminist Critiques of Structural Adjustment* (London: Zed Books, 1994); and Herman E. Daly and John B. Cobb Jr., *For the Common Good: Redirecting the Economy toward Community, the Environment, and a Sustainable Future* (Boston: Beacon Press, 1989).

36. UNDP, *Human Development Report 1999*, 2–3.

37. Ibid., 7.

38. For a helpful account of how financial markets work, see Doug Henwood, *Wall Street: How It Works and for Whom* (London: Verso, 1997).

39. UNDP, *Human Development Report 1999*, 25.

40. Greider, *One World*, 354.

41. Quoted in Nicholas D. Kristof, "Experts Question Roving Flow of Global Capital," *New York Times*, September 20, 1998, 18.

42. Ibid.

43. UNDP, *Human Development Report 1999*, 4.

44. Bennett Harrison, *Lean and Mean: The Changing Landscape of Corporate Power in the Age of Flexibility* (New York: Basic Books, 1994).

45. Ibid., 9.

46. Korten, *When Corporations Rule the World*, 216.

47. Bennett Harrison, *Lean and Mean*, 11–12.

48. Ankie Hoogvelt, *Globalisation and the Postcolonial World: The New Political Economy of Development* (London: Macmillan Press, 1997), 120.

49. Heretofore, Western societies have focused a great deal of energy on understanding and defining our universe through the concepts of *space* and *time*. In capitalist economies space is, in fact, expressed through time, space being the amount of time it takes to cover a particular distance.

50. Philosopher Anthony Giddens argues that the result is the "annihilation of space through time." Anthony Giddens, as quoted in Hoogvelt, *Globalisation*, 120.

51. Ibid., 121.

52. UNDP, *Human Development Report 1999*, 4.

53. Richard J. Barnet and John Cavanagh, *Global Dreams: Imperial Corporations and the New World Order* (New York: Touchstone, 1994), 168–69.

54. Ibid.

55. Ibid.

56. UNDP, *Human Development Report 1999*, 5.

57. "In the Shadows: Trafficking in Women," *The Economist* 356, no. 8185 (August 26, 2000): 38–39.

58. Ibid.

59. UNDP, *Human Development Report 1999*, 5.

60. Paul Hawken, *The Ecology of Commerce: A Declaration of Sustainability* (New York: HarperCollins, 1993), 37.

61. See ibid., esp. chap. 4, for a creative approach to internalizing the long-term costs of all manufactured products, which would include costs for recycling, reusing, or disposing of the product.

62. UNDP, *Human Development Report 1999*, 5.

63. For specifics see the UNDP's *Human Development Reports* beginning in 1990 as well as speeches by Joseph Stiglitz, former chief economist at the World Bank, esp. "Address to the World Institute for Development Economics Research," given at the 1998 WIDER Annual Lecture, Helsinki, January 7, 1998.

64. The criticism of the "traditional" or neoliberal model of development has been present in the World Bank for several years. See recent speeches by James Wolfensohn, esp. "The Other Crisis: 1998 Annual Meetings Address," given at the World Bank Annual Meeting, Washington, DC, October 6, 1998; "Foundations for a More Stable Global System," given at the Symposium on Global Finance and Development, Tokyo, March 1, 1999. Also see speeches by Joseph Stiglitz, esp. "More Instruments and Broader Goals: Moving toward the Post-Washington Consensus," given at the 1998 WIDER Annual Lecture, Helsinki, January 7, 1998; and "Towards a New Paradigm for Development: Strategies, Policies, and Processes," given at the 1998 Prebisch Lecture at UNCTAD, Geneva, October 19, 1998.

For a theological critique of the World Bank's recent attempts at transformation, see John C. Cobb Jr., *The Earthist Challenge to Economism: A Theological Critique of the World Bank* (New York: St. Martin's Press, 1999), esp. chaps. 7–10.

65. See Stiglitz, "Towards a New Paradigm," for more specific details and components of his new development strategy.

66. UNDP, *Human Development Report 1999*, 8.

67. The phrase "casino capitalism" comes from a book by Susan Strange that examines the phenomenon of a new form of capitalism that resembles high-stakes gambling and is intended to net large profits. Susan Strange, *Casino Capitalism* (Manchester, England: Manchester University Press, 1997).

68. UNDP, *Human Development Report 1999*, 8–9.

69. While it is true that even transnational corporations are still *legally* bound by the laws of their host countries, they have garnered positions of such power and influence that many are able to circumvent the laws and regulations.

70. UNDP, *Human Development Report 1999*, 9.

71. Chapter 6 addresses the undemocratic organization of the WTO more directly.

72. For a more detailed report from the UNDP on the development of some of these global agencies, see "A New Global Architecture," *Human Development Report 1994* (New York: United Nations Development Programme, 1994).

73. Donald K. McKim, "Responsibility," *Westminster Dictionary of Theological Terms* (Louisville, KY: Westminster/John Knox Press, 1996), 238.

74. As quoted in Marianne Gronemeyer, "Helping," *Development Dictionary*, ed. Sachs, 63.

75. Rich, *Mortgaging the Earth*, 83.

76. McNamara's strategies failed to reach the impoverished people whom he had felt so obligated to help. In fact, as it turned out, the lending strategies of the

World Bank during the McNamara years did two things that did damage to the poor. First, by lending mainly to the landowners and businesspeople of "two-thirds" world countries, the lending strategies increased the gap between the rich and the poor; and second, by pumping so many billions of dollars into already debt-burdened countries, the McNamara years set the stage for the debt crisis of the 1980s that would have devastating effects on the poor and marginalized.

77. Albert R. Jonsen, "Responsibility," *Westminster Dictionary of Christian Ethics*, ed. James Childress and John Macquarrie (Louisville, KY: Westminster/John Knox, 1986), 548.

78. Matthew 25.

79. As quoted in UNDP, *Human Development Report 1999*, 1.

80. Lawrence Summers as quoted in Cobb, *Earthist Challenge*, 134.

81. Charles W. Kegley, "Progress, Belief in," in *Westminster Dictionary of Christian Ethics*, ed. Childress and Macquarrie, 505.

82. Stiglitz, "Towards a New Paradigm," 1.

83. The "scientific" approach to development is apparent in such practices as mono-cropping, gene-splicing, and other agricultural "developments" in biotechnology. A critique of this approach follows in the next chapter.

84. Stiglitz, "Towards a New Paradigm," 1.

85. UNDP, *Human Development Report 1999*, 3.

86. Ibid., 37.

87. For a detailed account and moral defense of this position, see Daniel Finn, *Just Trading: On the Ethics and Economics of International Trade* (Nashville: Abingdon Press, 1996).

88. Douglas A. Hicks argues that the HDI is an incomplete alternative assessment of development because it does not reflect the distributional inequalities that exist within and among countries. He offers the "inequality-adjustment human development index," or IAHDI, as a way to promote equity by influencing the public policy discourse that is already consulting the UNDP's HDI. See Hicks, *Inequality and Christian Ethics*, esp. chap. 10.

89. Former World Bank chief economist Joseph Stiglitz included participation and ownership as key ingredients in the new development strategy that he offered for the World Bank in 1998. For details of his proposal, see Stiglitz, "Towards a New Paradigm."

90. The *Human Development Report 1999* emphasizes the necessity of increased global governance as the most important aspect of managing globalization. "What area of policy is most important for managing globalization? Harmonizing global competition and free market approaches with steady and expanding support for human development and human rights in all countries, developed and developing. This is at the heart of a new perspective, a new global ethic, a new approach to globalization." UNDP, *Human Development Report 1999*, 97. For a broader discussion of the issue of global governance, see chapter 5 in its entirety.

91. James Wolfensohn, "Globalization and the Human Condition," address given at "Symposium: Celebrating the 50th Anniversary of the Aspen Institute," Aspen, CO, August 19, 2000.

PART 3

THE RESISTANCE THEORIES OF GLOBALIZATION

Earthism and Postcolonialism

At the end of November 1999, a diverse array of people converged on the streets of Seattle to protest the World Trade Organization at its third ministerial meeting. The eclectic protesters represented a broad spectrum of political, theological, and social causes and beliefs, from anarchists to trade unionists, from socialists to "Veterans for Peace." While the unexpected crowds included people dressed as trees, ears of corn, bananas, clowns, monarch butterflies, and sea turtles and often used street theater and puppetry to depict their messages of the destructive and damaging nature of the WTO and corporate globalization, they also proved quite capable of achieving their goal of disrupting the meeting. Perhaps most importantly, their demonstrations and activities caught the world's attention and their voices and critiques were widely publicized by mainstream media.[1] This unlikely mix of people represents a critical aspect of the globalization debates, an aspect that was easily overlooked and dismissed prior to the Seattle confrontation and the wave of protests that followed in its wake.[2]

For most people in the "first" world, the two previous theories of globalization represent familiar philosophical themes, as the ideologies of neoliberalism and social equity liberalism arise from the collective consciousness of Western polities. For those of us who have grown up in cultures influenced by the Enlightenment philosophy of Descartes, Hobbes, and Locke, the emphasis on individualism and private property embedded in the dominant forms of globalization seems to be a natural and fundamental base for functional societies. As Western Christians we often read Scripture through these lenses, convincing ourselves that our religious traditions and sacred texts also promote individual thought and action and the possession of private property. However, limiting our perspective on globalization to familiar Western academic discourses of culture, politics, and economics causes us to miss the massive dissent that is being mobilized by grassroots people in communities around the world.

What we have heard thus far are the voices of those who sit within the halls of power, be they businesspeople or government officials or their appointees. These are the voices of the people who were safely ensconced inside the buildings in Seattle during the protests and riots. Now it is time to turn to the streets and listen to resistance voices from multiple locations around the world. Who are the people challenging and condemning globalization? Do they really believe they can escape the globalizing processes that currently dominate our world? These voices may not be so familiar; their ideas and ideologies may not resonate as well intellectually because they have not arisen from the mainstream intellectual traditions of the West. Despite their lack of "acceptability" within traditional academic circles (i.e., among economists and politicians) their messages are clear and their visions of the good life powerfully challenge the dominant positions we have already examined. These activists, academics, farmers, environmentalists, organizations, and agencies who are part of the resistance movements take a much more critical view of what is happening to people and the earth as a result of the dominant models of globalization.

Resistance to globalization is often criticized for its lack of central organization and its perceived lack of focus. These attributes are viewed by critics as evidence of the insignificance of globalization resistance and by supporters as a weakness that leads to ineffectiveness in achieving their objectives.[3] Indeed, even a cursory look at the globalization debates reveals a wide variety of perspectives, organizations, and individuals participating in resistance movements. Resistance to globalization does not follow traditional models of community organizing and social change that are often built on highly centralized organization models; rather, the resistance to globalization is truly grassroots. In fact, the strength of the resistance to globalization, right now, lies in the fact that it is such a diverse and widespread phenomenon. This, in and of itself, illustrates that the dominant model of globalization is not universally accepted as the only way forward. Ironically, many of the tools of capitalist globalization, such as the Internet, are being utilized to coordinate the resistance to corporate and development models of globalization.

Resistance to globalization has no guiding manifesto and cannot properly be considered a single movement. To the extent that resistance to the dominant forms of globalization is presently manifested in a wide variety of movements around the world, it is more like a network. As journalist Naomi Klein puts it, "What emerged on the streets of Seattle and Washington was an activist model that mirrors the organic, decentralized, interlinked pathways of the Internet—the Internet come to life."[4] These disparate groups are linked to one another by their common causes, much like "'hotlinks' connect their websites on the Internet."[5] These common causes include concern for the environment, frustration with the overweening power of corporations, outrage over the inattention to meaningful work and decent wages, disillusionment with the promises of capitalism to end poverty, and the desire to participate in organizing society more democratically. These groups also are linked by their alternative readings of history, which we will examine more closely below.

In examining a great many resistance voices and movements, two foci stand out: a move toward earth-centered, localizing resistance and a political critique of globalization as neocolonialism. While common agendas and strategies certainly bind these two resistance groups together, the next two chapters develop two slightly divergent themes—earthism and postcolonialism—that dominate the work of globalization resistance and transformation. While distinct, these two perspectives have enough overlap that it is best to treat the third and fourth theories of globalization as a continuum rather than as entirely discrete. Many people, organizations, and movements share elements of both these positions. As dominant trends emerge within the resistance forms of globalization, the need is less to draw a clear line of distinction between the two and more to elaborate the ideological bases of these positions.

Notes

1. Lynda Gorov, "The Varied Foes of WTO Unite in Seattle Protests," *The Boston Globe*, November 30, 1999, sec. A, p. 1; Patrick McMahon and James Cox, "'Stop the WTO': Protesters Say Goal Achieved," *USA Today*, December 1, 1999, sec. A, p. 19; Ellen Goodman, "Question from Seattle: Whose World Is It?," *The Boston Globe*, December 5, 1999, sec. D, p. 7.

2. For one perspective on how the Seattle protests marked a turning point in the resistance to neoliberal globalization see Walden Bello, "2000: The Year of Global Protest against Globalization," Focus on the Global South Web site, www.focusweb.org.

3. An example of this ineffectiveness was present in the World Bank/IMF protests in Washington, D.C., in April 2000. Initially protesters attempted to block access to the meetings by blocking the intersections surrounding the World Bank/IMF headquarters. When protesters realized that the meeting delegates had gotten inside despite their efforts there was disagreement over whether to stay and try to block their exit or to abandon their intersections and join the official march at the Ellipse. The spokescouncil decided that each intersection had autonomy and that each was to decide whether to stay locked down or to join the rest of the protesters at the Ellipse. While this logic was certainly fair and democratic, it made no sense as a tool for a coordinated political action. Some intersections stayed occupied and others disbanded, leaving a less than solid front to greet the delegates leaving the meeting.

This information was taken from Naomi Klein, "The Vision Thing: Were the DC and Seattle Protests Unfocused, or Are Critics Missing the Point?" *The Nation*, July 10, 2000, 18–21.

4. Ibid.

5. Ibid.

Globalization as Localization

Reconnecting to People and the Earth

A Different Historical Account of the Origins of Globalization

In the varied historical accounts of globalization so far explored, Bretton Woods has been identified as the birthplace of globalization. The alternative voices that challenge the dominant theories of globalization have a different historical starting place. The next two positions, earthism and postcolonialism, argue for the importance of locating the roots of contemporary processes of globalization within the context of European colonial conquest and control dating back to the fifteenth century. Resistance perspectives favor alternative readings of history, such as those offered by Fernand Braudel, Immanuel Wallerstein, and Giovanni Arrighi, as a more accurate explanation of why neoliberal economic globalization is gaining sway around the world.[1] This alternative historical approach argues that a careful reading of history reveals recurrent patterns of capitalist economic development tied to political power and authority. For a closer look at the implications of this thesis on contemporary globalization processes, we will examine Arrighi's reading of history as illustrative of this historical approach.

Arrighi argues that there are four different phases of capitalist economic development identified by the state or territorial power connected to each—the Genoese, the Dutch, the British, and the American. He chronicles each phase, illuminating a repeated pattern of capital accumulation[2] and knowledge accumulation (a new group ascends while the former power teeters to maintain control), followed by capital-intensive growth and market hegemony, followed by a period of high finance, consumerism, and excess wealth.

Each new phase marks a distinct break from the past and is made up of a new group of entrepreneurs/capitalists who offer a fresh approach to the changed social, political, and economic circumstances of each successive phase.

The first cycle of accumulation that Arrighi notes is that of the Genoese, who steadily gained ascendancy in the sixteenth century. The political economy of the region was dominated by localized city-states, and each of these city-states hosted a medieval fair that was known by the name of the city in which it was held. The Genoese created a new type of medieval fair, the fairs of Bisenzone,[3] which traveled from area to area and carried their name with them. By creating a traveling "market," the Genoese were able to disassociate capital and land. Arrighi claims that the Genoese diaspora of merchant bankers "was the prototype of all subsequent non-territorial systems of capital accumulation on a world scale."[4] By the later half of the sixteenth century, as nation-states began to take the place of city-states, the Genoese "nation" emerged as the most powerful market force in the region.

The Genoese success in capital accumulation lay in their disengagement from state-making and war-making functions. They preferred to develop alliances with other "states" so that they were able to focus on their strength and passion—markets, trade, and finance—while allowing their partners to engage in territorial disputes, expansion, and other military matters. In the end, it was this very cosmopolitan nature that turned out to be their downfall, as their political stability was ultimately dependent on the political stability of their trading partners. As the political landscape changed, the Genoese found themselves vulnerable to the rising power of economic forces rooted in stronger nation-states.

While the Genoese were busy making money, the Dutch had been fighting a long battle for their independence from Spain. Upon their success, the Dutch quickly established themselves as the leading power in a new form of exploration and trade that was based on the model of the joint stock company. These primitive "corporations" were first chartered by monarchs and governing bodies as business enterprises intended both to increase the wealth and capital of their nation and to carry out war-making and state-making activities on behalf of their governments.[5]

This emerging form of capitalism cemented Dutch political and economic hegemony in Europe in the seventeenth and early eighteenth centuries and was so successful that other European states began to imitate the Dutch model. There was, however, at least one major ideological difference between the way the Dutch and the other European states approached expansion. Dutch success was due largely to their privileging of capitalist accumulation over territorial accumulation, much like the Genoese before them. This emphasis on fiscal power filled the Amsterdam Bourse with ready capital to fund their joint-stock company ventures, but it also left them vulnerable to the economic success of other European states following the agreement of the Peace of Westphalia in 1648. This peace treaty stabilized the political atmosphere of Western Europe and allowed other European powers more time to focus their energies on mercantilist expansion. These countries eventually surpassed the Dutch capacity to continue their financial expansion through trade.

The Dutch trade strategies, which formed the second cycle of accumulation, were successful in the seventeenth century while the Dutch pursued trade in the areas of the Baltic and Indian Oceans. However, by the time trade routes expanded to the Atlantic, the Dutch no longer possessed the territorial or demographic base to compete with other European powers. Recognizing their inability to continue to compete successfully through trade, the Dutch concentrated instead on expanding their power in high finance in order to continue to benefit from the spread of mercantilism.

As Holland's hegemonic power in the European political economy began to waver in the mid-seventeenth century, England gained ascendancy. In the sixteenth century Queen Elizabeth had stabilized the pound, begun chartering joint-stock companies to compete with the Dutch, and begun the process of building up and stabilizing England's navy. By the eighteenth century, her actions had prepared England to surpass not only Holland but all the European states as the most powerful force in Europe. England's ascendancy heralded a new age for the chartered joint-stock company, or the emerging "corporation." As a formerly territorial expansionist state that had internalized important capitalist lessons from the Dutch, England became symbolic of the new age of expansion that wedded territorialism and capitalism in the devastating marriage known as colonialism. Joint-stock companies such as the English East India Company first functioned as the imperial governing bodies in many colonial states. With the authority to build forts, maintain military forces, engage in battle, levy taxes, and make and enforce laws, the joint-stock companies combined business and governmental functions as they both monopolized trade in and with the colonies and governed them as administrators of the British crown. In the eighteenth and nineteenth centuries these corporations invested mainly in extractive industries, which literally sucked the wealth out of Africa, India, and other colonial outposts. Often these raw materials were turned into manufactured goods in the imperial country and returned as expensive imports to their countries of origin. The methods of these corporations promoted high profit margins that enabled corporations and imperial governments of the period to amass great wealth, marking the third cycle of accumulation.

Just as the technological advances in European shipbuilding transformed prior economic dependence on medieval marketplaces, the advent of steam and machinery into the world of production in the nineteenth century again transformed the economic stage in ways that required new and innovative ways of thinking. Rather than the seventeenth- and early eighteenth-century world of exploration and trade or the colonizing world of the late eighteenth and early nineteenth centuries, the enterprises that emerged successfully in the late nineteenth and early twentieth centuries were strictly business ventures that served the primary purpose of concentrating and organizing the new forms of capitalism that steam and machinery made possible. In the mid-nineteenth century, the emergence of Fordism and factory production, as well as the nature of the industrial revolution, transformed the face of business in the United States.[6] The railroad, steel manufacturing, copper and oil production, and the mass production of consumer goods were all industries that were more profitably served by large business corporations rather than the traditional small-business enterprises of early America.

The post-Civil War years saw an increase in the consolidation of these industries as wealthy individuals and corporations aggressively sought to buy out their smaller competitors and monopolize various industrial sectors; these years of consolidation were known as the "first great merger wave." Two other factors contributed to this remarkable increase of corporate strength and power: extensive lobbying on the part of business to encourage states to be more willing to grant charters for corporations, and the friendliness of the courts in expanding the legal rights of corporations. Add to these factors the enormous growth potential represented by the North American continent, as well as the openness of a largely immigrant population to innovation and change, to see that the United States represented a unique set of historical conditions within which the development of the modern corporation proceeded. Indeed, historian David Landes remarks, "The 'American system' set standards of productivity for the rest of the industrial world."[7] Before long the successful U.S. corporations began to move beyond their own markets to pursue trade abroad, and by 1902 Europeans were already speaking of an "American invasion."[8] However, it would still be another century and two world wars before U.S. hegemony and the fourth cycle of accumulation would completely surpass European rivals.[9]

The Importance of Historical Antecedents of Globalization

These alternative theories of capital accumulation require us to think about globalization and capitalism in a much different way than the previous theories of globalization. While any critical historical account that is rooted in the long-term development of the structures of political economy is sometimes read as deterministic, resistance forms of globalization seek to use critical history as a tool for greater clarity and insight into the origins and patterns of capitalism and globalization. Theorists of the earthist position use critical history as a way of demystifying rather than objectifying history. Viewing twentieth-century economic developments in light of previous cycles of accumulation and hegemony offers us a number of insights into the issue of globalization. First, it allows us to see that the transnationalization of capital and the forced "opening" of economies in the "two-thirds" world to increased export and trade are part of a much longer history of capital accumulation. It also allows us to see that the $2 trillion that is traded in money markets around the world each day is reminiscent of previous eras of high finance.[10] Furthermore, it becomes clear that the excessive consumerism that is promoted and embodied by increasing numbers of people around the world has historical antecedents. By pointing out the precursors to some of the major elements of contemporary globalization, we are able to analyze some of the power dynamics inherent in the political and economic decisions that were made by particular groups or countries in the past. This enables us to see that rather than being inevitable, capitalism and the capitalist globalization we are now experiencing are the result of a particular set of political and economic decisions that played an important role in each new developing cycle of accumulation. In other words, a critical historical approach allows insight into the ways in which human agency has played an intergral role in capitalist development so that our analysis of contemporary economic globalization does not sink into the trap of historical inevitability.

Proponents of resistance models of globalization believe that studying and understanding the historical precursors of our contemporary situation empower us with important information that will enable us to change the present course of suffering that engulfs the majority of creation. Recognition of the essential role of human agency in the historical development of capitalism is a critical insight that informs the current resistance movements discussed in chapters 5 and 6. The political and economic decisions that are being made in our contemporary world also will shape the future of globalization in particular directions. Resistance theorists argue very strongly that close attention to both the structures of decision-making and the ideologies that inform those decisions will ultimately have a profound effect on the direction that globalization will take in the future.

Offering an Earthist Paradigm as an Alternative Ideology

The first two theories of globalization in this study—neoliberalism and development—can both be described as following an ideology of "economism" that holds that attention to the expansion of the economy should be the primary political, economic, and social consideration.[11] Process theologian John Cobb and others argue that this economic ideology is "morally bankrupt" because it privileges the accumulation of wealth over the well-being of people and the planet, and "functionally bankrupt" because its claims of a better life for people and the elimination of poverty through economic growth have not been borne out despite a decade of economic growth. In recent years, a number of theological and economic voices have challenged the hegemonic position of neoclassical economics in determining humanity's common economic future.[12] Among these heterodox voices are a cluster of people who align themselves with a new ideological perspective that recognizes the fundamental importance of the transformation of our relationship to the planet.

This new paradigm, which has arisen to challenge what is seen as the woeful inadequacies of economism, can best be described as "earthism."[13] Theorists who have adopted an earthist perspective have been deeply influenced by communities, families, and peoples whose lives have been rooted in the earth for generations and who are actively resisting current forms of economic globalization. In reflecting on the difference between economism and earthism, ecofeminist theologian Sallie McFague observes:[14]

> Both are models, interpretations, of the world; neither is a description. This point must be underscored because . . . the first model seems "natural," indeed "inevitable" and "true" to most middle-class Westerners, while the second model seems novel, perhaps even utopian or fanciful. In fact, both come from assumptions of different historical periods; both are world-pictures built on these assumptions, and each vies for our agreement and loyalty.[15]

When critically analyzing competing theories of globalization, we must acknowledge that each of these different theories is rooted in a specific ideology or worldview. Despite the fact that Western civilization has adopted and reified the model of economism, we must be willing to acknowledge that it is not a scientific proof but a mathematical theory, albeit one that has a long history of acceptance. Nevertheless, as we will see, the third and fourth theories of globalization offer substantive critiques of the sustainability and morality of all economistic approaches for the future of creation.

A number of contemporary ethicists and theologians are refusing to accept economic, social, political, or cultural models of society that do not take the earth and its distress centrally. This perspective is reflected in Christian ethicist Larry Rasmussen's normative standards of critique in his recent work *Earth Community, Earth Ethics*, which states clearly that "this volume judges as ethically valid only those human and religious energies that unapologetically serve earth's care and redemption."[16] In other words, prominent theo-ethical thinkers are challenging society to proclaim that profit is not king and that the earth and creation are far more centrally important to a sustainable moral vision for our future than any other criteria.

The proponents of earthism are concerned with practical issues of environmental or earth justice. Their primary considerations are three—the fate of their countrypeople, families, and friends; the land on which they live; and the creatures with which they share the land. Their starting point is the lived life of struggle, their own and their neighbors'. One of the most prominent themes of earthism is the notion that humanity is not separate from or higher than the rest of the created order (as for Augustine and Calvin). Rather, humanity is only one aspect of creation and all of creation is interdependent. Ecologist Thomas Berry describes the situation that faces us very simply as a need to move "from our human-centered to an earth-centered norm of reality and value."[17] Many ecofeminists feel that this notion of interdependence has been lost and that it can actually serve as a corrective model to help "heal" the sinful behavior that they see destroying the environment. In this way, earthists see creation as inherently good and even believe that creation holds within itself answers to the problems of the environmental crisis.

Valuing the Interdependence of Life

The ideologies of economism or liberalism (neo- and social equity) are deeply rooted in an anthropocentric worldview that can be traced back for millennia. This radical anthropocentrism has served to skew humanity's ability to see the interdependence of creation that is present and revealed in the natural world. This tendency has certainly been exacerbated by the Enlightenment shift toward individualism at the expense of the common good of the community. Earthists believe that this anthropocentric bias has prevented humanity from acknowledging not only that creation is dependent on us, but that we in turn are dependent on creation as well.

The interdependence of life is manifest all around us—from our own human life cycle of birth, childhood, adolescence, adulthood, and elderhood, to the damaging effects of our pollution on the climate, the creatures, and the plant life. The fact that we often only identify the ways in which humanity's actions affect the environment actually masks our dependence upon that which we are destroying. When put together, these two factors—creation's dependence on humanity and humanity's dependence on the created order—really represent the interdependence of all of life:

> A balance between I and thou, I and we, we and they, ourselves and the earth is the way to turn around and allow the human, as well as plants and animals and all the creative energies of the earth, to flourish anew. This new vision calls on us to see the universe as our body, the earth as our body, the variety of human groups as our body—a body that is in evolution, in creative ecstasy, in the midst of destructive and regenerative labor, of death and resurrection. Everything is our body . . . it is a continual tension and communion of multiplicity and unity, all within the ecstatic and mysterious adventure of Life.[18]

Furthermore, the anthropocentric tendencies of Western liberal thinking have been reinforced by Christian theological orientations that serve to mask our planetary interdependence in ways that ultimately harm all of creation. A theological anthropology that elevates "man" above the rest of creation lends itself toward a theology of controlling the environment that betrays humanity's lack of humility as well as our lack of respect for the world around us. This kind of hierarchical model of creation also has a tendency to patronize other groups of people who are less fortunate in the world. If theology supports the notion that there is a divine "order" in the world, then the existence of poverty runs the risk of being overlooked as a justice issue. Any attitude toward the poor based on this type of hierarchical theology is bound to be one of charity and beneficence rather than justice. Earthists' desire for justice in the world—justice for all of creation—requires a radical overturning of hierarchical structures that maintain order for some at the expense of others.

Respecting the Sacred Quality of Creation

A distinct spirituality underlies and supports the earthist orientation toward interconnectedness. It is a spirituality that is rooted in a deep belief that all of life is imbued with sacredness. This theological perspective may be traced to ancient texts as in Judaism or Christianity, or it may have its roots in tradition and sacred story as in many indigenous cultures around the world. Regardless of where this spirituality originates, it generates a reverence and respect for life that cause believers to act differently toward creation. If someone deeply believes that the trees are living beings whose very existence is both blessed and, in part, constitutive of their own existence—then movements such as the Chipko become a profoundly spiritual quest championing respect for life.[19] Chipko poet Ghanshyan 'Shailani' reflects these very ideas in her song:

A fight for truth has begun
At Sinsyari Khala
A fight for rights has begun
At Malkot Thano
Sister, it is a fight to protect
Our mountains and forests.
They give us life
Embrace the life of the living trees and streams
Clasp them to your hearts
Resist the digging of mountains
That brings death to our forests and streams
A fight for life has begun
At Sinsyaru Khala.[20]

The type of earthist ideology described in this chapter is the predominant worldview underlying the work of a wide variety of social activists, ecofeminists, and indigenous peoples who often work for change through nongovernmental organizations.[21] NGOs gained international attention in the 1980s when many began to challenge the policies and practices of the World Bank and the IMF.[22]

Labor activists Jeremy Brecher and Tim Costello credit coordinated NGO resistance with the saving of the Amazon rainforest, or at least portions of it.[23] While the original resistance was begun in the 1970s by Amazonian rubber tappers who opposed the loggers felling vast swaths of the rainforest, environmental NGOs in the United States joined the fight and added their considerable organizational skills to the project. They persuaded Congress to hold hearings on how the World Bank projects contributed to the "destruction of the rainforests, contamination of the rivers, and forced displacement of indigenous people."[24] NGOs mobilized anthropologists, environmentalists, and indigenous people to testify at these hearings. As a result, the World Bank projects in the Amazon underwent extensive outside scrutiny by a joint U.S.-Brazilian research team that documented the devastation being perpetrated by the Bank in the name of development. Brecher and Costello describe the results:

> Thirty-two non-governmental organizations (NGOs) from eleven countries sent the results of this research to the World Bank with a demand for emergency measures to protect indigenous people and the environment. In response to pressures from NGOs and the U.S. Congress, the World Bank finally cut off the loan—the first time a public international financial institution had terminated a loan for environmental reasons.[25]

Earthist activists and the NGOs with which they work do more than just function as defensive agencies working to protect the earth. While this is a vitally important task, and perhaps the one with which most people are familiar, there is a second and equally important agenda that concerns the environmental community and earthist activists. This second agenda is oriented toward fighting the excesses and domination of neoliberal globalization through efforts to contain and foreshorten the power and authority of transnational corporations and their allied institutions (the World Trade Organization, International Monetary Fund, and World Bank). A major victory on this front was the defeat of the Multilateral Agreement on Investment, or MAI, an international treaty that was being negotiated by the Organisation for Economic Co-operation and Development (OECD) to facilitate the ease of direct foreign investment across international borders.[26] Carrying out organized opposition to neoliberal economic policies and the institutions of economic globalization is balanced in the earthist community by sowing seeds of hope and promise in the grass roots in the form of alternative businesses, cooperatives, thinking, and ways of life. These strategies of localization will be taken up more fully later in the chapter.

An Earthist Critique of Economistic Globalization

An important part of understanding each theory of globalization is understanding its criticisms and warnings regarding the effects and potential effects of the current wave of globalization sweeping our globe, both in its neoliberal and development forms. In chapter 4 we examined the development community's concerns about the neoliberal model of globalization that presently dominates our world. As we turn to examine an earthist critique of economistic globalization, we will see that while some of the areas of concern overlap those raised by the development community, earthist thinkers often see the problems differently from development workers and consequently offer different solutions.

Broadly speaking, there is general agreement among proponents of the earthist position that the survival of our planet and the life forms it sustains (including our own) is in peril. There is also broad consensus among earthist activists that there is a hole in the ozone layer, that climate change is happening, that desertification and pollution are increasingly destroying the sustainability of life on our planet, and that all of these environmental problems share one thing in common—their causes all lie in irresponsible human behavior.

The Ideological Roots of Environmental Degradation

Proponents of earthism argue that the breadth and depth of the environmental damage is so vast that it is impossible to conclude that the late capitalism of the twenty-first century is simply the next stage in an "evolutionary ladder" that continues to "advance." Rather, earthist critics see human behavior that has led to rampant environmental degradation as rooted in three ideological postures that disregard life, community, and the earth in favor of comfort (of the few, the wealthy), profit, and productivity. These postures include overconsumption, environmental racism, and economic models that promote producing for export.

The first ideological posture, which earthist proponents argue implicitly undergirds all of the planetary devastation, is the "first" world's increasing appetite. Environmental researchers repeatedly remind us that the planet itself cannot sustain many more countries that consume at the level of the "first" world. Earthist activists argue that the overconsumption of the world's wealthy elite (the majority of the "first" world and the wealthy in the "two-thirds" world) requires a change of our behaviors and lifestyles in radical ways in order to return our communities and countries to sustainable relationships with the earth and the environment.

While the transnational corporations and their media affiliates may be blamed for "brainwashing" or "conditioning" people into believing that we need to buy more and consume more, ultimately, we as individuals, families, and communities must acknowledge our responsibility for the products we buy and the circumstances surrounding the production of those items. While we may live in a consumer society, consumers must learn how to make educated decisions about our purchases; this implies a prior step that requires us to think about our purchasing power and our consumer behavior.

Earthist activists argue that middle-class, mainstream people will have to change the way that we have become accustomed to living. McFague points out that North Americans are "privileged players in the global economic game. Just as we do not deliberately harm nature, so most of us do not set out to make other people poor. But those of us who are citizens of the United States benefit from our accident of birth: in the growing global divide between the rich and the poor, most of us end up on the plus side."[27]

Environmental racism refers to the reality that poor, disadvantaged, and minority communities or "two-thirds" world communities receive the brunt of exposure to environmental toxins and waste.[28] Researchers and activists who have exposed the racist nature of environmental dumping and environmental waste exposure also have revealed statistics to support their claims that poor, minority communities are disproportionately at risk for environmental illness and exposure to deadly toxins. Studies have shown that children of color are disproportionately at risk for lead poisoning, regardless of income level. Out of the three to four million children in the United States affected by exposure to lead, most are African American and Latino/a Americans living in urban areas.[29] The United Church of Christ's 1987 landmark study entitled *Toxic Wastes and Race* found "race to be the most important factor (i.e., more important than income, home ownership rate, and property values) in the location of abandoned toxic-waste sites."[30]

Environmental racism is also evident in relations between the "first" and "two-thirds" worlds as corporations move their production facilities to poorer countries in Asia, Africa, and Latin America where environmental regulations and workers' rights are almost nonexistent. In addition to corporate pollution, the United States Environmental Protection Agency has plans to send sludge and other wastes from East Coast states to Central and South America.[31] A highly publicized and controversial memo written by then chief economist of the World Bank, Lawrence Summers, reveals the attitude of many who view pollution in terms of cost-benefit analysis.[32]

> In a 1991 internal memorandum . . . Summers argued for the transfer of waste and dirty industries from industrialized to developing countries. "Just between you and me, shouldn't the World Bank be encouraging more migration of the

> dirty industries to the LDCs [lesser developed countries]? . . . I think the economic logic behind dumping a load of toxic waste in the lowest wage country is impeccable and we should face up to that. . . . I've always thought that underpopulated countries in Africa are vastly under polluted; their air quality is vastly inefficiently low [*sic*] compared to Los Angeles or Mexico City.[33]

To grasp the depth of Summers' statement fully, we need to recognize that Los Angeles and Mexico City rank as two of the seven most polluted cities in the world.[34] While Summers later apologized, claiming that the memo was intended to be ironic, not many earthist activists believed him.

By naming the racist and classist tendencies of the environmental strategies of corporations, governments, and even international "aid" agencies, the earthist community is attempting to show the highly prejudicial behavior of people who buy into globalization theories that privilege profit and efficiency over people and the planet. It is not just the racism of neoliberal and social equity liberal theories of globalization that elicit objections from earthist proponents; they also fundamentally object to the promotion of export-oriented growth for "developing" countries as dangerous to the earth and its inhabitants. Details of these problems unfold below.

The Devastating Consequences of Biotechnology

The drive for profits has combined with the scientific and technological developments of the late twentieth and early twenty-first centuries to create an entirely new field of research and development that is commonly referred to as biotechnology. We will take a glimpse at only three aspects of the biotechnology revolution that are of concern to the earthist perspective—genetically modified crops, seeds, and the patenting of life forms. At the outset we must note that biotechnology is inherently risky and expensive. Consequently, most of the research is funded by transnational corporations that are largely interested in boosting their profit margins in agribusiness. The five largest companies involved in biotechnology research and development are DuPont, ICI, Monsanto, Sandoz, and Ciba-Geigy.[35] According to a 1985 World Bank study, 92.5 percent of all biotech research is done in the United States, the European Economic Community (EEC), and Japan.[36]

Ostensibly, gene splicing is intended to create "super" strains of genetically modified crops that are sturdier, grow faster, produce their own fertilizer, or are resistant to pests or that exhibit any of a host of other miraculous traits. The basic procedure allows scientists to "snip" genes from one organism and "insert" them into the gene sequence of another, thereby transferring a "valuable" trait from one life form to another.

Recent examples include pigs engineered with human growth genes to increase their size; tomatoes engineered with flounder genes to resist cold temperatures; salmon with cattle growth genes spliced in to increase their size;

tobacco plants engineered with the fluorescent gene of fireflies to make them glow at night; and laboratory mice encoded with the AIDS virus as part of their permanent genetic makeup.[37]

Scientists and some members of the development community claim that genetically modified crops will both help solve the world's hunger crisis and help poor farmers increase their crop yields and thus their profit margins. The United States passed a law in the early 1960s that allowed scientists and corporations the right to patent the seeds they created through centuries-old processes of plant breeding.[38] Since that time, there has been a rush on the U.S. patent office to be the first person to register a patent on every conceivable type of life form, including the human genome. May 1983 saw the production of the world's first genetically modified plant—a tobacco plant resistant to herbicide.[39] As we know, though, researchers did not stop with plants.

> Pig number 6707 was meant to be "super"—super fast growing, super big, super meat quality. It was supposed to be a technological breakthrough in animal husbandry, among the first of a series of high-tech animals that would revolutionize agriculture and food production. Researchers at the USDA implanted the human gene governing growth into the pig while it was still an embryo. The idea was to have the human growth gene become part of the pig's genetic code and thus create an animal that, with the aid of the new gene, would grow far larger than any before. To the surprise of the bioengineers, the human genetic material that they had injected into the animal altered its metabolism in an unpredictable and unfortunate way. Transgenic pig 6707 was in fact a tragicomic creation, a "super cripple." Excessively hairy, riddled with arthritis, and cross-eyed, the pig rarely even stood up, the wretched product of a science without ethics.[40]

The impact of genetically modified biotechnology on farming in the "two-thirds" world has been far-reaching. The combination of the development of high-yielding seed varieties with the urging of farmers to produce crops for export rather than for local consumption has produced disastrous results. Bioengineered seeds are one form of undermining the ability of local farmers to continue practicing sustainable agriculture. For centuries, farmers have saved some seeds from each harvest to plant for the next year's crops. Transnational biotech corporations that have invested millions of dollars in the research and development of their "new" seeds are trying to make it illegal for farmers to save seeds. Monsanto is in the process of developing a new type of gene, known as the "Terminator," which can be spliced into the gene sequence of any seed, allowing the production of a seedless crop.[41]

This commodification of seeds is a direct result of U.S. patent laws and the legal enactment of the right to "own" seeds. Seeds have a long history of being part of the "commons" available to all, traveling "on the wind, in birds' bellies, in traders' caravans, conquerors' pockets, and immigrants' knapsacks."[42] Behind every food crop, from rural peasant farmers to the industrial farms of "ag colleges," are seeds that have been carefully selected and cultivated by someone. In the case of the rural peasant farmers, their choices of which seeds to save and which to reject in planning for the next season's crops are not respected as legitimate forms of knowledge by the system that created intellectual property rights. "With the passage of GATT, farmers all over the world will be forced to adhere to U.S.-style law and pay royalties to companies that hold patents on the genetic material they or their ancestors helped to shape."[43] The patenting of life forms has been vigorously opposed by a host of earthist activists and NGOs from all corners of the globe who object to the commodification of life that is inherent in the ability to patent nature's essence in the life form of genes, bacteria, and even mammals.[44]

Additionally, local economies are no longer self-sufficient because they are forced to rely increasingly on imported food products. Earthist advocates argue that this process is detrimental to the community to the extent that the transportation involved in exportation increases the ecological impact of the product[45] and the community becomes disassociated from both the food that it produces and the food that it consumes. The process is further detrimental to the farmers, they argue, when farmers are convinced to transfer farmland from traditional, locally consumed crops to monocrops (e.g., coffee, vanilla, tea) for export and then the bottom drops out of their market. Vanilla bean growers, primarily in Madagascar, Reunion, and Comoros have recently experienced the devastating consequences that more and more traditional farmers are likely to face as biotechnology continues to invade traditional agricultural terrain. Two U.S.-based biotechnology firms recently developed a way to produce vanilla flavor in the laboratory. "While natural vanilla sells on the world market for about $1200 per pound, Escagenetics, a California biotechnology company, says it can sell its genetically engineered version for less than $25 per pound."[46] One NGO estimates that "more than one hundred thousand farmers in the three vanilla-producing countries are expected to lose their livelihood over the next several years."[47]

Some predictions include the possibility that genetically engineered and artificially created food will replace food production and consumption as we know it. With the use of enzymes, crops would be harvested and converted to sugar solution. The solution would then be piped to urban factories and used as a nutrient source to produce large quantities of pulp from tissue cultures. The pulp would then be reconstituted and fabricated into different shapes and textures to mimic the forms associated with traditionally grown crops.[48]

It seems that a twenty-first century version of Star Trek's food replicator may not be too far-fetched. The issues raised by earthist proponents regard the safety and nutritional quality of food; the spiritual consequences of disassociating ourselves from the earth and the production of our food; the displacement of hundreds of thousands of farmers worldwide; and the dangers of losing generations of wisdom and knowledge about the land, the growing seasons, the soil, and traditional crops that would disappear with the farmers. All of these concerns bear serious ethical and moral weight in any decision-making process about whether or not the human population wishes to pursue a bio-engineered version of globalization. As yet, the concerns of the earthist community have not been adequately heard or discussed.

The Physical Destruction of Our Planet

Earthist activists point out that biotechnology is not the only threat to farming advanced by the dominant theories of globalization. The degradation of the earth, wrought by new agricultural practices that are touted as "improving" production through various shifts in traditional farming practices, has proven to be enormous. Once again the ideological pressure to maximize profits through export-driven agricultural production is what underlies these shifts.[49] Traditional sustainable cultural practices of crop rotation, the balancing of livestock and crops, mixed cropping, and shallow and superficial plowing were abandoned as researchers, scientists, development workers, and other "experts" convinced local farmers around the world to buy into the "green revolution" by promising stronger crops, better yields, and less manual labor.[50] Physicist and ecologist Vandana Shiva describes how the so-called "green revolution" transformed the very meaning of agriculture in rural communities in the "two-thirds" world: "It was no longer an activity that worked towards a careful maintenance of nature's capital in fertile soils and provided society with food and nutrition. It became an activity aimed primarily at the production of agricultural commodities for profit."[51]

The genetically modified seeds that were introduced in the traditional farmlands of India and parts of Africa were largely intended to function as high-yielding monocrops. For maximum production and efficiency, the green revolution urged farmers to practice intensive use of fertilizers and pesticides. Often the new seed varieties were quicker growing as well, which allowed for more than one harvest in a field per year. Traditional labor-intensive practices of caring for the land were dismissed as primitive and unnecessary in the new world of the green revolution.

Unfortunately, the new techniques did not prove to be as advantageous as promised. While it is true that farmers often harvested bumper crops in the first few years of adopting the new techniques, there were dire consequences for the soil that may prove to be irreversible. As tropical ecologist Robert Goodland points out, "Land that degraded thousands of years ago in the valley of the Tigris and Euphrates rivers or on the Greek Isles remains unproductive today."[52] He also points out that currently 35 percent of the earth's land is degraded and that soil loss exceeds soil formation by at least ten times.[53] Topsoil is one of creation's most fragile miracles. Shiva relates how the women of the Chipko movement refer to the soil as the "skin of the earth."[54] What farmers found after utilizing the seeds, fertilizers, and pesticides of the green revolution was that the high-yielding seeds absorbed the rich nutrients of the soil at a higher rate than their traditional crops. Additionally, the crops demanded a higher intake of water, and the runoff from the fertilizers and pesticides often contaminated local sources of drinking water. Shiva notes that the result has been "increased soil and nutrient loss, water-logging, salinisation and drought and desertification."[55]

Similar problems have plagued the United States as transnational agribusiness firms have pressured farmers into the creation of what has been called the "factory farming" approach to livestock such as pigs, chickens, cattle, and particularly veal.[56] Increasingly the environmental effects of the waste produced by these farms are becoming the subject of controversy in rural communities. According to the *New York Times*, a farm in Missouri owned by Premium Standard, the third-largest pork producer in the United States, keeps 550,000 hogs in close quarters and the neighbors are not pleased with the arrangement.[57] In addition to the vast amount of pork products generated by the farm, the amount of manure it produces rivals that of midsized cities but without a sewage treatment facility. In 1996, forty manure spills in three states killed several hundred thousand fish.[58] "Elsewhere, manure from chicken sheds is suspected as a factor in recent blooms of the toxic algae pfiesteria in the Chesapeake Bay, and the lack of dissolved oxygen in the Gulf of Mexico off Louisiana is linked to nutrients washed off agricultural land."[59] Often local activists and environmental organizations call for regulations or organize to prevent new factory farms from relocating to their area.[60] In addition to the environmental impact, many earthist advocates argue that the living conditions in which animals exist in these factory farms constitute cruel and unusual punishment that no living creature should be forced to endure.

Of course, the systemic destruction of our planet cannot be described without reference to the increasing elimination of our forests through logging. We have already mentioned the struggles to save the Amazonian rainforest. Similar struggles are being waged in all parts of the globe as logging companies move from place to place in search of ever cheaper and more accessible timber. Half of the forest area in the "two-thirds" world was cleared between 1900 and 1965, and the logging has accelerated in recent decades.[61] In addition to the soil erosion, loss of biodiversity, and increased flooding that logging often causes in tropical forests, the introduction of "invader" species are threatening the livelihood of indigenous flora and fauna in places such as South Africa.[62] Invader species are those trees that arrived with the colonial invaders or that have been brought in since, such as the pine trees planted by timber and paper companies.

Another problem that threatens our planet's well-being is the degradation of the atmosphere caused by various forms of pollution and the resultant climate change. We have already noted some of the concerns regarding the disproportionate effects of pollution on marginal communities due to environmental racism. Mexico City has long topped the list as the most polluted city in the world. In December 1998 the Mexican government had to twice declare pollution "emergencies" due, for the first time, to dismal clouds of particles rather than the ozone.[63] In addition to the toxic concentration of ozone in the air, these particle clouds are made up of bus exhaust, industrial smoke, garbage, and fecal matter. Within a week after these emergencies were declared, official surveys showed that half of the city's 18 million residents became sick with some respiratory ailment.[64] Similar stories of pollution and disease reverberate around the globe as the expansion of the industrial revolution continues with wanton disregard for air quality, the ozone layer, or the health of the earth's inhabitants.[65]

In the last years of the twentieth century, heightened attention was paid to the advanced pace of the climate changes that are transforming the present face of our planet.[66] In a strongly earthist-oriented study addressing the crisis of climate change, the World Council of Churches opened with the following words:

> Scientifically-based evidence tells us that human activity is altering the conditions of life on Planet Earth. Changes in the atmosphere caused by the emission of greenhouse gases . . . are expected to lead to an increase in average global temperature, sea-level rise, and far-reaching climatic changes. The evidence comes to us as an unprecedented, extraordinary sign of this present time. Our interpretation of the sign is fraught with implications for the future well-being of human and other life and for the faithfulness of Christians to the Creator of all that is. Accelerated climate change represents not only a threat to life but also an inescapable issue of justice. It throws into sharp relief the unjust imbalances of wealth, resources and economic power between the rich and poor that characterizes the world today.[67]

These words reflect broadly the fact that many of the issues related to the destruction of our planet are embraced by earthist activists, including some church groups, as issues deeply rooted in a profound injustice that has accompanied the dominant forms of globalization that perpetrated this destruction.

The degradation of the world's water is manifesting itself in the forms of scarcity, contamination, and the viability of various water creatures. The issue of water scarcity is prevalent in the western states of the United States as well as in India and parts of Africa, albeit for vastly different reasons. In the United States, water usage goes beyond the subsistence necessities of drinking and cooking, bathing and cleaning, and watering crops. Earthist proponents point out that millions of gallons of water are used to keep golf courses and trophy lawns green in the middle of deserts and for other vain and superfluous purposes. According to Shiva, drought in "two-thirds" world countries is

> an outcome of reductionistic knowledge and modes of development that violate cycles of life in rivers, in the soil, in mountains. Rivers are drying up because their catchments have been mined, deforested or over-cultivated to generate revenue and profits. Groundwater is drying up because it has been over-exploited to feed cash crops. Village after village is being robbed of its lifeline, its sources of drinking water, and the number of villages facing water famine is in direct proportion to the number of "schemes" implemented by government agencies to "develop" water.[68]

We have already seen how pesticides and fertilizers as well as manure and other waste products are contaminating groundwater in "first" and "two-thirds" world countries alike. Another factor that contributes to the degradation of the water is fishing and shrimp production.[69] Both of these livelihoods used to be practiced by communities of coastal people who had been fishing for generations. With the increasing appetite of the "first" world for sea creatures of all stripes, the oceans became a new growth industry. In chapter 3, we read about the encroachment of large-scale fishing in the tuna industry and how commercial tuna fishers were killing dolphins as well as edging local fishermen out of the market. Like all of the issues we have examined in this chapter, the problem has multiple layers. Just as corporate agribusiness stands poised to destroy the small-scale farmer, corporate fishing interests stand likely to destroy hundreds of fishing communities around the world—not just by pricing them out of the market but through their unsustainable practices that have resulted in the depletion of the world's fish sources. "Today, nine of the world's seventeen major fishing grounds are in decline, and four are already "fished out" commercially."[70]

People grounded in the alternative ideology of earthism realize that a crisis is inherent in the liberal tradition's models of globalization because these models are inherently unsustainable. The recent salmon crisis in the Pacific Northwest spurred the following earthist response from local inhabitant Robert Sullivan:

> Unlike other environmental crises here in the Pacific Northwest, the salmon crisis is one none of us can escape. . . . Back when the controversy over logging was at its height, you could sit at home and write a check (preferably printed on recycled paper) and vote for a forestry reform candidate. . . . Now, with the salmon crisis, you step out the door and the rain that's running off your front lawn, awash in fertilizer, is a problem. You drive to work (alone) and you are adding to the oil and other chemicals that all eventually drain into

> the streams. You work for a company that wants to expand its offices into what is a salmon habitat, which describes just about every wetland within a day's drive of Seattle. At home, you turn on a light that is fed cheaply by the very dams that make it nearly impossible for salmon to swim upstream. For us to change this chain of events requires more than just writing checks. It requires changing our life styles, which is something most Northwesterners have always seemed loath to do.[71]

At the root of the earthist globalization paradigm is an acceptance of the need to change behaviors, to change lifestyles, to enact a particular moral vision. Many earthist proponents in the "first" world are of European descent and many come from lives of privilege. Within this group, most of these people grew up in the liberal culture that formed the first two theories of globalization, but each has ultimately rejected these models as unsustainable. They have been transformed by the ideology of earthism or by their recognition of their shared humanity with the people from the "two-thirds" world or perhaps by some other personal life experience. What matters, though, is that this group of people has come to recognize that with the different worldview they have adopted comes a different lifestyle they also must adopt. This is not to say that most of these people woke up one day and turned in their Lexus for a bicycle, or that any of them follow all of the public policy strategies that will be shared in the pages that follow. What it means is that these people remind us of the feminist liberation claim made earlier in this study that the way we live in the world is a testimony to our moral vision and values."[72]

An Earthist Revisioning of Globalization as Localization

In addition to a critique of the dominant form of globalization, earthist proponents also share a vision of a different future for globalization. That vision holds that if we keep the earth as the center of our attention, then our social, economic, and political policies will reflect a respect for our interdependence with all of creation. Ultimately, earthist proponents call for a future that is rooted in smaller economies of scale in which a turn toward the local is prioritized. The freedom and creativity that often accompany the work of resistance have allowed for a space in which earthist thinkers have been able to generate a wide variety of public policy strategies that challenge the self-centered and greed-oriented model of capitalism that they feel currently dominates society.

This earthist paradigm calls for an ardent need to shift away from a model of globalization as export-oriented trade and mass-produced food and consumer products and back toward a model of globalization as localization. We have already seen that an important part of this strategy is to expose the inadequacy of an economic model that privileges wealth creation over care for creation. One alternative model is being developed in the form of ecological economics[73] that, as McFague describes it,

> begins with the viability of the whole community, on the assumption that only as it thrives now and in the future will its various members, including human beings, thrive as well. In other words, ecological economics begins with sustainability and distributive justice, not with the allocation of resources among competing individuals. . . . Ecological economics does not pretend to be value-free; its preference is evident—the well-being and sustainability of our household, planet Earth.[74]

Herman Daly, a pioneer in the field of ecological economics, describes ecological economics as being based on an understanding of the human economy as existing within a closed ecosystem. This description means that while humans take resources from the environment and return them as waste (an open system), all matter within the ecosystem circulates internally (a closed system). While human populations and waste were small enough to be absorbed by the ecosystem, humans posed no threat. As our population increases and our behaviors create more waste than the ecosystem can subsume, we face dangerous problems. Daly argues that we must strive for a "steady-state" economy, which means "that the input of raw materials and energy to an economy and the output of waste materials and heat must be within the regenerative and absorptive capacities of the ecosystem."[75]

Achieving a steady-state requires that the price of consumer products more adequately reflect all of the actual costs associated with that product. In contrast to the neoclassical model of economics that encourages the externalization of costs in order to increase efficiency, the model of ecological economics requires that all potential costs—not just production costs, but waste and environmental costs as well as disposal costs (especially for big-ticket items such as cars, washing machines, etc.)—be incorporated into the price of an item.[76] The externalization of the pollution and recycle or waste costs of most products has led to those costs being borne by the earth and the general public. Paying for bottled drinking water rather than drinking polluted tap water is just one example of how our commons and our environment are being both destroyed and commodified simultaneously.[77] Corporations benefit both from externalizing their environmental costs and from developing new products to replace items from the commons that have been destroyed by corporate negligence and greed.

Ecological economics is deeply rooted in an earthist ideology that recognizes that "we cannot survive . . . unless we acknowledge our profound dependence on one another and on the earth."[78] It is an economic model that starts with the understanding that our economic life is not separate from our cultural and political life—indeed, it is a profound expression of the interconnectedness of human society and "other" society; namely, the earth and all the living beings that coexist. In addition to rethinking economic theory, the earthist position offers the following strategic principles to help guide its vision of globalization as localization.

The Principle of Local Production for Local Consumption

One of the biggest public policy interests of earthist proponents is to shift our economies back toward the production of food and products for local consumption. In recent years a distinct bias in agriculture has tipped the scales against family farms. We have already seen the role that agribusiness and biotechnology have played in changing the face of agriculture. With the push to produce higher yields and for small farms to grow, grow, grow (and I do not mean their crops), those who were unwilling or unable to expand their production have mostly disappeared. Between 1910 and 1920, one-third of the people in the United States lived on farms, by 1991, fewer than 2 percent were left.[79]

In 1944 anthropologist Walter Goldschmidt conducted a study of two rural California communities. Dinuba and Arvin were quite similar except that one was surrounded by family farms, the other by corporate farms. Goldschmidt found that the family farm community of Dinuba was "more stable, had a higher standard of living, more small businesses, higher retail sales, better schools and other community facilities, and a higher degree of citizen participation in local affairs."[80] The United States Department of Agriculture (USDA), which had commissioned the study, invoked a clause in Goldschmidt's contract that prevented his findings from becoming public for thirty years. "Meanwhile the USDA continued to promote research that rapidly transformed the Dinubas of our country into Arvins."[81]

This kind of research is not limited to the 1940s or to the context of the United States. With regard to subsistence agriculture, several studies have shown that it is efficient and sustainable and that it adequately provides for the food needs of its local producers.[82] Even the World Bank, which has spearheaded the modernization of agriculture in the "two-thirds" world, admitted in one of its more notorious reports that "smallholders in Africa are outstanding managers of their own resources—their land and capital, fertilizer and water."[83] Then why modernize agriculture and push the smallholders into the slums? The answer, as the report fully admits, is that subsistence farming is incompatible with the development of the market.[84]

Despite the fact that subsistence farming is not the best way to "develop the market," earthist proponents argue that it is best for the environment, for the community, and for the earth. Their position is supported by the increased environmental costs associated with widespread trade as well as Goldschmidt's findings regarding the increased community identity and stability corresponding to family farming. While "first" world consumers have become accustomed to eating strawberries in January, earthist proponents argue that "first" world consumers must take a serious look at what price is being paid for the imported food on our tables, and they do not mean the price paid at the grocery store. Those same strawberries are being grown on land that could be raising food for the migrant workers who pick it because they no longer have sustainable communities and farmlands of their own. Our increased appetite for beef has resulted in the destruction of rainforests in Central America. The problem of food supply in our world is not one of quantity but rather one of distribution. Earthist advocates argue that a return to local food production for local consumption would greatly increase poor people's access to food, both through trading in local markets and through encouraging and aiding poor communities in developing garden plots. Practices like these have been common in rural communities in Africa and other parts of the world for generations, but they have been increasingly abandoned as rural populations have flocked to the cities in search of paid work.

Small-scale farming—known as "farming with a face on it" in Japan, subscription farming in Europe, and community supported agriculture (CSA) in the United States offers one model of how we might return to local food production for local consumption.[85] CSAs are a growing phenomenon in which a group of persons pay a farmer up front for fresh produce to be delivered over a prescribed number of weeks. This arrangement allows a small farmer the capital necessary to produce a crop and gives the mostly urban customers a concrete connection with the food they eat. More importantly, by connecting consumers directly with the farmer, people know where and how their food is being grown and the environmental impact of their consumptive behavior is greatly reduced. The transportation costs (including the environmental costs) are reduced, and because most CSAs practice sustainable farming methods, the use of chemicals, fertilizers, and bioengineered seeds are eliminated. While it is true that the prices for the produce tend to be higher than those at many grocery stores, these prices are more reflective of the "true" cost of production in a steady-state economy.

The Principle of Bioregionalism

Of course, most proponents of the earthist position recognize that it would be virtually impossible as well as prohibitively expensive for local communities to produce all of their own goods. So it is important to recognize that they are not against trade per se, but rather they are against an economic model that promotes international trade as the primary mode of economic exchange. Most earthist proponents would argue, as did Adam Smith, that local communities should produce what they can in order to meet their needs and trade for the rest. The issue then arises as to how that trade should be organized.

One suggestion is that trade should be oriented around the principle of bioregionalism. Bioregionalism is rooted in a model of economic self-sufficiency that flies in the face of economic models promoting the increased economic interdependence of nations through the institutional structures of corporations and the World Trade Organization.[86] Bioregionalism is promoted as one way society might organize itself under a model of ecological economics. The basic principle advocates that bioregions would be established along either naturally occurring boundaries or along established political boundaries. Environmental activist Kirkpatrick Sale explains that a bioregional economy "would seek first to maintain rather than use up the natural world, to adapt to the environment rather than exploit it or manipulate it, and to conserve not only the resources but also the relationships and systems of the natural world. . . . Sustainability, not growth, would be its goal."[87]

French financier and politician James Goldsmith offers a somewhat less radical version of bioregionalism that holds that regions should be empowered to decide "whether and when to enter into bilateral agreements with other regions for mutual economic benefits. We must not simply open our markets to any and every product regardless of whether it benefits our economy, destroys our employment, or destabilizes our society."[88] Goldsmith argues that the freedom of movement of capital is not the problem; rather, the transnationalization of capital causes problems. In other words, capital needs to be rooted in communities in order for communities to continue to be viable. Goldsmith contends that if Japan (or any other country) wants to sell its products in U.S. markets, it should "bring its capital and its technology, build factories in America, employ American people, and become a corporate citizen of America."[89]

Another practical step toward creating sustainable economic bioregions is the development of regional currency, a grassroots practice that already has an impressive track record in parts of Britain, the United States, Canada, and Australia.[90] The principle behind regional currencies is to keep money invested in local communities rather then having it fill the coffers of transnational corporations with no interest in community well-being. While the numerous programs are set up in a variety of ways, they all function on a trade or barter system (the true basis for any currency). People perform tasks for others (e.g., carpentry, plumbing, cooking, child care) and either receive a local currency that can only be spent in the community or a certain amount of banked credit. These people are then able to trade their currency or credit for goods or services that they require. While a traditional barter system requires that each individual possess a skill or product that the other person wants or needs, local currencies widen the pool by allowing people to receive payment for services, but in a form that ensures that the money will be reinvested in their local community.

The Principle of Environmental Justice

The reality of community outrage and protest against the environmental racism described earlier is an integral facet of an earthist revisioning of globalization. By her own account, Lois Gibbs, wife and mother, had bought into the "American Dream."[91] She had a house, two children, a husband, and HBO. The problem was that her dream home was located in Love Canal. While she had never considered herself an activist or an organizer, Lois became both when her son developed epilepsy and her daughter almost died from a rare blood disease. She describes how mothers all over the country have been galvanized into action as their children have fallen ill from the harmful effects of factories and plants located in their communities.

> Women in Texas . . . organized against the pollution they believed was causing brain cancer in their children. A mother of a child born severely retarded became a leader in a movement against a battery recycler in Throop, Pennsylvania, that contaminated her neighborhood with lead. A mother of two autistic children in Lemonster, Massachusetts, discovered that there were over one hundred autistic children in her community, a statistic she believes is the result of policies at a nearby Foster-Grant sunglasses plant.[92]

People all across the United States, and increasingly in other countries, have mobilized their neighbors and their resources to clean up their communities. These activists and their organizations have come to be known as the "environmental justice" movement. Gibbs writes that "a major goal of the grassroots movement for environmental justice is to rebuild the United States, community by community."[93] What sets environmental justice advocates apart from many other environmental or ecological agencies is their ability to locate their own particular issue or problem within a broader context of societal structural injustice. Richard Hofrichter, executive director of the Center for Ecology and Social Justice, describes how environmental justice advocates recognize that marginalized peoples' inability to receive adequate health care, clean water and air, affordable shelter, and a safe workplace is not an accident but a result of "institutional decisions, marketing practices, discrimination, and an endless quest for economic growth. Environmental problems therefore remain inseparable from other social injustices such as poverty, racism, sexism, unemployment, urban deterioration, and the diminishing quality of life resulting from corporate activity."[94]

Persons living in marginalized communities have come to realize that the dump or incinerator scheduled to be located in their community is just a symptom of a larger structural problem and that even if they successfully manage to keep it out of their neighborhood, it will be located somewhere else unless they work to change the system.

The Principle of Voluntary Simplicity

The idea of voluntary simplicity is increasingly becoming a significant part of resistance to globalization in the "first" world and among many earthist activists. It involves individuals and families making personal lifestyle choices that reduce the adverse impacts of their behavior on the environment. There are a wide range of behaviors that people adopt in the voluntary simplicity movement—from the farmers setting up a sustainable lifestyle running an organic CSA to the urban CSA shareholders who may recycle, compost, walk to work, and otherwise try to "simplify" their lives.

Some personal lifestyle choices—such as leaving a high-paying corporate job for community-based work or giving large portions of your income to organizations and agencies working toward an alternative vision of society—also are aimed toward addressing the issues of distributive justice in our society. One of the most attractive aspects of voluntary simplicity is that it is a mode of resistance that is easily accessible. It also reflects the kind of behavioral changes that the majority of "first" world people will have to adopt if human life on earth is going to continue.

An Earthist Vision of the Good Life

Those who adhere to an earthist ideology have a very definite vision of what constitutes the good life, and it is a vision that differs quite substantially from the two previous theories. Reverence and respect for life (and not just human life), as well as for the whole of God's creation, are evident both in the earthist position's criticisms of globalization and in its public policy proposals. Wealth and prosperity are not goals in and of themselves, but rather are viewed as means toward achieving a particular quality of life that is respectful of the interconnected essence of planetary existence. McFague points out that this vision of the good life is marked by moderation, a quality absent from the two previous globalization theories.[95] She explains: "Just as the good life for human beings rests on distributive justice—all must have the basics—so also the planet must have the basics. The earth itself must have the conditions necessary to support us and, increasingly, this means we must live so that these conditions are possible. In other words, the good life for all human beings and for the planet is a whole—it is one good thing."[96] As we have seen in this chapter, the three core values that constitute the earthist vision of the good life are mutuality, justice, and sustainability.

Mutuality as the Context for Moral Agency

In direct contradiction to the first globalization position, earthist proponents define human existence in non-individualistic terms. People are fundamentally understood as relational and as a part of a larger ecosystem. Our interdependence functions to create a sense of moral agency that requires individual decision-making to occur within the context of respect for mutuality. In other words, while the first position finds people making decisions based on individual self-interest and the second position finds people making decisions based on a sense of responsibility or obligation toward others, this position defines moral agency more broadly than individual decision-making. Decisions cannot be thought about merely from the perspective of the person making a decision and how they will be affected, or even how their decision might affect others. Rather, in an earthist worldview, moral agency, or the capacity to know what is good and to act on it, is influenced by fundamental beliefs about the relationships that exist between different aspects of creation.

Within religious perspectives this understanding of moral agency as dependent upon mutuality has been referred to as "the integrity of creation."[97] Rasmussen contrasts mutuality and the integrity of creation with the dominant modes of moral agency, which he labels "apartheid thinking," which "assumes that some worlds can be separated from other worlds (other humans' and otherkinds'), and these can pursue separate development because they are not internally related."[98] Recognition of the integrity of creation represents a "refusal to separate human from nonhuman worlds," an insistence that the fate of creation rests in respect for our relationships and interconnectedness.[99] These relationships are both social and ecological as the WCC noted, "The integrity of creation has a social aspect which we recognize as peace with justice, and an ecological aspect which we recognize in the self-renewing, sustainable character of natural ecosystems."[100] When we value mutuality and the integrity of creation, we exercise our moral agency in fundamentally different ways than when moral agency is based on individualism or notions of responsibility.

In an earthist paradigm, an understanding of the good is defined by a common good. What is good can only be good if it respects the integrity of creation, if it does not harm others or our world. What may, at first glance, seem good for the individual might actually be harmful to another species or to the streams or the air if we look at the issue from an earthist perspective. Mutuality implies respect for others in the form of neighbor, creature, ocean, wind, and earth. This requires that decision-making becomes a discernment process in which both the social and ecological aspects of human relatedness with creation must be balanced. This does not necessarily make for easy decisions, but it certainly makes for better ones.

Justice as Humanity's Telos

Building on a model of decision-making shaped by the radical experience of mutuality and interrelatedness is the earthist position's understanding of humanity's telos as rooted in the task of justice. If our moral world is constituted by respecting the integrity of creation, then in a world where this integrity is being violated right and left, the most pressing task bearing down on us is the struggle to establish right-relatedness where there is brokenness and justice where there is injustice.

The conception of justice that marks the earthist position is one that requires attention to the concrete relationships of our contemporary world. This position is closely aligned with the notions of justice sought by feminist ethicists and theologians; it is concerned with issues of social power and oppression. In this paradigm of justice, the rights and well-being of the poor and exploited are often privileged as a means toward rectifying their marginalized position within society. Theologically speaking, attempts to ameliorate situations of exploitation are attempts to approximate the relationships of justice and care that earthist proponents believe God intended for creation.

The behavior and actions of earthist activists often are motivated by their recognition of particular violations of right relation. Indeed, as we have observed throughout this chapter, the lives of the earthist activists are given over to the struggle for justice, whether in movements to save trees and the forests, or dolphins and whales, or the soil and the streams, or our neighbors and their children being poisoned by toxic waste. We can see clearly the values of the proponents of earthism being lived out on a daily basis in their lives. The search for justice is one of the most important motivating factors behind resistance to globalization and the concomitant move toward localization.

Here, within the earthist paradigm, living as if justice were our calling is a critical way of defining what it means to be human. This call to justice is described by Rasmussen as meaning "essentially that we share one another's fate and are obligated by creation itself to promote one another's well-being."[101] This negation of self-interest in favor of caring for others is a fundamental redefinition of the good life from the previous two positions. It is a sense of justice that is quite different from the Western liberal tradition's notion of justice as liberty, which provides the conditions for wide-ranging individual choice, or justice as equality, which ensures the distribution of rights and goods at a humane level among the largest number of people possible.[102] Rasmussen's notion of justice as "comprehensive right-relatedness means the rendering, amid limited resources and the conditions of a still chaotic world, of whatever is required for the fullest possible flourishing of creation in any given time and place."[103]

The calling toward justice that defines this position's vision of the good life is an important moral norm because it stands in opposition to the hubris of anthropocentrism and human greed that mark contemporary models of globalization. Given the potential climatic and planetary catastrophes that threaten to transform the earth as we know it, earthist proponents hold that it is humanity's responsibility to work toward the reparation of creation through seeking to establish justice and right relation.

Sustainability as What Constitutes Human Flourishing

Of course, the flourishing of creation itself is what defines this position's response to the final question of what constitutes human flourishing. In this third theory of globalization, the anthropocentrism of this typology is completely unraveled; earthist advocates are interested not merely in what constitutes human flourishing because the question does not make sense within their own worldview. Earthist advocates see themselves not as independent from the rest of creation but as existing within a relationship of mutuality with their surroundings; the question must necessarily be reframed as "What constitutes the flourishing of creation?" The answer, as we have seen repeatedly throughout this chapter, is undoubtedly sustainability.[104]

Over and over again the critiques of the neoliberal model of globalization echo a similar theme—the green revolution is causing ecological damage, loggers and timber companies are destroying the world's forests, corporate pollution is choking our air—in a word this behavior is unsustainable. This behavior is killing creation as we know it. Proponents of an earthist ideology hold up for us another model of what global interaction and global connectedness could look like. The globalization-as-localization theory holds that sustainability should mark our vision of the good life.

Sustainability as a value that constitutes the flourishing of creation refers to a world in which steady-state economic values are respected and there is a balance between what humans take from the planet and what we return as waste. It refers to a world in which humans, the earth, and other creatures are able to live together in mutually supportive and complementary ways. This vision of sustainability is interested not in sustainable growth or sustainable development, but in sustainability as a value that seeks to eliminate poverty and conflict, hunger and homelessness, the extinction of species, and the pollution of our planet through care for creation.

The alternative vision of globalization outlined in this chapter seeks to challenge what its proponents see as the abusive and exploitative versions of globalization that we have previously examined. The vision here is grounded in the reality of human existence and strives to transform relationships of hierarchy and domination into relationships of mutuality and justice. Earthist proponents argue that it is through a vision of the good life as mutuality, justice, and sustainability that our world can be transformed into a world of people who care more about the dignity and well-being of other human beings and the care of our planet than about wealth and its illusions of satisfaction.

Notes

1. This is not to imply that proponents of the first two globalization theories would *deny* the historical events that scholars such as Wallerstein, Braudel, and Arrighi lift up. Rather, it is to point out that when we tell our history, it is important to note what is included and what is left out.

2. This approach to history is informed by Karl Marx's theory of primitive accumulation, which holds that the accumulation of capital is a necessary precursor

to the development of capitalism. Marx compares his primitive accumulation to Adam Smith's notion of "previous accumulation." Both ideas are rooted in the belief that the emergence of capitalist production is dependent on a certain amount of previously accumulated wealth, which provides the necessary start-up funds for the development of capitalist means of production. Marx ties the bourgeoisie's ability to accumulate wealth to the transformation of the means of production by which the agrarian proletariat lost their access to the land. Braudel, Wallerstein, and Arrighi all use the concept of accumulation theory to explain the historical patterns of capitalist development. Karl Marx, *Capital: A Critique of Political Economy*, vol. 1, trans. Ben Fowkes (1867; repr., London: Penguin Books, 1990), esp. chaps. 25 and 26.

3. These fairs were named after the town of Besancon where they were first held. Giovanni Arrighi, *The Long Twentieth Century: Money, Power, and the Origin of Our Times* (London: Verso, 1994), 82.

4. Ibid., 83.

5. At the time corporate charters emerged, debt was inheritable. David Korten describes the situation: "Those who sailed forth from England to trade for spices in the East Indies faced not only the inevitable perils of the dangerous sea voyage but also the prospect that they and their families could be ruined, even into future generations, if their cargo were lost to bad weather or pirates. The corporation represented an important institutional innovation to overcome this barrier to international commerce. . . . Specifically, the corporate charter represented a grant from the crown that limited an investor's liability for losses of the corporation to the amount of his or her investment in it—a right not extended to individual citizens." David C. Korten, *When Corporations Rule the World* (West Hartford, CT: Kumarian Press, 1995), 54.

6. See David S. Landes, "The Nature of Industrial Revolution," chap. 13 in *The Wealth and Poverty of Nations: Why Some Are So Rich and Some So Poor* (New York: W. W. Norton, 1998), for a solid capitalist historical account of the technological developments that led to the industrial revolution.

7. Ibid., 304.

8. Ibid., 241.

9. Since we have already rehearsed the post-World War II historical situation as it affects globalization, we will not revisit that here. See pp. 41 and 43.

10. Maude Barlow and Tony Clarke, *MAI: The Multilateral Agreement on Investment and the Threat to American Freedom* (New York: Stoddart Publishing, 1998), 9.

11. See John B. Cobb Jr., *An Earthist Challenge to Economism: A Theological Critique of the World Bank* (London: Macmillan, 1999); and McFague, *Life Abundant: Rethinking Theology and Economy for a Planet in Peril* (Minneapolis: Fortress Press, 2001) for an elaboration of economism and earthist alternatives.

12. For theological voices in addition to Cobb and McFague cited above, see Ivone Gebara, *Longing for Running Water: Ecofeminism and Liberation* (Minneapolis: Fortress Press, 1999); Leonardo Boff, *Cry of the Earth, Cry of the Poor* (Maryknoll, NY: Orbis Books, 1997); Larry Rasmussen, *Earth Community, Earth*

Ethics (Maryknoll, NY: Orbis Books, 1996); and Ulrich Duchrow, *Alternatives to Global Capitalism: Drawn from Biblical History, Designed for Political Action* (Utrecht, Netherlands: International Books, 1995). For economic voices see Edward J. Nell, *Making Sense of a Changing Economy: Technology, Markets, and Morals* (London: Routledge, 1996); and Oscar Nudler and Mark A. Lutz, eds., *Economics, Culture, and Society—Alternative Approaches: Dissenting Views from Economic Orthodoxy* (New York: Apex Press, 1996). For a combined approach see Herman E. Daly and John B. Cobb Jr., *For the Common Good: Redirecting the Economy toward Community, the Environment, and a Sustainable Future* (Boston: Beacon Press, 1989).

13. While the term "earthism" has been coined by Cobb to name this ideology, the values and beliefs of this earthist ideology are shared by a multitude of grassroots activists, people of faith, economists, ethicists, and theologians. In fact, in economic circles the terms "steady-state economics" and "ecological economics" are often used to describe economic theories that value care for people and the planet above strictly growth- and profit-oriented models.

14. It is important to point out that while McFague does not use the same terminology as Cobb (economism and earthism) the two distinct worldviews that she describes in her book correspond to these categories of Cobb. See McFague, *Life Abundant*, esp. chaps. 4 and 5.

15. McFague, *Life Abundant*, 72–73.

16. Rasmussen, *Earth Community*, 10.

17. Thomas Berry, *The Great Work: Our Way into the Future* (New York: Bell Tower, 1999), 56. This book focuses on developing an earthist ideology and pointing the way toward what he terms an "Ecozoic" Era.

18. Ivone Gebara, "The Trinity and Human Experience: An Ecofeminist Approach," in *Women Healing Earth: Third World Women on Ecology, Feminism, and Religion*, ed. Rosemary Ruether (Maryknoll, NY: Orbis Books, 1996), 22.

19. The Chipko movement started in India in the 1970s as a protest against the logging of Indian forests. Women and children placed their bodies between the loggers and the trees by "hugging" the trees and refusing to leave.

20. Vandana Shiva, *Staying Alive: Women, Ecology, and Development* (London: Zed Books, 1989), 210.

21. The term "nongovernmental organization" (NGO) refers to a plethora of non-state and voluntary groups, agencies, and civil society organizations that function as "nonprofit" agencies and that pursue social agendas related to health, human rights, education, peace and justice, and the environment. These organizations are characterized as "nongovernmental" in order to distinguish them from both official governmental agencies as well as for-profit business interests.

22. For a more detailed look at the role of NGOs in World Bank history, see Bruce Rich, *Mortgaging the Earth: The World Bank, Environmental Impoverishment, and the Crisis of Overdevelopment* (Boston: Beacon Press, 1994); and Catherine Caulfield, *Masters of Illusion: The World Bank and the Poverty of Nations* (New York: Henry Holt & Co., 1996).

23. Jeremy Brecher and Tim Costello, *Global Village or Global Pillage: Economic Reconstruction from the Ground Up* (Boston: South End Press, 1994), 90–94.

24. Ibid., 91.

25. Ibid., 91–92.

26. For a detailed analysis of the MAI, see Barlow and Clarke, *MAI.*

27. McFague, *Life Abundant*, 73.

28. For more detailed studies of environmental racism, see United Church of Christ Commission for Racial Justice, *Toxic Wastes and Race in the United States: A National Study of the Racial and Socioeconomic Characteristics of Communities with Hazardous Waste Sites* (New York: United Church of Christ, 1987); Richard Hofrichter, ed., *Toxic Struggles: The Theory and Practice of Environmental Justice* (Philadelphia: New Society Publishers, 1993); and Jace Weaver, ed., *Defending Mother Earth: Native American Perspectives on Environmental Justice* (Maryknoll, NY: Orbis Books, 1996).

29. Robert D. Bullard, "Anatomy of Environmental Racism," in *Toxic Struggles*, ed. Hofrichter, 26.

30. As cited in ibid., 27.

31. Rasmussen, *Earth Community*, 78.

32. In honor of the absurd nature of Summers's remarks, the monthly publication *Multinational Monitor* has a regular feature titled "The Lawrence Summers Memorial Award" in which they highlight similarly inappropriate statements.

33. As quoted in *Multinational Monitor* 21, no. 6 (June 2000): 9.

34. Professor James R. Fleming of Colby College. Online: www.colby.edu/sci.tech.

35. Henk Hobbelink, "Biotechnology and the Future of Agriculture," in *Biopolitics: A Feminist and Ecological Reader on Biotechnology*, ed. Vandana Shiva and Ingunn Moser (London: Zed Books, 1995), 227.

36. Ibid.

37. Andrew Kimbrell, "Biocolonization: The Patenting of Life and the Global Market in Body Parts," in *The Case against the Global Economy and for a Turn toward the Local*, ed. Jerry Mander and Edward Goldsmith (San Francisco: Sierra Club Books, 1996), 132.

38. Karen Lehman and Al Krebs, "Control of the World's Food Supply," in *Case against the Global Economy*, ed. Mander and Goldsmith, 129.

39. Robin McKie and John Arlidge, "The GM Controversy: How Seeds of Doubt Were Planted," *The Observer*, May 23, 1999.

40. Kimbrell, "Biocolonization," in *Case against the Global Economy*, ed. Mander and Goldsmith, 137.

41. Sarah Anderson and John Cavanagh with Thea Lee and the Institute for Policy Studies, *Field Guide to the Global Economy* (New York: The New Press, 2000), 35.

42. Lehman and Krebs, "Control of the World's Food Supply," in *Case against the Global Economy*, ed. Mander and Goldsmith, 128.

43. Ibid., 129.

44. For more details see Kimbrell, "Biocolonization"; and Vandana Shiva, *Biopiracy: The Plunder of Nature and Knowledge* (Boston: South End Press, 1997).

45. Lehman and Krebs note that food travels an average of 2,000 miles before it lands on our plate. Lehman and Krebs, "Control of the World's Food Supply," 122.

46. Jeremy Rifkin, "New Technology and the End of Jobs," in *Case against the Global Economy*, ed. Mander and Goldsmith, 111.

47. Ibid., 112.

48. Ibid.

49. For more detailed treatment of an earthist critique of how export-oriented trade harms the environment, see Edward Goldsmith, "Global Trade and the Environment," in *Case against the Global Economy*, ed. Mander and Goldsmith.

50. For an excellent critique of the green revolution, particularly as it has affected women, see Shiva, *Staying Alive*, esp. chap. 5.

51. Ibid., 103.

52. Robert Goodland, "Growth Has Reached Its Limit," in *Case against the Global Economy*, ed. Mander and Goldsmith, 213.

53. Ibid.

54. Shiva, *Staying Alive*, 140.

55. Ibid., 143.

56. For a detailed account of the conditions for animals within this growth industry, see C. David Coats, *Old MacDonald's Factory Farm: The Myth of the Traditional Farm and the Shocking Truth about Animal Suffering in Today's Agribusiness* (New York: Continuum, 1989).

57. John H. Cushman Jr., "Pollution by Factory Farms Inspires Industrial Approach to Regulation," *New York Times*, March 6, 1998, sec. A, p. 12.

58. Ibid.

59. Ibid.

60. "Kathy Bloom, vice president of Citizens for a Healthy Environment, the Seward County citizens' group that led the fight against the pork industry, said that her county already had 80,000 hogs and that voters did not want to add 400,000." As quoted in "Rural Opposition to Hog Farms Grows," *New York Times*, September 22, 1997, sec. A, p. 18.

61. Martin Khor, "Global Economy and the Third World," in *Case against the Global Economy*, ed. Mander and Goldsmith, 52.

62. Donald G. McNeil Jr., "Woodman, Don't Spare That Tree! It Doesn't Belong in South Africa," *New York Times*, June 15, 1998, sec. A, p. 10.

63. Julia Preston, "A Fatal Case of Fatalism," *New York Times*, February 14, 1999, sec. WK, p. 3.

64. Ibid.

65. See also, "Asian Pollution Widens Its Deadly Reach but Many Are Oblivious," *New York Times*, November 29, 1997, sec. A, pp. 1, 7.

66. William K. Stevens, "Dead Trees and Shriveling Glaciers as Alaska Melts," *New York Times*, August 18, 1998, sec. F, pp. 1, 5; William K. Stevens, "Surveys Uncover Substantial Melting of Greenland Ice Sheet," *New York Times*, March 5, 1999, sec. A, p. 13; Andrew C. Revkin, "Report Forecasts Warming's Effects: Significant Climate Changes Predicted for the Country," *New York Times*, June 12,

2000, sec. A, pp. 1, 25; Bob Herbert, "The Danger Point," *New York Times*, July 6, 2000, sec. A, p. 27; Bob Herbert, "Cold Facts of Global Warming," *New York Times*, July 10, 2000, sec. A, p. 25; Walter Gibbs, "Research Predicts Summer Doom for Northern Icecap," *New York Times*, July 11, 2000, sec. F, p. 2; Andrew C. Revkin, "Study Faults Humans for Large Share of Global Warming," *New York Times*, July 14, 2000, sec. A, p. 12.

67. World Council of Churches, "Accelerated Climate Change: Sign of Peril, Test of Faith" (New York: WCC U.S. Office, 1994).

68. Shiva, *Staying Alive*, 179.

69. For more details see Edward Goldsmith, "Global Trade and the Environment," in *Case against the Global Economy*, ed. Mander and Goldsmith.

70. Alex Wilkes, as quoted in ibid., 83.

71. Robert Sullivan, "And Now, the Salmon War," *New York Times*, March 20, 1999, sec. A, p. 15.

72. See p. 18 above.

73. For a more in-depth look at ecological economics, see McFague, *Life Abundant*, esp. chap. 5.

74. McFague, *Life Abundant*, 100.

75. Herman Daly, "Free Trade: The Perils of Deregulation," in *Case against the Global Economy*, ed. Mander and Goldsmith, 232.

76. For a detailed examination of this issue, see Hawken, *The Ecology of Commerce: A Declaration of Sustainability* (New York: HarperCollins, 1993).

77. Edward Goldsmith, "The Last Word: Family, Community, Democracy," in *Case against the Global Economy*, ed. Mander and Goldsmith, 503.

78. McFague, *Life Abundant*, 99.

79. Wendell Berry, "Conserving Communities," in *Case against the Global Economy*, ed. Mander and Goldsmith, 407.

80. The story of Dinuba and Arvin is told in David Morris, "Free Trade: The Great Destroyer," in *Case against the Global Economy*, ed. Mander and Goldsmith, 226.

81. Ibid.

82. Goldsmith, "The Last Word," 509.

83. Ibid.

84. Ibid.

85. For a more detailed account of this movement see Daniel Imhoff, "Community Supported Agriculture: Farming with a Face on It," in *Case against the Global Economy*, ed. Mander and Goldsmith.

86. For more detailed treatments of bioregionalism, see Kirkpatrick Sale, "Principles of Bioregionalism," in *Case against the Global Economy*, ed. Mander and Goldsmith; and Daly and Cobb, *For the Common Good*, esp. chap. 14.

87. Sale, "Principles of Bioregionalism," 480.

88. James Goldsmith, "The Winners and the Losers," in *Case against the Global Economy*, ed. Mander and Goldsmith, 178.

89. Ibid.

90. For more specific details about several programs, see Susan Meeker-Lowry, "Community Money: The Potential of *Local* Currency," in *Case against the Global Economy*, ed. Mander and Goldsmith.

91. See Lois Gibbs, foreword to Hofrichter, *Toxic Struggle*.

92. Ibid., ix–x.

93. Ibid., x.

94. Ibid., 4.

95. McFague, *Life Abundant*, 115.

96. Ibid., 117–18.

97. This phrase was first raised at the Vancouver assembly of the World Council of Churches (1983) where it was added to the themes of justice and peace as a major focus for the work of the WCC. For an extensive explication of six different dimensions of the phrase "integrity of creation," see Rasmussen, *Earth Community*, 98–110.

98. Ibid., 105.

99. Ibid.

100. Ibid., 104.

101. Ibid., 260.

102. Ibid.

103. Ibid.

104. It should be noted that there is some discrepancy regarding the use of the term "sustainable," particularly when it is associated with the terms "growth" and "development." For details of these debates, see Boff, *Cry of the Earth*; and Rasmussen, *Earth Community*, 127–73.

6

Globalization as Neocolonialism

The Struggle of People's Movements for Global Solidarity

People's Movements as a Locus for Transforming Globalization

The final theory of globalization identified in this study, postcolonialism, shares many of the concerns for the land and for creation that are advocated by earthist proponents. Proponents of a postcolonial theory of globalization often are grassroots people from the global South who share a deep commitment to sustainable agriculture and other forms of local production for local consumption; however, at least two features distinguish this theory from the earthist paradigm. First, this position is characterized by social movements that reflect a postcolonial ideology.[1] These movements represent networks of resistance that have arisen either to combat oppressive forms of globalization or to create new pathways of globalization. Second, these networks are either located in the "two-thirds" world or share their postcolonial perspective that globalization is a new form of colonialism that is reinscribing dependency and control over politically weak and economically impoverished countries. The social location of marginalization that partially defines this position gives rise to a theoretical perspective that is inherently political. Recognition of the deeply political nature of the transformation that is necessary to overturn dominant forms of globalization is largely what distinguishes the postcolonial position from the earthist paradigm.

Proponents of postcolonialism are largely people in poverty, the disenfranchised, those who feel that their traditions and cultures are being destroyed by the neocolonial practices of the dominant form of globalization, and their allies. This chapter highlights voices from those groups and coalitions, formal and informal, that are working together to effect transformative social change in their local settings. Because these groups are made up of grassroots people seeking the power of communal self-determination and the ability to improve their own lives and the lives of their communities, I will refer to these groups as "people's movements." By this designation I mean to capture the grassroots nature of the resistance as well as the dynamic and ever-changing reality of networking and coalition work. The work being accomplished by people's movements serves as a model for how global solidarity can support and strengthen the local work of resistance and transformation. Investigating the activity of people's movements also illustrates how resistance groups are able to learn from each other's local struggles and resistance strategies in ways that can inform their own local situations and struggles.

Many of the strategies that people's movements pursue for transforming globalization are rooted in a concern for local communities, a concern that is shared by the earthist position. Earthists seek localization through the reconnection of people's daily lives with local communities so that they are able to participate in subsistence-oriented economies that provide for the majority of people's needs. Because people's movements are grassroots groups seeking social transformation, localization manifests itself in their work in their focus on resolving local problems by creating local solutions. The efforts of NGOs may have defeated the passage of the Multilateral Agreement on Investment through a coordinated international campaign, but people's movements are what are behind many of the localized actions around the world, including striking for better working conditions, fighting the infiltration of corporations into their communities, and resisting the development agendas of outside forces. In their book *Grassroots Post-Modernism*, Gustavo Esteva and Madhu Suri Prakash argue, "Since 'global forces' can only achieve concrete existence at some local level, it is only there—at the local grassroots—that they can most effectively and wisely be opposed."[2]

Rereading History with Postcolonial Eyes

Proponents of postcolonialism usually take a highly critical view of traditional historiography as fundamentally Eurocentric.[3] Indeed, as we have seen in the three previous theories of globalization, the historical narratives of these positions have centered on the behavior and activities of Europe. In other words, many of the historical accounts of globalization position Europe as the central actor on the historical stage. While the alternative theories of the origins of globalization describe the exploitative system of contemporary international relations in a way that is sympathetic to the "two-thirds" world, they still use Eurocentric concepts and theory.[4] As an academic discipline arising from the European tradition of the "university," history has quintessentially been shaped by the thought and experiences of Europe. In essence, all other histories are told in relation to the master narrative and assume a "subaltern"[5] position.[6] Europe functions as a "silent referent" for the elaboration of postcolonial[7] history.[8] Postcolonial historian Dipesh Chakrabarty challenges historians to "write into the history of modernity the ambivalences, contradictions, the use of force, and the tragedies and ironies that attend it."[9] The aim is for a more rigorous historical inquiry that will yield historical narratives that are no longer Eurocentric, but that rather function to "provincialize" Europe in a manner that places Europe in an appropriately relativized relationship with other countries.[10]

On the other hand, postcolonial critic Arif Dirlik cautions his peers about focusing too much energy on issues of Eurocentricity at the expense of addressing the material conditions of grassroots people in the global South.[11] Dirlik is fearful that the focus on combating Eurocentrism will divert attention away from the critique of capitalism and capitalist ideology that he believes is fundamental to challenging the inequality, exploitation, and oppression that are a direct result of colonialism and, now, neocolonialism. Viewed from this perspective, capitalism itself is fundamentally Eurocentric, and at heart the capitalist system is what is destroying people's livelihoods, not merely the cultural hegemony of Europe. As Dirlik writes, "Without capitalism as the foundation for European power and the motive force of its globalization, Eurocentrism would have been just another ethnocentrism."[12] Proponents of this position argue that what is needed is a critical theory that problematizes the examination of the inequality of the "two-thirds" world by focusing attention on the relationship between power, culture, and economics. Dirlik challenges the postcolonial intelligentsia by pointing out that they themselves are complicit in the perpetuation of Eurocentrism because they define their subdiscipline in relation to it and are its beneficiaries by virtue of their acceptance within academia and their considerable role in shaping academic critique.

Viewing the history of colonialism from a subaltern position yields a fundamentally different story. Subaltern history must be a reading done through the eyes of the people who lived in the lands that were conquered. It is a pluriform history of tribes, peoples, cultures, and nations and their experiences of encounters with foreigners and the exploitation and abuse that resulted from that contact.[13] One of the major challenges of postcolonial theory is to the "objectivity" that is assumed by mainstream historiography. Postcolonialists point out that historians who purport merely to "tell" the story of history are, in fact, guided by their own ideological predispositions that affect their choice of what is to be included and what excluded as well as the perspective from which the story itself is told. While traditional historical accounts of colonialism may disapprove of some of the methods that were used (e.g., slavery, theft of land), they generally share the overall assessment that the results have proven to be positive overall for former colonized countries. Postcolonial writers, on the other hand, tell the story in a much different way. They begin by labeling the ideological motivation of colonialism as imperialism and proceed from there to describe the material effects of imperialist policies and colonial presence on the people and the land.[14]

An example of postcolonial history is found in Gwendolyn Mikell's *Cocoa and Chaos in Ghana*, which traces how the colonial imposition of cocoa production for export devastated not only the local economy, but also the cultural stability of the Ashanti people.[15] Mikell begins by giving a critical anthropological analysis of the Ghanaian cultures before the European invasion. She argues that cultures such as the Ashanti were matrilineal cultures in which women participated in the economic, political, and decision-making processes and in which the family lineage descended through women. The economic systems were clan-based, and most agricultural efforts were directed toward subsistence farming. There was no private ownership of land; instead, the royals allocated land for farming. The British colonial authorities imposed their own culturally specific practices of social hierarchy, private property, and export-oriented agriculture on the Ashanti. These practices created social stratification that placed women and slaves at the bottom of the ladder. It also destroyed the clan-based economies and social organization, resulting in class stratification and inadequate food production. While the introduction of cocoa in Ghana led to the inclusion of Ghana in the global market, the intensification of cocoa production coincided with the replacement of communal, clan-based structures with state bureaucracy. Greed for land increased and more and more people became displaced and unable to feed themselves. The Ghanaian agricultural system shifted from subsistence to export. As a result, local and transnational slave labor increased.

The history of the Ashanti is only one example of a familiar pattern of imperial domination, colonial rule, and the transformation of the lives of self-sufficient local and regional tribes and peoples into lives of dependency and poverty. Colonial history reads differently from the perspective of the colonized than from that of the colonizer. Postcolonial theorists often compare the dependency of colonies on their colonizers to the dependency that presently exists between contemporary countries and the International Monetary Fund, the World Bank, and transnational corporations that dominate an individual country's decision-making powers regarding its own domestic economic policies. Postcolonial critics argue that the dependency of the global South on the economic models and policies of the global elite has created a new situation in which they describe globalization as neocolonialism. Those initial patterns of intellectual and cultural superiority that accompanied colonialism laid the groundwork for the "monocultural" aspects of the neocolonial model of globalization that is presently dominating our world.[16]

Experiencing Globalization as Neocolonialism

Local people around the world are rising up to resist the persistent threat to their culture, language, lifestyle, and land that is posed by economic globalization. This resistance is not a new development, but rather the most recent form of challenge to threats of assimilation, destruction, and irrelevance that have accompanied Western colonialism. As we have seen, postcolonial critics are engaged in alternative theorizing that challenges traditional academic assumptions. Even though postcolonial theorists are often Western-trained intellectuals from the "two-thirds" world who are working and writing in academic posts in elite "first" world institutions, the theory that they articulate is representative of the actions and practices of many people's movements. That is to say, the activist nature of the resistance to globalization that is foundational to this position is rooted in a postcolonial reading of history.

Proponents of postcolonialism argue that globalization is re-presenting the familiar threat of colonialism in a new, sophisticated, and highly seductive package that promises wealth, possessions, and comfort, but that remains neocolonialism nonetheless. Media images of wealth, prosperity, and adventure often lure rural young people to the cities to seek their fortunes. The appeal of Western-style affluence has been heightened in recent years by the declining sustainability of traditional lifestyles in many rural communities around the world as peasants and indigenous peoples have been dispossessed of their land or had the productivity of their land compromised through drought or desertification. What most of the youth do not realize is that job opportunities in urban centers of the "two-thirds" world are increasingly scarce. Many of these rural youth end up in prostitution or low-wage jobs that will never be able to offer them the kind of lifestyle they came to the city seeking nor even the ability to provide the basic necessities for themselves, much less a family.

The grassroots postcolonialists argue that a capitalist political economy is intrinsically a colonizing paradigm and that while the former relationships of colonization were based on extracting raw materials, the more recent move is toward an integration of the "developing" world into political and economic relationships that are dominated by the West. From this perspective, it is essential to recognize that contemporary globalization is a re-entrenchment of the political and economic domination of the global South by the global North under a new guise. Colonialism has functioned as a threat to indigenous communities at all social levels—economic, political, and cultural. In what follows we will look at the ways in which postcolonialists see twenty-first century globalization processes as again attempting to dominate these three areas of life.

How Neoclassical Economic Policies Reinscribe Colonialism

We have already seen how both the neoliberal and development models of globalization function to reinforce the neoclassical economic goals of growth and trade. The postcolonial position holds, in general terms, that these are the economic policies that continue to keep the "two-thirds" world enslaved to the wealthy countries of the world. Specifically, three sets of economic policies—the "opening" of economies, stabilization, and "free trade"—will be examined from a postcolonial perspective to see how they function to control the economic activities of poorer countries. While proponents of the neoliberal and development theories of globalization argue that these policies are intended to assist poorer nations in their development, proponents of postcolonialism argue that these policies merely function to keep them enslaved to capitalism.

Controlling the "Two-thirds" World by Opening Its Economies

Rapidly increasing inequality around the world suggests that wealth might be a more accurate indicator of the divisions that separate people than the more traditional divides of geography (North-South) or economics (industrialized-developing). Increasingly the poor around the world have more in common with one another than they do with the wealthy in their own countries. Leaders of people's movements argue that a wealthy and powerful transnational social class that benefits from the structures of capitalism is driving the spread of the dominant model of globalization, which is sometimes referred to as "elite globalization" precisely because it benefits so few members of society.[17] Postcolonial theorists argue that the creation of a global elite within the "two-thirds" world has rendered the need for colonial administrators obsolete.[18] In effect, the colonial powers discovered that traditional colonial relationships are no longer necessary when local citizens have been thoroughly assimilated into Western thinking. Western-trained indigenous bourgeoisie are able to further the cause of capitalism, as well as neoliberal and development globalization, in ways that lend an air of authenticity to an essentially foreign ideology. When foreign-trained intellectuals enter governmental posts, particularly those dealing with economic decision-making, they are in excellent positions to embed their countries further in the types of neoclassical economic solutions promoted by the first two theories of globalization.

This happened in Latin America in the 1970s and '80s when a group of Harvard, MIT, Yale, Stanford, and Chicago Ph.D.s returned to their home countries and moved into positions of power and influence in government and business. These young men were market-oriented economists, with a flair for politics, who had adopted the philosophy of the "open economy" as the best way for their countries to achieve economic success and prosperity, particularly as the prospect of their countries' defaulting on their loans loomed large. Many of these men were also the sons of the wealthy elite in Latin America, and their families stood to profit handsomely from the increased flow of money that direct foreign investment and structural adjustment loans offered. These influential economists encouraged their governments to embrace the advice of their U.S. friends, leading economists such as Jeffrey Sachs and Lawrence Summers, to undergo austerity measures and to open their economies. Though these Western-trained intellectuals were born in Latin America, the economic programs they supported were thoroughly neoliberal and often opposed by the vast majority of the local people.[19]

Postcolonial theorists note that the financial dependence of debtor nations on the Bretton Woods institutions, as well as the corporate money necessary to ensure continued payments on their loans, is reminiscent of the dependency of the colonized countries on their colonizers in years past. While the balance-of-payments crisis of the 1970s was real in Latin American countries and other "two-thirds" world countries, the "solution" offered by the World Bank and the IMF in the form of structural adjustment loans functioned to deepen the debt of those countries rather than alleviate it. Ecologist Edward Goldsmith describes the situation in the following way:

> Once in debt, they inevitably become hooked on further and further borrowing rather than cutting down on expenditure and thus fall under the power of the lending countries. At this point the latter, through the IMF, can institutionalize their control over the debtor country through structural adjustment programs . . . that, in effect, take over its economy to ensure that interest payments are regularly met. This arrangement leaves the borrowing country as a de facto colony.[20]

For the governments of many countries in the global South, foreign loans have promised an appealing solution to economic problems, but the consequent economic policies that accompany those loans require participation in a particular economic model that is heavily invested in external trade. So while countries may seek out help for addressing the material needs of their citizens, help comes with a prepackaged formula for how "development" should proceed. Proponents of postcolonialism argue that the development model of globalization undermines economic self-sufficiency, political autonomy, and creative indigenous solutions to local problems. In fact, Filipino activist Walden Bello points out that analysis of the World Bank's own data has shown that the strategy of import substitution, which promotes local self-sufficiency, has been effective at fostering productivity.[21] Feminists also have noted that women bear a disproportionate amount of the brunt of structural adjustment due to the gender bias of neoclassical theory and the consequent effect of export-oriented policies that do not incorporate adequate gender analysis in their formation.[22]

Perhaps the strongest critique that postcolonialists offer to the economic model of what the dominant ideologies call the "open" economy, and the foreign loans that supports it, is a demystification of its promises of economic prosperity through their examination of its actual effects. While it is true that austerity policies have been implemented in some of the poorer countries around the world, their promised economic relief and reduction of poverty have not materialized. Time has shown what theoretical economic models cannot. The indebtedness of "developing" countries has continued to increase, and trade-oriented economies are not reducing poverty but rather exacerbating it in most areas of the world. As Bello points outs, the result has been that "two-thirds" world countries "have become more tightly integrated into the capitalist world market and thereby made increasingly dependent for their sustenance on the northern powers and the transnational corporations that effectively control them."[23]

Exposing Stabilization Policies as Paternalistic Control

The policies of structural adjustment were originally described as aid packages aimed toward helping struggling economies get back on their feet again. The unspoken assumption that accompanied structural adjustment was that these "developing" economies were not sophisticated enough to be in charge of their own economic policy and this "crisis" served as an excellent opportunity to turn these economies onto the "right" track; namely, an economic track of export-oriented growth. This process is referred to as "stabilization," and it is also used more directly between countries when direct aid is transferred to help "stabilize" an economy that economists fear will "spiral out of control." The unofficial practice of "bailing out" countries is usually implemented under the auspices of aiding the people and the local government.

An infamous case in point was the recent U.S. bailout of Mexico. That bailout was sold as a public relations plan to "help out" the Mexican people. Compassion and concern for our "neighbor to the South" were repeatedly invoked as moral justification for intervening in the political and economic governance of the Mexican economy. Postcolonialists are quick to point out that the real objective of these "bailouts" is to protect the massive investments of "first" world banks and corporations as well as the private investors who all stand to sustain heavy losses in the event of loan defaults or collapsing currencies.[24]

In December 1994 after the Mexican government allowed an overvalued peso to float on world trading markets, the value fell by 40 percent. This sudden devaluation threatened the recently passed NAFTA trade agreement as well as the confidence of the Organisation for Economic Co-operation and Development, which had just recently welcomed Mexico into its ranks. President Bill Clinton quickly arranged an economic aid package to stabilize the Mexican peso. Critics of the plan charged that the neoliberal economic vision had not worked thus far for Mexico and that a further infusion of money without a shift in policy would not stabilize the country. Authors

Carlos Heredia and Mary Purcell list three glaring oversights of the current model of stabilization that will continue to spell poverty for millions of Mexican workers: First, Mexico lacks an income-generating strategy for the poor and working class; second, Mexico currently lacks the productive capacity to provide the basis for growth; and third, Mexico lacks a democratic system by which citizens can participate in national debate and decision-making about the future of their country.[25] Postcolonial critics such as Heredia and Purcell argue that bailouts function to protect the wealth of the North while turning a blind eye to the failure of austerity measures to achieve their stated goals to "restore 'sustainable' economic growth and make lasting progress in alleviating poverty."[26]

To see the extent to which bailouts are used to rescue wealthy investors, we need look no further than Long Term Capital of Greenwich, Connecticut.[27] In 1998 the imminent failure of this enormously influential hedge fund threatened a possible stock market crash. Long Term Capital was simply "too large to fail." The economic fallout from such significant financial losses, even though the investments were speculative, was deemed too dangerous to risk. In the end the New York Federal Reserve orchestrated a bailout of the investors of Long Term Capital to the tune of $3.6 billion.[28]

Ultimately, the most damning moral aspect of such economic bailouts is that the speculative trading of those same wealthy elite often precipitated the economic crises that prompted the bailouts. In the case of Long Term Capital, the highly sophisticated economic models on which investments were based had worked wonderfully for years before their failure. While speculative investment obviously carries with it the possibility of failure and loss, the high finance of globalization seems to imply that if a person is wealthy enough, failure is impossible.

Exposing "Free Trade" as a Mechanism for Exploitation and Wealth Extraction

The contemporary model of "free trade" was first attempted in the 1970s and '80s in the form of free trade zones or export processing zones.[29] These zones are specially designated areas in which normal governmental regulation of trade is suspended in a variety of areas to promote investment and industrial growth. The *maquiladoras* in Mexico are some of the most familiar free trade zones. Journalist Alexander Goldsmith points out that free trade zones often share the following characteristics: "lax social, environmental, and employment regulations; a ready source of cheap labor; and fiscal and financial incentives that can take a huge variety of forms, although they generally consist of the lifting of custom duties, the removal of foreign exchange controls, tax holidays, and free land or reduced rents."[30] With the popularity of deregulation and the advent of the World Trade Organization and regional trade blocs such as the European Union and NAFTA, whole countries now share these same features Goldsmith describes in the hopes of making themselves attractive to the roving capital that has accompanied economic globalization.

"Free trade" was the economic trend of the 1990s as neoliberal policy makers pushed countries and their citizens to accept the wisdom of regional trading markets. Promoters of free trade argued that the discipline of the market would assure that any relocation of jobs would increase efficiency and that capitalist innovation would create new jobs to fill the gap. In the end, consumers would benefit from lower prices, and producers and stockholders would benefit from increased profits. The assumptions of comparative advantage, capitalist innovation, and division of labor that underlie the free trade movement ultimately require a global trading market.

Just as a "free market" is, in fact, a fiction,[31] so "free trade" can never in fact be free from the realm of regulation. What is at stake when it comes to "free trade" is who is being protected and who (or what) is not. Proponents of the postcolonial position argue that for the most part, free trade agreements function to protect corporate interests while eliminating governmental controls protecting the environment, workers, and other marginalized groups.[32] Critics of the current model of globalization argue that the externalization of the environmental and social expenses of capitalist production for the sake of efficiency does not allow for prices that accurately reflect an item's cost.[33] Consequently, the workers in the "two-thirds" world and the environment bear the burden of the lower prices that free trade supposedly produces.

Postcolonialism holds that so-called free trade agreements function as a mechanism of neoclassical economic ideology and that they continue to reward producers who can offer the lowest prices, even if they do so at the expense of child labor, unsafe working conditions, and the destruction of our environment. Furthermore, as promoters of free trade seek to "open up" economies by arguing that increased domestic production will increase efficiency by making these countries' products more competitive, postcolonial critics counter that we still must seek to discern who reaps the material rewards from this increased production. Given the fact that it is generally transnational corporations rather than local or national business interests that are able to compete in the international trade arena, these profits are not being repatriated into the local economies of the "two-thirds" world where the goods are being produced. Rather, critics point out that the majority of these profits are being extracted and deposited in banks in Geneva, New York, or London or they end up in the bonus and dividend checks of the CEOs and stockholders, most of whom reside in the "first" world. Because this extractive model of business and trade is so reminiscent of the colonialism of the eighteenth and nineteenth centuries, this neoclassical model of "development" is often referred to as neocolonialism.

How Political Power Is Being Usurped by Corporations

The political control of colonial states has long been one of the most powerful weapons of colonial authority. In the colonial era, power was enforced by colonial armies and the threat of force they provided was viewed as a legitimizing tool of colonial administrations. In the neocolonial era, the political power that threatens to challenge the self-sufficiency of democratically elected governments resides in the unlikely form of transnational corporations. Corporations are an unlikely form of political power because business is normally thought of as a sphere of society separate from politics. Historically, however, this has not been the case, as seen with the joint-stock companies of the eighteenth and nineteenth centuries; nor is it the case in today's globalizing economic arena.

Increasingly the wealth of transnational corporations is surpassing that of the world's smaller countries, and corporations are finding it in their interest to garner as much political power as possible.[34] In fact, these institutions appear to be in a position to replace nation-states as the dominant political, economic, and social force of the twenty-first century.[35] "In 1991, the ten largest businesses in the world had collective revenues of $801 billion, greater turnover than the smallest one hundred countries in the world."[36] In the context of a global capitalist economic order, this wealth carries with it an enormous amount of power, influence, and authority for corporate business leaders and their institutions.

The growing political influence of corporations over nation-states is reflected in the situation of Nigeria, a country described by local human-rights attorney Oronto Douglas as a country designed by corporations for corporations that "simply disregards the people who live there."[37] Corporate interest in Nigeria dates back to the 1800s, but oil exploration did not begin until 1937. In the mid-1950s the Niger Delta was found to be rich in oil reserves, and by 1958 Shell was exporting tremendous quantities of oil. Douglas links Nigeria's civil war to the struggle for control of oil reserves, and evidence has even been uncovered that executives from oil multinationals were involved in the development of Nigeria's "independent" constitution.[38] This multinational interest in controlling Nigeria is concerned solely with the extraction of the country's natural resources as the poverty of the region and the problem of pipeline explosions attest. While the oil companies certainly have brought jobs to the region, they also have exploited corrupt government officials and contributed to a situation of social and economic chaos in the local communities. Official figures indicate that more than 2,000 women, men, and children died in pipeline explosions in Nigeria between 1998 and 2000.[39] These explosions are due not to accidents, but to oil spills left by organized rings of thieves, frequently escorted by corrupt military officials, who knock holes in the pipeline and siphon large quantities of oil into waiting trucks. Invariably it is the desperately poor local villagers attempting to gather oil to sell on the black market who are killed by the explosions.

Corporations play a major role in the neocolonizing aspects of globalization in a variety of ways as their practices recreate many of the problems once associated with colonial powers. Through their trading practices, corporations can force small farmers and producers out of business, causing them to sell or abandon their land and become dependent on wage labor, thereby radically changing the traditional ways of life in rural communities.[40] With the increase of production facilities in low wage areas, transnational corporations import "foreign" work values and practices, often exploiting the labor through poor working conditions and substandard wages.

With this newfound political power has come a shift in the self-understanding of corporations that can best be described as their ability to transcend national allegiance and the concomitant responsibilities of a corporate "citizen." Just as colonial powers once recognized some minimal level of responsibility toward their subjects, businesses rooted in local communities have a sense of place and responsibility that is evaporating in an increasingly globalizing economy.

The World Trade Organization (WTO) represents one of the most recent developments in corporate power as well as one of the most threatening to the political power of smaller nation-states. Increasingly activists from the "two-thirds" world are exposing the undemocratic procedures of the WTO as a front for the increasing power of transnational corporations to force weaker nation-states into compliance with business and trade policies that benefit big business at the expense of the environment, workers, communities, and cultures.[41]

Threats to Traditional Ways of Life

A form of cultural colonization can be seen in the process of Americanization. This involves the proliferation of American television, music, videos, movies, clothing, attitudes, and culture that is inundating the rest of the world. Americanization represents a convergence between the capitalist economic spirit and the American culture that it exports. This convergence produces a form of globalization that seeks uniformity and threatens to destroy the difference and distinctiveness it encounters in other cultures. The ease of communication in the age of the Internet and computers has certainly facilitated the spread of Americanization through the growth of global markets.

Consumerism and Culture

One of the driving forces behind the spread of globalization has been the ability of advertising departments and public relations campaigns to manufacture global consumers and manipulate their very wants and desires. McDonald's is not spreading across the globe because it provides families with access to a cheap and nutritional meal. Nor is it gaining popularity because its food is superior in quality to the local eating establishments. The success of

McDonald's can be understood only in the context of the creation of the global consumer. McDonald's sells itself as a symbol of the United States, and part of its appeal is generated by people's desire to emulate "America." The myth of American opportunity, success, wealth, power, and satisfaction is being marketed in multiple ways by transnational corporations—from soap operas and movies to music videos and ad campaigns. McDonald's hamburgers and Coca-Colas are only symbols of that myth, but they are small, accessible symbols that allow people around the world to feel as if they are able to grab hold of the "American Dream," even if only fleetingly.

These products represent more than just commercial consumption; in their symbolic representation of the cultural ethos of the "American way of life," products like these have fused consumerism with culture in such a way that what is being bought is not just a hamburger or a drink. When people buy a Coke or a McDonald's hamburger, particularly in the "two-thirds" world, they are attempting to buy access to U.S. culture. The message that has been sent by the media and that is quickly being absorbed by global consumers is that culture is not something indigenous to a particular group of people, but can be bought and sold. Culture has become commodified through the marketing of music, food, clothing, jewelry, behavior, religion, and values. The underlying assumption in a global marketplace is that people are basically the same everywhere and that the trappings of culture can be uprooted and sold to anyone in the name of globalization, cultural diversity, and the free market. This assumption is grounded in a fundamental denial of cultural specificity and a misunderstanding of the relationship between cultural symbols and their spiritual or historical meaning.

A young white man who was intrigued by indigenous religious traditions approached Native American theologian George Tinker when he was pastoring a small rural church. The young man asked Tinker if he would guide him in learning the rituals and ways of those traditions. Tinker responded, "I can teach you the songs and dances that will call upon the spirits of the ancestors, but what will you do when they come?"[42] Tinker's words reveal the depth of misunderstanding that can emerge among people who approach the cultural traditions of others as if they were merely something to be shared, learned, and ultimately practiced by anyone.

The fact that the dominant religious tradition in the United States is Christianity allows the proselytizing nature of Christianity to influence how people view other religious traditions. New Age religions and many religious seekers in the United States (and other predominantly Christian countries) approach religion as if it were a buffet from which they can pick and choose the practices and beliefs that make sense to them and reject the ones that offend or bore and "create" their own religions. Unfortunately for these people, the consumer approach to spirituality prevents them from studying any particular religious tradition deeply enough to understand its historical and theological origins and to grasp the connection between its rituals, practices, ethics, and origins.

Globalization threatens traditional ways of life to the extent that it is able to commodify, trivialize, or supplant local culture.[43] The loss of tradition and indigenous forms of art, speech, song, and dance are one of the greatest fears of many older generations of people around the world. As they watch their young people dance to techno music and wear the latest fashions out of New York, the elders are aware of the youths' dismissal of their own cultural traditions as embarrassing and backward. In many countries elders in the community worry that their traditional music and dances will die out because their young people listen only to "popular" music imported from the West.

An MTV executive once said, "Kids on the streets in Tokyo have more in common with kids on the streets in London than they do with their parents."[44] Sociologist Frank Alford begs to differ: "No, the kids . . . only think they do. Or perhaps we only think they do."[45] Alford is pointing out that, at least at this point in the development of globalization, the cultural lens through which we view the world still renders most young people more closely aligned with their parents than with other young people from halfway around the world. People everywhere may be watching *Dallas* and *Baywatch*, but for most of them the behavior is bizarre and decidedly "foreign." People in their own cultures do not behave like the people in these TV shows nor would it be acceptable or appropriate for them to do so. At least for now, most people are able to read U.S. culture through the lenses of their own particular, local cultures. Nevertheless, postcolonial theorists argue that the threat to local culture is real and that the consumer ideology being promoted through the global media is a significant factor in shaping and changing cultural values.

Media

The well-orchestrated media campaigns of many corporations have affected the traditional values and cultures of many peoples around the world as the promotion of the global consumer is sold to people who can barely afford food for their families but are convinced they need to drink Coke or wear Levi's or own a television. While neoliberals argue that corporations are interested in using advertising only to sell their products, not to destroy cultures, there is a correlation between the two. This correlation is illustrated in the following story that Sherif Hetata, an Egyptian doctor, tells about a friend:

> In my village, I have a friend. He is a peasant and we are very close. He lives in a big mud hut, and animals (buffalo, sheep, cows, and donkeys) live in the house with him. Altogether, in the household, with the wife and children of his brother, his uncle, the mother, and his own family, there are thirty people. He wears a long galabeya (robe), works in the fields for long hours, and eats food cooked in the mud oven.

> But when he married, he rode around the village in a hired Peugeot car with his bride. She wore a white wedding dress, her face was made up like a film star, her hair curled at the hairdresser's of the provincial town, her finger and toe nails manicured and polished, and her body bathed with special soap and perfumed. At the marriage ceremony, they had a wedding cake, which she cut with her husband's hand over hers. Very different from the customary rural marriage ceremony of his father. And all this change in the notion of beauty, of femininity, of celebration, of happiness, of prestige, of progress happened to my peasant friend and his bride in one generation.[46]

Television shows and advertising, Hollywood movies, billboards, magazines—all of these different forms of media and advertising project particular images—images of success and the good life that are defined by money, possessions, and particular forms of beauty and body size. As Hetata points out, these images conflict with culturally specific notions of success and the good life in traditional cultures around the world. It is difficult to hold on to traditional notions of beauty and wealth while being inundated with a barrage of U.S. (or European, or Australian) images that are so fundamentally different. While there is certainly some question about the moral depth and long-term value of the Western images of success promoted through the media, postcolonial theorists are more concerned with the threat that these culturally foreign models of "success" pose to traditional ways of life.

Education

Education is another aspect of globalization that threatens to undermine traditional ways of life. While education is widely regarded as a significant and important aspect of development, the way that education is conceived and implemented in the "two-thirds" world reflects the biases and predilections of the West. Two examples help to illustrate how external notions of the benefits of education fail to address the real needs of local people in culturally distinct situations.

Helena Norberg-Hodge has lived among the Ladakhi people of Kashmir for thirty years.[47] As a Western "outsider" who has maintained long-term contact with this remote indigenous culture, she has observed a great deal of change in both their perception of the world and their self-perception. One of her most trenchant observations is the disconnect between the education offered in the "modern" schools accompanying development, and the local knowledge that is necessary to sustain life in the Himalayas. In her own words:

> No one can deny the value of real education—the widening and enrichment of knowledge. But today in the Third World, education has become something quite different. It isolates children from their culture and from nature, training them instead to become narrow specialists in a Westernized urban

> environment. This process has been particularly striking in Ladakh, where modern schooling acts almost as a blindfold, preventing children from seeing the very context in which they live. They leave school unable to use their own resources, unable to function in their own world.[48]

Instead of learning about soil conservation, indigenous planting techniques that have been developed over generations, and how to build and maintain the mud and stone houses of their people, the Ladakhi children learn about math, science, culture, and custom in ways that were originally intended to educate British children. The Eurocentrism of the Ladakhi educational system is evident from the assumptions made about what constitutes essential life skills down to the actual textbooks and teaching curricula. Norms and standards for education that were agreed upon by European educators, and that adequately educate Western children, have been adopted and implemented in many postcolonial communities without sufficient thought being given to the actual needs and life goals of local families. Not only are these educational resources often irrelevant to the material lives of people in the "two-thirds" world, but their inherent bias toward Western culture, behavior, and knowledge often prejudice children away from the ways of life that have molded their communities for generations, including sustainable agriculture, rural living, and self-sufficiency.

In addition to Western-style primary and secondary schools, globalization and development have brought a proliferation of trade-oriented schools that focus on teaching young people proficiency in skills that will allow them to find jobs. Once again, an underlying Western assumption in these models reflects a bias toward urban life and the development of marketable skills for city dwelling. Most of the trade schools for young African girls teach two skills—cooking and sewing—when there is already an overabundance of women with trade skills in both cooking and sewing. The likelihood of these young women finding jobs sewing and cooking that will provide a livable wage is marginal at best. A postcolonial model would pay more attention to discerning the needs of the local communities and figuring out how to meet those needs, rather than contributing to the continued overcrowding of cities in the "two-thirds" world.

People's Movements Struggle for Globalization as Global Solidarity

Various people's movements around the world are engaged in a wide variety of mobilization and protest against globalization as neocolonialism. Even when most of their followers have never undertaken formal educational training, many of these movements are influenced by an organic ideological conception of postcolonial theory. What draws them together to form a discrete theoretical category within this study is not a common idea of what the world should be, but rather a vision of a world where individual communities of people are able to articulate their own version of the good life and where those communities possess the political, economic, and social capital to realize that goal. These communities have an alternative vision of globalization as global solidarity. Increasingly they are rejecting the capitalist models of globalization that have been defined by the West and are demanding a voice in defining the future of globalization. People's movements seek increased democratic processes that will provide for their participation in the political forces that affect their lives. Global solidarity increasingly offers practical and psychological support to disparate groups that are struggling to challenge forces of oppression within their local communities.

In a world where globalization is understood as global solidarity, the focus would be on an awareness of humanity's diversity that is rooted in respect for difference rather than on the forced unity and uniformity promoted by contemporary globalization processes. A striving for global solidarity goes beyond the superficial celebration of ethnicity—a mark of the current models of globalization in their eagerness to trade on the market of cultural capital—to a deeper and more nuanced approach to engaging difference. That deeper approach requires and reflects a particular set of values that molds the postcolonial vision of the good life. But before we explore the ethical landscape of this alternative conception of global solidarity, let us look at two concrete examples of people's movements that represent different approaches to achieving global solidarity. In the first example, a variety of people's movements worked together to affect the development of a public policy agenda for sustainable development in the Philippines. In the second example, a marginalized indigenous community waged war on the Mexican government primarily through words, media images, and a groundswell of support from people around the world.

The Role of Civil Society in Strengthening Democracy

The two dominant interpretations of globalization focus primarily on relationships between nation-states and markets. Neoliberals argue that the market should remain unfettered by governmental intervention, while social equity liberals argue that governmental regulations are necessary to protect the interests of the people. Either way, the end result is a theater of power in which only two major characters—the state and the market—are recognized as the authentic and valid sources of public policy action and direction. A postcolonial theory of globalization attacks this fundamental theoretical claim by arguing that a third sector is active in the formation of society; namely, civil society.[49] The postcolonial position understands civil society to be the arena in which grassroots people are able to mobilize, organize, and vocalize their concerns regarding the neocolonization of the "two-thirds" world through the machinations of big business and its institutions—the WTO, the IMF, and the World Bank.

People's movements in the "two-thirds" world are using the term civil society to indicate a sector of society that exists independently from the realms of business and government and that serves as a unique locus for enforcing the accountability of both corporate interests and elected officials.[50] The concept of "civil society" offers a space to locate the voices of the marginalized, which are often excluded from business and governmental discourse. Individuals and groups working within the civil society arena are able to mobilize and articulate their concerns collectively and often are able to collaborate with other grassroots organizations. The power of civil society lies in the fact that it is not institutionalized, but rather remains fluid. Issues arise from the concern and passion of local citizens, and loose networks of people's movements are able to respond as interest dictates. Civil society does not wait to be recognized as a valid participant in scheduled debates, but rather asserts its authority as a democratic expression of the will of the people. Proponents of the postcolonial position argue that the growing protest movements that are challenging the legitimacy and authority of the WTO and other multilateral institutions are an expression of the ability of civil society to call unchecked authoritarian power into accountability.[51]

Notions of civil society that are rooted in postcolonial thinking are also unique in their insistence that the driving force of civil society is located within the realm of culture. Just as business is reflective of the economic sphere of life and government is reflective of the political sphere of life, the notion of civil society draws its meaning and legitimacy from the cultural sphere of life.

> Culture is that realm which intuits the guiding comprehensive ideas of any society. Culture is the realm that gives identity and meaning, and is the realm that develops the full human potentials of individuals and enables them to be competent participants in the economy, in political life, in culture, and in society-at-large. . . . Culture deals with the realm of ideas in its various diverse forms including worldviews, knowledge, meanings, symbols, identity, ethics, art, and spirituality, among others.[52]

This affinity with the cultural roots of grassroots people is what allows for a distinctively different assessment of globalization from that found in most orthodox economic and political communities. Civil society's connection to people's cultural heritages allows for a perspective that prioritizes human and community concerns as opposed to profit, efficiency, and expediency.

Attempts to formalize the accountability of business and government to civil society have been foremost in the struggles against globalization in the

Philippines. Filipino activist Nicanor Perlas describes the Philippine Agenda 21 (PA21) as "a countervailing force in Philippine society to the initiatives of the state and the market that civil society has viewed as problematic."[53] PA21 was born out of the protests of civil society organizations in the Philippines to the neoliberal model of globalization that was being forced upon them by the international banking community. The long history of community organizing in the Philippines led to an invitation by Philippine President Fidel V. Ramos to eighteen civil society leaders to participate in a dialogue on sustainable development as a follow-up to the United Nations Conference on the Environment and Development held in Rio de Janiero in 1992.[54] The very participation of civil society leaders in the dialogue from its inception ensured that the conversation would include the voices and concerns of grassroots Filipino citizens. Not surprisingly, when leaders from government, business, and civil society sat down to hash out their understanding of just what sustainable development is, differences of opinion became apparent immediately.

It took the committee, known as the Philippine Council on Sustainable Development, two years to come to consensus on a definition for sustainable development.[55] From there the Council was able to develop Philippine Agenda 21 as a formal plan for implementing sustainable development in the Philippines. The prior active work of civil society over a number of decades in the Philippines laid the groundwork for PA21 to incorporate civil society into its process as an established and credible component of Philippine society. The collaboration of politicians, businesspeople, and grassroots leaders allowed the Council to forge a unique agenda that seriously grapples with both the benefits and the dangers of globalization. Perlas notes, "PA21 recognizes that the solution cannot simply be an economic solution or simply an environmental solution. PA21 seeks a kind of solution that is able to address the multidimensionality of the problems of Philippine society, its people, and its environment."[56]

The forward-thinking approach that the Philippines has taken toward sustainable development has placed Philippine leaders in strategic political positions over the last five years in the Asia-Pacific Economic Cooperation (APEC) as well as the Rio+5 deliberations and the United Nations Commission on Sustainable Development. These leadership positions have allowed the Philippines' concern for the incorporation of civil society as a formal partner in public policy strategy to have a wider influence. The model of direct dialogue between leaders of business, government, and civil society marks a new form of public policy discourse that holds the promise of empowering grassroots people through the venue of civil society.

Armed Rebellion as a Means to Communal Autonomy

In the highlands of Chiapas, Mexico, another people's movement is actively in rebellion against the neoliberal model of globalization being hoisted on

Mexico primarily via the North American Free Trade Agreement. The Zapatista Army of National Liberation, or EZLN, is composed of a rag-tag group of peasant and indigenous communities that are deeply rooted in a post-colonial ideology. These people are the poorest of the poor in Mexico, and their movement has taken a different tack from the Filipino civil society movement.

The Zapatistas declared war on Mexico on January 1, 1994, citing Article 39 of the Mexican constitution as justification: "National Sovereignty essentially and originally resides in the people. All political power emanates from the people and its purpose is to help the people. The people have, at all times, the inalienable right to alter or modify their form of government."[57] Defending themselves against the economic, social, and political policies that they felt were condemning their people to poverty and death, the Zapatistas rose up in resistance with the intent of altering their form of government. Like many of the armed rebellions in Central America in the last two decades, the Zapatistas' motivations stemmed from their commitment to their land, their families, and their communities. As one observer observed, "The message was not new, not a surprise to anyone living here: we want land so we can grow food, access to health care, free schools, a decent wage, an end to racism. Our lives are not worth living if things do not change. We would rather die fighting than watch our children die of malnutrition or curable diseases."[58] One thing that distinguishes the EZLN from recent rebellions in neighboring countries is its lack of desire for political power and rebel control. As Andrew Flood describes it:

> The common feature of all the Zapatista communities is not a common and worked out political program but rather a commonly agreed structure of decision making. It is not at all clear that there exists any program beyond the demands for dignity, liberty and justice. However, what is agreed upon is the decision making structures which combine a radical democracy with more traditional indigenous assemblies.[59]

The Zapatistas have not declared war on Mexico so they can be in charge; they only desire to have local autonomy in order to be able to achieve self-sufficiency and a level of sustainable living that provides the basics of "work, land, housing, food, health care, education, independence, freedom, democracy, justice and peace."[60] In their declaration of war, the Zapatistas call for their army to advance on the capital to overcome the Mexican army, but their intent is to permit "the people in the liberated area the right to freely and democratically elect their own administrative authorities."[61] The EZLN is a people's movement that has arisen to demand justice from the oppressive political and economic sectors of Mexico; it is fundamentally a social movement rather than a political party. Nevertheless, it is a social movement with a highly sophisticated analysis of the political barriers that stand in the way of achieving justice.

Other characteristics that set the Zapatistas apart from previous revolutionary uprisings in Latin America are their sophisticated use of language as a strategy of war, their extensive use of the Internet to spread their message and rally support for their cause, and their surprising lack of interest in using force to achieve their goals. Their model of rebellion is thoroughly postmodern and an excellent example of the fact that postcolonialists are not against progress, development, technology, or change. What they desire is an opportunity to participate in the democratic processes that are shaping their collective lives and futures. What they demanded was recognition of their status as an independent and sovereign nation of indigenous peoples with subsequent rights for self-determination and participation in the democratic process.

One of the most amazing aspects of the Zapatista rebellion is the enormous surge of energy and support that it has received since its declaration of war in 1994. People from around the world have offered support, traveled to Mexico, and met with the rebels—many of them seeking to gain inspiration for the struggles of their own people's movements back home. The Zapatistas' message of *Basta!* (Enough!) has resonated with alienated and marginalized people around the world, and their willingness to stand up for their beliefs, even at the cost of death, has been a compelling witness to the dignity in the struggle for life in the face of injustice and oppression. The Zapatista movement does not pretend to hold up a universal solution to the problems of neoliberalism, democracy, and injustice in our world; what it does seek to accomplish is to create new spaces in which new solutions to old problems might begin to emerge through a process of deliberation that is rooted in the material lives of grassroots people. No decision is made in the Zapatista movement until each local community has been given the opportunity to discuss the issue and weigh the consequences. The ability for local communities to function autonomously with regard to social, political, economic, cultural, and other decisions that will significantly affect their lifestyles and ways of being in the world is of fundamental importance to the Zapatistas and their postcolonial supporters. The radical democracy this model represents is also a direct challenge to the autocratic decision-making practiced by the dominant forms of globalization in our world today.

A Grassroots Vision of the Good Life

The vision of the good life for the grassroots people who make up the variety of people's movements that constitute this fourth theory of globalization is not a clearly defined and singular conception of the good life. Rather, it is better understood as a set of values oriented around community, culture, and autonomy that creates an atmosphere in which individual communities are able to create and enact their own understanding of the good life in ways that honor the integrity and authenticity of their own particular tribe, people, clan, or culture. For Western audiences that are a step or two removed from historical identification with a particular tribe or clan, this type of orientation can be confusing at best and irrelevant at worst. What is important to remember at this point is that the vast majority of the world's population are still connected to their people of origin closely enough for this approach to have far-reaching implications for the future construction of models of globalization and their impact on the majority of the world's people.

Community as the Context for Moral Agency

The defining value for the exercise of moral agency in postcolonialism is that of community. For postcolonial thinkers, one's position as a member of a community is the most significant factor in evaluating personal choices and decisions. Ethicist Elizabeth Bounds describes the emphasis on a community orientation as "an effort to assert the value of solidarity in the midst of forces eroding connection."[62] Bounds is alluding to the fact that the value of community has taken on specific urgency in the era of globalization as the forces of capitalism, consumerism, and homogeneity threaten to undermine the survival of existing communities. In other words, as Western interpretations of prosperity and progress dominate the social construction of globalization, the power and authority that support these particular notions make it increasingly difficult for grassroots people with alternative interpretations of progress and prosperity to actualize their visions for their own future.

Under these circumstances, many groups are drawing on one of the most important and powerful resources at their disposal—their very identity as a community. We have already seen how the Zapatistas banded together as a community to organize and mobilize their resistance to the oppression of globalization that threatened their survival, and similar situations of rebellion can be found in a variety of communities around the world who have nothing but their faith in themselves and a commitment to their people and their way of life to guide them.[63]

For many people living in the "two-thirds" world, and particularly for indigenous people and people living in poverty, the relationship in their community is the basis of survival—in terms of both their cultural identity and their material well-being.[64] For these people, identity is forged within the context of particular communities, and it is from the locus of these communities that young people come to learn about the world around them. The traditional education of the Shona tribe of Zimbabwe illustrates how identity is formed through a network of relationships that teach children both their connection to other people and life forms as well as their responsibility within that web of relationships. Missiologist Tumani Mutasa Nyajeka describes the

Shona worldview at the turn of the nineteenth century as holistic and community-oriented.[65]

Beginning at an early age, children are taught about the Mutupo principle. This theological principle, which holds not only that all life is sacred, but that all life is interconnected and interdependent, undergirds the way of life of the Shona people. Each clan among the Shona is identified with a specific water or land animal known as its totem. It is viewed as their spiritual kin. The Shona believe that whatever happens to the human community will affect their totem and vice versa. Stories are passed on to the young to teach them about behavior, ethical decision-making, and the ways of the world; these stories feature not only their own clan's totem, but the whole of the natural world. In fact, in most of the stories, humans end up learning from the animals that are depicted as full of wisdom and knowledge. If children wander off and get lost in the forest, the people ask the forest to look after the children and bring them back home safely.

The Mutupo principle teaches the Shona children a particular cosmological orientation that encourages them to view the world in which they live in a holistic way. The Shona imagine themselves as part of a larger universe in which they still have much to learn from the living world around them. Their totem connections with a variety of species make the abstract principle of interconnectedness concrete in a meaningful and practical way. It forms a basis for their moral decision-making that is fundamentally rooted in an understanding of community that privileges neither the human community over the animal community, nor their own well-being over the well-being of their natural environment. While Nyajeka is describing the religious and educational practices of the nineteenth- and early-twentieth-century Shona people, contemporary evidence indicates that the Shona retain a strong sense of communal identity.[66]

Throughout this chapter we have seen reverberations of the foundational role that community plays within the postcolonial ideology. The emphasis on culture and the effects of colonialism and neocolonialism on local communities underscore the centrality of community in this fourth theory of globalization. Community is important because it is the locus within which culture has arisen and in which culture is nurtured and transmitted. By acknowledging that moral agency can be rightly exercised only within the context of community, postcolonialists recognize a moral universe fundamentally different from the individualism of neoliberalism. It is a moral universe in which individual actions are understood to have communal effects—for good or ill—and in which the well-being of the community is taken into consideration before individual decisions are made.

Culture as Humanity's Telos

In addition to the emphasis on community relationships, the importance of culture is paramount to the grassroots individuals who make up the people's movements. From a postcolonial perspective, the arena of culture is one of the most threatened. We have already noted how corporations and media campaigns are marginalizing traditional cultural expressions and identities. As we explore the postcolonial vision of the good life, we need to recognize that for postcolonial thinkers, humanity's purpose is understood as the ability to be authentically human, however individual communities choose to define that. In other words, humanity's purpose is to live authentically, something that is inevitably expressed in culture.

In proposing culture as the teleological end of postcolonialism, it is necessary to suspend Western conceptions of telos in order to comprehend fully how culture can be understood as humanity's purpose. That is to say, traditional Western conceptions of telos (as evidenced by the three previous theories of globalization in this study) are goal oriented in the sense of understanding teleology as something that is actively pursued. An action quality is present even in the language we use to describe telos—purpose connotes conscious, intentional activity aimed toward a particular goal.

In examining the notion of telos embodied in the postcolonial theory of globalization, we must let go of our Western, competitive, achievement-oriented philosophy. Rather than thinking of our telos as something that we *do*, or an end that we work toward achieving, let us try to think of our telos as something that we *are*. In this way we can more easily see the connection between telos and culture in this fourth theory of globalization.

Culture-building is a value to the extent that it expresses what postcolonialism views as a "good" or "right" response to the question of humanity's purpose. For people who hold this theory of globalization, culture is an expression of the lifeblood and identity of a particular group of people; it is the way in which a people are able to stay connected to their past and to construct their future in a way that honors their beliefs. While most of us are familiar with the most apparent trappings of culture—namely, music, art, clothing, and language—various subtle and often unobserved behaviors, actions, and patterns also form a significant part of a culture. The total combination of these expressions is what forms a particular culture.

For proponents of postcolonialism, this theory holds no sense of ideological authority by which the rest of humanity is informed of what their individual or collective purpose should be. Rather, the vision of the good life is understood in such a way that all communities and cultures around the world are respected as equally valuable and authentic. Each community is charged with the responsibility of caring for and maintaining its own cultural identity within the context of a globalizing world. At the same time, most postcolonial proponents would argue that this individualism does not give license to traditional and cultural behaviors that infringe on the human rights of community members or others. In the most positive vision of postcolonial proponents, invoking culture as humanity's telos is not a license for a reactionary and controlling vision of culture as expressed by groups such as the Taliban, for culture is not a static entity. People desire the space and freedom to shape their own cultures in response to their engagement with new ideas, peoples, and cultures. An eloquent expression of the foundations of this vision of the good life is found in a powerful statement made by Subcomandante Marcos, the unofficial spokesperson for the Zapatistas, at the 1996 Encounter for Humanity and against Neoliberalism held in Mexico:

> Considering that we are:
> Against the international order of death,
>   against the globalization of war and armaments.
> Against dictatorships,
>   against authoritarianism,
>   against repression.
> Against the politics of economic liberalization,
>   against hunger,
>   against poverty,
>   against robbery,
>   against corruption.
> Against patriarchy,
>   against xenophobia,
>   against discrimination,
>   against racism,
>   against crime,
>   against the destruction of the environment,
>   against militarism.
> Against stupidity,
>   against lies,
>   against ignorance.
> Against slavery,
>   against intolerance,
>   against injustice,
>   against marginalization,
>   against forgetfulness.
> Against neoliberalism.
> Considering that we are:
> For the international order of hope,
> for a new, just, and dignified peace.
> For a new politics,
>   for democracy,
>   for political liberties.

For justice,
for life, and dignified work.
For civil society,
for full rights for women in every regard,
for respect for elders, youth, and children,
for the defense and protection of the environment.
For intelligence,
for culture,
for education,
for truth.
For liberty,
for tolerance,
for inclusion,
for remembrance.
For humanity.[67]

Communal Autonomy as What Constitutes Human Flourishing

While it is true that for some communities or individuals, the responsibility of maintaining their culture might translate into a Luddite approach to globalization represented by a rejection of technology, science, and other modern innovations, for the most part postcolonialists are not interested in withdrawing from the world.[68] In fact, many people's movements rely heavily on the Internet and other advanced technology for their own organizing efforts. Nevertheless, they are concerned about their ability to mediate and control the way in which their interaction with global authorities and powers will transpire. This desire to be an active participant in the processes of globalization that affect their own communities is the reason that the postcolonial answer to the question "What promotes human flourishing?" is communal autonomy.

Autonomy comes from the Greek words *autos* (self) and *nomos* (law or rule) and bears the consequent general meaning of "self-rule." While modern usage of the word often is focused on the meaning and limits of individual autonomy, the postcolonial perspective hearkens back to the original Greek usage of the word *autonomia* for the independent self-rule of city-states and their desire to determine their own laws.[69] The desire for *autonomia* or autonomy by people's movements that are experiencing the oppressive control of hegemonic globalization is that same desire for the communal right to self-determination that was present in ancient Greece.

The practical value of autonomy as a defining element in the expression of human flourishing is evident in the experience of the Indian people in rejecting colonial rule.[70] In 1930 Gandhi led the poor of India in the nonviolent resistant act of taking over the production of salt in deliberate violation of British colonial law. Salt production was administered under the authority of colonial rule, and a salt tax was imposed on all citizens. As salt is an essential ingredient for cooking in India, this tax became a symbolic representation of the oppressive force and control that the British Empire held over the Indian people. The act of regaining some measure of autonomy for India's masses by defying the British laws regarding the production of salt and later the production of traditional clothes facilitated the move toward independence and autonomous self-rule.

Contemporary people's movements strive for similar experiences of communal autonomy as a way of regaining a sense of power and control over their futures. In a world where the defining power of colonialism and neocolonialism has led to human poverty and degradation for the majority of people in the "two-thirds" world, the promise of autonomy over their own economic, social, political, and cultural resources and enterprises offers the promise of a new vision of human flourishing. This vision of human flourishing has already been articulated by the Zapatistas as a life free from want, disease, and premature death; a world where everyone has land to grow food, access to health care, access to education, and a decent wage and where racism has been eliminated. While the exact picture of the good life may differ from culture to culture and community to community, human flourishing requires respect for basic human rights and some degree of autonomy for communities that allows them to participate in the sociopolitical processes that affect the health and well-being of their people.

Notes

1. I will be following Elleke Boehmer's distinction between the hyphenated "post-colonial," which is used to designate the historical period after World War II and the nonhyphenated "postcolonial," which is used to "denote the dynamic textual and political practices that critically examine the colonial relationship, practices through which colonized people seek to assert themselves as subjects of history." Elleke Boehmer, *Colonial and Postcolonial Literature* (Oxford: Oxford University Press, 1995), 3; as quoted in Wong Wai Ching, "Negotiating for a Postcolonial Identity: Theology of 'the Poor Woman' in Asia," *Journal of Feminist Studies in Religion* 16, no. 2 (fall 2000): 5.

2. Gustavo Esteva and Madhu Suri Prakash, *Grassroots Post-Modernism: Remaking the Soil of Cultures* (London: Zed Books, 1998), 25.

3. See Dipesh Chakrabarty, "Postcoloniality and the Artifice of History: Who Speaks for 'Indian' Pasts?" in *Contemporary Postcolonial Theory: A Reader*, ed. Padmini Mongia (New York: Oxford University Press, 1996).

4. Immanuel Wallerstein describes the world economy as functioning with a core, periphery, and semiperiphery. The core areas dominate the system while the peripheral areas provide cheap materials and labor that function to enrich the core. Nevertheless, Europe and the neo-Europes (Canada, New Zealand, Australia, the

United States) are still conceptualized as the "center" of the system. What a postcolonial critique objects to is the way Wallerstein's theory marginalizes the role of the people and countries in the "periphery" in his model.

5. The term "subaltern" is used in postcolonial studies to refer to a subjective position of inferiority that exists within a dominant framework of hegemonic control—usually maintaining European biases.

6. Chakrabarty, "Postcoloniality," 223.

7. One of the intellectual sources for this fourth globalization position is the sub-discipline known as "postcolonial" studies. The rhetorical usage of the words "postcolonial," "neocolonial," and "Third World" is currently one of the topics under debate by theorists. For more detail on different arguments regarding the use of these terms, see Ankie Hoogvelt, *Globalisation and the Postcolonial World: The New Political Economy of Development* (London: Macmillan, 1997); Arif Dirlik, "The Postcolonial Aura: Third World Criticism in the Age of Global Capitalism," in *Contemporary Postcolonial Theory*, ed. Mongia; Ella Shohat, "Notes on the 'Post-Colonial,'" in *Contemporary Postcolonial Theory*, ed. Mongia; and Sherif Hetata, "Dollarization, Fragmentation, and God," in *The Cultures of Globalization*, ed. Fredric Jameson and Masao Miyoshi (Durham, NC: Duke University Press, 1998).

8. Chakrabarty, "Postcoloniality," 224–25.

9. Ibid., 242.

10. While Chakrabarty is specifically addressing Europe and European theorists, the argument can easily be extended to apply to North America and its Eurocentric biases.

11. Dirlik, "Postcolonial Aura."

12. Ibid., 307.

13. For more details regarding postcolonial critiques of history see Arif Dirlik, Vinay Bahl, and Peter Gran, *History after the Three Worlds: Post-Eurocentric Historiographies* (Lanham, MD: Rowman & Littlefield, 2001); and Bill Ashcroft, Gareth Griffiths, and Helen Tiffin, *The Post-Colonial Studies Reader* (London: Routledge, 1995), esp. 355–88.

14. A distinction can be made between imperialism and colonialism in that the former can refer to the domination of distant territory by a metropolitan center while the latter can refer primarily to the establishment of settlements in those territories. However, because the establishment of territories has historically been intrinsically related to the oppression and subjugation of the indigenous peoples and their land by the colonizing people, this study will use the words interchangeably.

15. Gwendolyn Mikell, *Cocoa and Chaos in Ghana* (Washington, DC: Howard University Press, 1992).

16. The term "monoculture" refers to one of the tendencies of the current model of globalization to promote uniformity (usually conforming to Western, and mostly U.S., cultural standards) at the expense of diversity.

17. Nicanor Perlas, *Shaping Globalization: Civil Society, Cultural Power, and Threefolding* (Quezon City, Philippines: Center for Alternative Development Initiatives, 1999), esp. chap. 2.

18. Edward Goldsmith, "Development as Colonialism," in *The Case Against the Global Economy*, ed. Jerry Mander and Edward Goldsmith (San Francisco: Sierra Club Books, 1996), 257.

19. Daniel Yergin and Joseph Stanislaw, "Playing by the Rules: The New Game in Latin America," in *The Commanding Heights: The Battle between Government and the Marketplace That Is Remaking the Modern World* (New York: Simon & Schuster, 1998).

20. Edward Goldsmith, "Development as Colonialism," in *Case Against the Global Economy*, ed. Mander and Goldsmith, 262.

21. Import substitution relied on local production for local consumption and was the common practice in Latin America from 1960 to 1973. Walden Bello, "Structural Adjustment Programs: 'Success' for Whom?" in *Case Against the Global Economy*, ed. Mander and Goldsmith, 288.

22. For an excellent collection of feminist critiques of structural adjustment policies from "two-thirds" world women, see Pamela Sparr, ed., *Mortgaging Women's Lives: Feminist Critiques of Structural Adjustment* (London: Zed Books, 1994). For good examples of feminist analysis of gender and economics, see Bina Agarwal, *A Field of One's Own: Gender and Land Rights in South Asia* (Cambridge: Cambridge University Press, 1994); and Lourdes Beneria and Martha Roldan, *The Crossroads of Class and Gender: Industrial Homework, Subcontracting, and Household Dynamics in Mexico City* (Chicago: University of Chicago Press, 1987).

23. Bello, "Structural Adjustment Programs," 293.

24. Ibid., chap. 25; and Carlos Heredia and Mary Purcell, "Structural Adjustment and the Polarization of Mexican Society," in *Case Against the Global Economy*, ed. Mander and Goldsmith.

25. Heredia and Purcell, "Structural Adjustment," 274.

26. Ibid., 276.

27. Michel Lewis, "How the Eggheads Cracked," *New York Times Magazine*, January 24, 1999, 24–31, 42, 67, 71, 77; Gretchen Morgenson, "Seeing a Fund as Too Big to Fail, New York Fed Assists Its Bailout," *New York Times*, September 24, 1998, sec. A, p. 1, sec. C, p. 11; and Peter Truell, "An Alchemist Who Turned Gold into Lead: Financial Wizard Done In by His Smoke and Mirrors, *New York Times*, September 25, 1998, sec. B, pp. 1, 5.

28. Lewis, "How the Eggheads Cracked," p. 69.

29. Alexander Goldsmith, "Seeds of Exploitation: Free Trade Zones in the Global Economy," in *Case Against the Global Economy*, ed. Mander and Goldsmith.

30. Ibid., 267.

31. See p. 38.

32. As the big business institution responsible for promoting "free trade," the World Trade Organization reveals a strategy much more closely aligned to "managing" trade. Under its management, trade ends up benefiting the strongest players in the game, namely, transnational corporations. The governmental negotiating teams for GATT that were privy to the inner circle that negotiated the treaty leading to the WTO were advised by a team of business leaders that represented the

interests of the largest and strongest transnational corporations in the world. The advisory team included no representatives from small business, farms, churches, environmental organizations, or unions. Paul Hawken points out that the treaty is "full of loop-holes, concessions to special interest groups, variable tariffs, and outright giveaways to industries that happened to be sufficiently wealthy and strongly represented in the negotiations." Paul Hawken, *The Ecology of Commerce: A Declaration of Sustainability* (New York: HarperCollins, 1993), 97.

33. Herman Daly, "Free Trade: The Perils of Deregulation," in *Case Against the Global Economy*, ed. Mander and Goldsmith.

34. One example of the increasing political role of transnational corporations can be seen in the relatively recent practice of hiring mercenary armies to protect their plants and workers.

35. Ninan Koshy, "The Political Dimensions and Implications of Globalization," *Voices from the Third World* 20 (1997): 26–48.

36. Hawken, *Ecology of Commerce*, 92.

37. Oronto Douglas, "The Case of Nigeria: Corporate Oil and Tribal Blood," in *Views from the South*, ed. Sarah Anderson, *Views from the South: The Effects of Globalization and the WTO on Third World Countries* (Chicago: Food First Books, 2000), 159.

38. Ibid., 161–62.

39. Details of this story are taken from Norimitsu Onishi, "In the Oil-Rich Nigeria Delta, Deep Poverty and Grim Fires," *New York Times*, August 11, 2000, sec. A, pp. 1, 8.

40. For an excellent, in-depth study of how this happened in Senegal, see Maureen Mackintosh, *Gender, Class, and Rural Transition: Agribusiness and the Food Crisis in Senegal* (London: Zed Books, 1989).

41. For an insightful set of essays on this topic, see Sarah Anderson, ed., *Views from the South.*

42. As relayed in a course George Tinker taught at Union Theological Seminary in 1998.

43. For an analysis of how globalization uses culture as a weapon of neocolonization, see K. N. Panikkar, "Globalization and Culture," *Voices from the Third World* 20 (1997): 49–58.

44. As quoted by Benjamin Barber in C. Fred Alford, *Think No Evil: Korean Values in the Age of Globalization* (Ithaca, NY: Cornell University Press, 1999), 148.

45. Ibid.

46. Hetata, "Dollarization, Fragmentation, and God," 278.

47. Helena Norberg-Hodge, "The Pressure to Modernize and Globalize," in *Case Against the Global Economy*, ed. Mander and Goldsmith.

48. Ibid., 36.

49. For an example of this approach, see Perlas, *Shaping Globalization.*

50. For two examples see Perlas, *Shaping Globalization*; and Esteva and Prakash, *Grassroots Post-Modernism.*

51. The shift in the nature of the globalization debates in recent years suggests that the postcolonial theorists are right. Web sites, promotional material, and public

policy discourse have shifted in the wake of the Seattle protests toward convincing people why neoliberal and development globalization are the best courses of action.

52. Perlas, *Shaping Globalization*, 53–54.

53. Ibid., 124.

54. Ibid., 129.

55. Ibid.

56. Ibid., 122–23.

57. "First Declaration from the Lacandon Jungle." Online: http://flag.blackened.net/revolt/mexico/ezln/ezlnwa.html.

58. Observations from Jenna, an organic farmworker living nearby, as quoted in Peter Rosset with Shea Cunningham, "Understanding Chiapas." Online: http://flag.blackened.net/revolt/mexico/reports/back94.html.

59. Andrew Flood, "Understanding the Zapatistas: Five Years of Rebellion in Mexico." Online: http://flag.blackened.net/revolt/ws99/ws56_zapatista.html.

60. "First Declaration from the Lacandon Jungle"; see n425.

61. Ibid.

62. Elizabeth M. Bounds, *Coming Together/Coming Apart: Religion, Community, and Modernity* (New York: Routledge, 1997), 3.

63. For the powerful story of indigenous Guatemalans and their rebellion against the tyranny of the state, see Rigoberta Menchu, *I, Rigoberta Menchu: An Indian Woman in Guatemala*, ed. Elisabeth Burgos-Debray, trans. Ann Wright (London: Verso, 1984).

64. The issue of community is fundamentally different in the "first" world where the most serious issues related to community stem from the perceived loss or disintegration of community. Larry Rasmussen describes how the morality of a capitalist market has slowly replaced the noncapitalist moral sentiments on which capitalism was initially envisioned. The results are societies marked by the ideologies and moral values of neoliberalism and social equity liberalism—societies in which an individual's wants and needs take precedence over communal well-being and in which a personal sense of individual responsibility creates a paternalistic approach to care-taking and justice. The struggle for community in the "first" world is caught up with the task of exposing the moral vacuousness of capitalist morality and struggling to recreate a context and meaning for the concept of community among a population that has drifted into anomie. See Bounds, *Coming Together/Coming Apart*; and Larry Rasmussen, *Moral Fragments and Moral Community* (Minneapolis: Fortress, 1993).

65. Information regarding the Shona and the Mutupo principle is taken from Tumani Mutasa Nyajeka, "Shona Women and the Mutupo Principle," in *Women Healing Earth: Third World Women on Ecology, Feminism, and Religion*, ed. Rosemary Ruether (Maryknoll, NY: Orbis Books, 1996).

66. Elias Mpofu, "Exploring the Self-Concept in an African Culture," *The Journal of Genetic Psychology* 155, no. 3 (1994): 341–54.

67. Online: http://www.ezln.org/documentos/1996/19960803.en.htm.

68. The term "Luddite" refers to a group of English workers who protested the introduction of machinery into the textile industry because they feared that they

would replace human skill and labor. The term now commonly refers to people who are wary about technological innovation.

69. James F. Childress, "Autonomy," in *The Westminster Dictionary of Christian Ethics*, ed. James F. Childress and John Macquarrie (Philadelphia: Westminster, 1986), 51–52.

70. Esteva and Prakesh, *Grassroots Post-Modernism*, 29.

PART 4

MOVING FORWARD

7

The Good Life for Whom?

Critiquing the Four Theories of Globalization

Americans have labeled September 11, 2001, as "the day the world changed." Indeed, something unprecedented did happen when the tactics of terrorism shifted from hijacking planes to utilizing them as weapons of mass destruction. In other ways, the loss that the United States experienced of over three thousand lives to forces of death and destruction parallels the loss of lives to forces of death and destruction from poverty, malnutrition, disease, and armed conflict that people around the world have been experiencing for years as the direct and indirect results of globalization in our world. The resounding denunciation of capitalism and the West symbolized by the al-Qaeda terrorists in their attack on the symbols of Western political, military, and financial power (the Capitol, the Pentagon, and the World Trade Center towers) reflects the desperation, anger, resentment, and fury that are present in some of the opposition to globalization around the world. While the path that was chosen by the terrorists is unconscionable to a human community that values justice, it is incumbant upon us, particularly those of us in the United States and other "first" world nations, to ask if the increasing economic and social inequality around our world is responsible for untold death and destruction to innocents whose lives we will never see. Before we can begin to envision our future, we must acknowledge the sins and culpabilities of the present form of globalization and the profound social, economic, and political inequality that it generates around the world.

On July 18, 2000, two articles appeared in the *New York Times* that exemplify the vastly different faces of globalization in our world. The front page carried a story of how builder Jay Lieberman had finished a home in the Hamptons that he hoped to sell for $8 million, preferably cash.[1] The individually handcrafted shower heads of the house's nine and a half bathrooms were just the beginning of the no-holds-barred extravagance that characterized this mansion. The excessive wealth generated by economic globalization and the stock market excesses of the 1990s caused an unprecedented boom in the housing and construction markets on the eastern end of Long Island as an elite group of Manhattanites sought refuge from the city. This group of global elite epitomizes the picture of the good life as painted by neoliberalism. Their very success and existence offers hope to others that global capitalism and market success hold the secret to accessing the good life. After all, the unemployment rate in Southampton fell to 2 percent by 2000 and the area experienced a shortage of skilled labor. Miguel Velasquez, a Salvadoran immigrant who grossed almost $90,000 a year working construction,[2] seemed to be proof that "trickle-down" economics works, although the fact that he worked twelve hours a day, seven days a week begs the question as to the quality of life this version of the good life offers to day laborers and other working-class people.

Six pages later the *New York Times* shared the story of Rogelio and Maria Luz Ochondra, who lost three of their four sons in a massive garbage landslide that killed over 200 people in Manila's "Promised Land," the ironic name given to the fifty-foot mountain that is the city's main dump.[3] The Ochondras are part of a community of peasants who live in shanties built around the edges of the smoking mountain of garbage whose methane gases are perpetually burning. The "Promised Land" shows the other face of capitalism, the face that is invisible in corporate boardrooms, ministerial meetings of the World Trade Organization, and the mansions of the Hamptons. But walk through the dumps in Manila, Mexico City, Rio de Janeiro, or countless other cities and you will also see capitalism at work. In a money economy, people require cash to get by. The "market" does not care if they have lost their land or are unable to find work, nor does it care that there are still hungry mouths to feed. The impoverished often turn to whatever means are available to earn money. For some that means prostitution, the black market, or other forms of illegal gain; for others society's refuse offers the possibility of a few pesos to buy bread or beans or milk for a baby's bottle. In a capitalist economy, when people like the Ochondras cannot find work, often the only choice open to them is to become scavengers, living off the waste of human existence. They may be free to exercise their individuality in search of prosperity, but to what end?

Assessing the Dominant Theories of Globalization

Now that we have identified and described each of the four theories of globalization, it is time to return to some of the questions with which we started. What knowledge and insight can the task of Christian ethics bring to bear on these competing ideologies? What do these theories tell us about living in the world? What sort of moral order do they offer humanity? And what would it be like to live in the world that each of them is trying to create? In short, it is time to evaluate the moral standing of these four theories. Each position will be examined in light of the three normative criteria offered in chapter 2 as a Christian ethical guide to a morally just model of globalization—a democratized understanding of power, care for the planet, and the social well-being of people.

Critiquing Neoliberal Globalization

The vision of the good life offered by neoliberalism is indeed attractive and highly sought after by many people around the globe. Individualism, prosperity, and freedom are three values that in and of themselves have a great deal of merit. The problem is that this particular vision of the good life imagines as its primary constituent that illusive *Homo economicus* we encountered earlier—an atomistic, male individual who exists outside of time and space, with no obligations to family or community that might impinge on his freedom to pursue prosperity through hard work. Unfortunately, as we have seen throughout this study, this idealized vision of life simply does not correspond to the reality of the global economy or to the lives of the majority of the world's workers. Given the scarcity of meaningful jobs at a living wage, this vision of the good life is truly available only to the global elite. Furthermore, most of the world's women continue to exist within complex relational networks that often require caring for children, aging relatives, husbands, and many times other relatives and friends as well. *Homo economicus* has always reflected the male gaze of society and the economy, a fact that continues to affect the world's women who are expected to conform as "workers" to a theoretical model that has always marginalized them. But the fact that this vision of the good life is only accessible to the top 10 percent of the world's people is only the tip of the iceberg.

The call in this study toward power-sharing stems from a belief that human moral agency is best exercised within the context of community. In the present globalizing context of our world, decision-making is increasingly being transferred from the grass roots, from local governments, and even from nation-states to the larger transnational powers that dominate our world. This ceding of power from the local to the global, which is part and parcel of both the neoliberal and development theories of globalization, compromises the ability of individuals and communities to share in decision-making and the exercise of power that often have deep and lasting effects on local communities.

In examining whether the neoliberal position meets the criteria of caring for the planet, we must begin with the knowledge that environmentalists have been telling us for years: The earth cannot sustain a world full of "first" world countries as they are now constituted. Even if all the world's people were able to live the neoliberal good life, or a lifestyle comparable to the world's wealthiest 10 percent, the burden on the earth would be too great; we would destroy our ecosystem. We have seen clearly the ways in which neoliberal globalization encourages public policy initiatives of growth and trade that create an enormous burden on the resources of the planet. The sustainability of planet Earth under the conditions of present patterns of economic globalization is highly dubious.

Neoliberals have suggested that technological developments will be created to address the environmental disaster threatening creation; but these developments have not, in fact, materialized, despite their assurances that we can be confident that the "market" will give rise to solutions. Furthermore, the work toward colonizing other planets, creating self-sufficient biospheres, or manipulating the weather raises a whole new set of ethical dilemmas that have not been adequately acknowledged or addressed within the scientific community. Successfully creating virtual atmospheres or abandoning this planet once we have rendered it unsustainable for human life, and many other forms of life in the process, sidestep the deeper moral question of our responsibility as part of *this* world to recognize and respect our interdependence with the life around us.

Finally, in examining whether this position attends to the social well-being of people, we can see that the value of freedom that is constitutive of human flourishing in the neoliberal paradigm has allowed for a situation in which an individual's "right" to make decisions eclipses a community's or society's right to determine the moral and behavioral standards that can protect them, their people, and the larger community from harm.

In the global North people are not allowed to drive or hunt or practice medicine without a license. To a similar degree, people who have children are required to care for them or face the possibility of losing them. In many situations, there are agreed-upon standards of behavior to which people are held accountable. Yet when these standards come in the form of limitations on behaviors that are currently harming our environment and consequently people's social well-being (e.g., burning fossil fuels, over consumption of meat), individuals claim the right of "freedom" to justify their behavior, regardless of the consequences. While the complicated nature of environmental degradation may make it more difficult to locate the proverbial "smoking gun," scientists do know what kinds of behavior are destroying the ozone shield, causing desertification, and speeding up global warming. Limitations on behavior, which are perfectly acceptable under other circumstances, are denounced as "barriers" to economic growth and "free trade." Although it is true that the value of freedom promoted by neoliberalism is an important democratic value, justice requires that we pay more attention to ways in which human flourishing can thrive under conditions of freedom that allow communities to achieve autonomy and self-sufficiency than to a model of freedom as nonconstraint for individuals.

Fundamental assumptions of neoclassical economics allow for a discourse in which the effects of growth and trade on the human community and the environment are rendered peripheral. The burning moral question that is rarely acknowledged within economic discourse is this: Are there human commitments and values that ought to take precedence over profit margins? Simply raising questions like this challenges the neoclassical economic assumptions that economics is rational and value-free. As we have seen, engines of neoliberalism such as the World Trade Organization continually reinforce these neoclassical assumptions through trade dispute negotiations that strike down the very kind of regulations meant to protect people's lives and the integrity of the environment. Governments have a moral responsibility to ensure a certain level of welfare for their citizens. Governments ought to be able to institute public policy measures that guarantee the health and security of their people and their habitats.

In addition to being able to protect their communities from the callousness of big business, governments should provide for the welfare of their citizens through adequate education for all members of society, adequate child-care policies and facilities for working families, and job training, retraining, and placement programs that would ensure that citizens were able to become contributing members of society. Even if all of these programs were offered, the plagues of unemployment; illness; racism, sexism, classism, homophobia, and other barriers to fair employment; insufficient health care coverage; a lack of decent, affordable housing; and a number of other factors make it clear that governmental involvement in securing the welfare of its people will not readily be rendered obsolete. In short, striving to achieve the social well-being of people is an ongoing task in a world that seeks to promote human flourishing.

Even if we could disregard the fact that the neoliberal vision of the good life is an exclusive ideal reserved for the world's privileged class and the fact that it fails to meet the test of the three criteria offered in this study, I would still argue that the vision of the good life that it offers is morally bankrupt on the grounds that it is incompatible with the image of the good life rooted in the Christian tradition that is oriented toward caring for our neighbor and for creation in addition to ourselves. These three moral norms—individualism, prosperity, and freedom—each of which has a potentially important role to play in the ethical life of the human community, somehow work together to create a community of people who are more concerned about their own welfare and freedom to do what they want than what will advance the common good. Individualism is certainly important, but sometimes it must be tempered by the needs or best interest of the community. Likewise, prosperity is not something to be disdained, but if achieving it becomes the most important goal in our life—our telos—then think of all the other aspects of life that we would miss. The bankruptcy of thinking of prosperity as our life's goal is even more true when we measure our understanding of prosperity solely by the wealth that we amass. The fact that these three values take precedence over community, care for the neighbor and the earth, compassion, and many other values means that the moral world created by the neoliberal vision of the good life, even if it were accessible to everyone, would be a world of greed, strife, envy, and callousness.

Critiquing Development Globalization

While the perspective of development globalization shares the neoclassical economic assumptions and agenda of neoliberalism, its approach to globalization is different in morally significant ways. The values of the development vision of the good life themselves—responsibility, progress, and equity—reveal a certain concern for some of the moral criteria of this study that was simply absent in the neoliberal model.

With regard to the challenge of this study that globalization processes need to move toward a democratization of power, the branches of the development community examined here—the World Bank and the United Nations Development Programme—are attempting to move in the direction of consulting local communities in their development protocols and plans. Nevertheless, the hierarchal and bureaucratic structures of institutions like the World Bank continue to privilege traditional development models that rely heavily on "experts" at the expense of genuine models of shared partnership working toward development goals generated by local communities. Additionally, the development theorists' emphasis on responsibility as the driving force behind moral agency precludes the kind of respect and collaboration that democracy requires. An ethic of moral agency fueled by feelings of responsibility generates a social ethic of paternalism that undermines true democratic participation. A theory of globalization rooted in noblesse oblige conceptions of responsibility is fundamentally antithetical to the democratization of power.

Because the neoliberal and development models of globalization share the presuppositions of neoclassical economics, it is clear that development globalization will fail to meet the criterion of caring for the planet based on the same grounds we saw in the critique of neoliberalism. The arguments from the development community that placing controls and regulations on big business will be adequate to address the environmental crisis ignore the fact that the capitalist model that is being touted as the best avenue toward development is based on a model of industrialization that is simply unsustainable. It is true that we cannot justify denying others the right to the kind of social development that will ease their burdens by providing employment, improving health care, and generally making life more livable for them. What is disputable is whether a development model of globalization that is committed to capitalist economic integration is an adequate theory of either development or globalization.

The moral norms posited here suggest that what is required is not more growth, not more profit, not more unexamined excess even under the guise of "social development." What is required is a transformation of our ideological orientation that would place the earth and all of creation at the center of our moral world. Taking care of the planet becomes humanity's teleological calling, if you will. If we acknowledge this to be the case, two things become evident. First, we in the global North must alter our lifestyles to a level that would be sustainable if shared with others around the globe. This undertaking will undoubtedly include the development of alternative, sustainable energy sources as well as a reduction in our consumerism. Second, social development does not have to be dependent on the capitalist model that has dominated development theory since World War II. Communities of scholars, civil society groups, and even heterodox economists are already engaged in developing alternative sustainable economic models to challenge the presumed inevitability of economic globalization.[4]

To the extent that the value of equity promoted by the development community as constitutive of human flourishing is focused on improving the conditions of economic globalization in such a way that the benefits of development become more accessible for more people, it does meet the criterion of attending to the social well-being of people. This approach fails, however, in that it uncritically accepts the possibility that capitalism can be regulated in ways that allow for justice. Given the history of capitalism and development in contributing to a world marked by increasing class stratification and economic inequality, the burden of proof in demonstrating the capacity for capitalism to promote justice lies with its proponents. Furthermore, the development model is not concerned with the redistribution of the world's resources in concert with a valuing of equality, but is rather concerned with equity, a value that provides for the possibility of continued severe inequality so long as basic human needs are met. This leaves open the possibility that we in the "first" world do not need to change our behavior so long as we help provide for the subsistence of the "two-thirds" world. The fact that the development vision of the good life allows for some measure of inequality, in and of itself, undermines the work of justice.

Theologically the ongoing necessity of striving for justice is a reflection of the brokenness of the corporeal world. This brokenness is a deeply rooted religious belief that is perhaps most well-known in the mythical story of the garden of Eden. In this biblical account, God places Adam and Eve in the paradisiacal garden to care for it with the sole proviso that they do not eat from the tree of the knowledge of good and evil. Adam and Eve disobey God's order by eating the fruit from this tree and God casts them out of paradise.[5] This story symbolizes humanity's recognition of the brokenness of our world and our attempt to try to make sense of it. In the story God does not curse Adam and Eve; rather, the relationships between God, humanity, and the rest of creation *change*. This story can be seen as an ancient way of grappling with the questions of what constitutes human flourishing and why life is so difficult. Within the biblical narrative, this story sets the stage on which the rest of God's story unfolds. And in that story, God does not abandon humanity because humans have sinned, nor does God allow our sinfulness to be an excuse for our behavior. Human flourishing is set in the context of struggle and of interdependence—with others, with God, and with the rest of creation. The biblical call to human flourishing requires that we understand human existence as part and parcel of a larger world, a world valued and loved by God in its entirety, not hierarchically.

The stories that unfold in the Hebrew Bible and in the New Testament are stories of human accountability and responsibility. While many of these stories open with the mistakes or failings of the characters, Scripture uses these failures as a heuristic device for teaching responsibility. In a similar vein, the brokenness of our world is not an excuse for giving up on justice or for ceasing to be responsible people. Our task is to recognize and name the injustices in our world and, in the case of globalization, to strive toward a model of globalization that honors and cares for creation.

In the end, while the theory of globalization as social development is preferable to neoliberalism, it does not represent a "middle ground" between the proponents of neoliberalism and the resistors of globalization. To the extent that development globalization accepts the assumption that trade-oriented growth can solve the problems of poverty, the world that it would create would differ very little from the world of today. As a stopgap measure between the world of today and a transformation of globalization into a life-affirming movement of solidarity and knowledge-sharing, some of the attempts of the development community can serve an important purpose. Some development ideas and strategies do offer a check on the extreme abuses of neoliberalism, and we should recognize the value of alleviating suffering in the immediate present as we continue to work toward a future of social democracy that honors the normative criteria laid out in this study. But as a long-term strategy of survival, we have already seen that the good life offered by the development community is incompatible with the Christian ethical vision of globalization set forth in this study.

Acknowledging Our Ideological Blind Spots

This study has highlighted the importance of the role that ideology plays in the formation of different theories of globalization. We also need to acknowledge the ways in which ideology functions on the individual level to prevent people from either seeing or participating in transformative action. We have already seen that many of the crises of the global South are borne out of the dominant ideologies that drive U.S. culture. In addition to the business world, most of our news media, entertainment industries, government officials, and even religious leadership not only buy into the status quo, but also reproduce it in their own ways for their constituencies. In our present culture, it is almost impossible to escape the religion of the market.[6] It affects and influences us in ways of which we are not always even aware. To return to the language of standpoint theory, our vision is limited by our perception of reality. Mired in a capitalist economy and a capitalist cultural identity, we often are unable to see beyond the possibilities of the present. We become stuck in an attitude of reform that limits our imagination. These limitations can blind us to the potential for change offered by alternative ideologies, or even worse, they can blind us to the recognition of the need for change.

An example of this kind of ideological "blind spot" is evident in a recent book on globalization by *New York Times* Foreign Affairs columnist Thomas Friedman. In *The Lexus and the Olive Tree*, Friedman spends a great deal of time arguing that globalization has divided the world into two competing groups symbolized by the Lexus and the olive tree. Those in the Lexus group are "dedicated to modernizing, streamlining and privatizing their economies in order to thrive in the system of globalization."[7] Those in the other half of the world spend their time fighting over who owns the olive trees that represent "everything that roots us, anchors us, identifies us and locates us in this world."[8] Unfortunately, rather than moving toward an analysis of globalization that questions the values and priorities of the Lexus model, Friedman falls into an uncritical acceptance of a definition of globalization that requires this kind of behavior in order to survive. By accepting the neoliberal definition of globalization, Friedman is unable to see the possibilities of transformation that were undoubtedly right in front of him as he traveled, talked, and worked with the "olive tree" people. Consequently, his own proscriptive agenda is unable to move beyond a call for minimizing the excesses of globalization, because the concepts of transformation and revolution are not acknowledged as viable options within his own worldview. This limitation is evident in the following excerpt:

> Analysts have been wondering for a while now whether the [countries and people] who are left behind by globalization, or most brutalized by it, will develop an alternative ideology to liberal, free-market capitalism. . . . [I]n the first era of globalization, when the world first experienced the creative destruction of global capitalism, the backlash eventually produced a whole new set of ideologies—communism, socialism, fascism—that promised to take the sting out of capitalism, particularly for the average working person.

> Now that these ideologies have been discredited, I doubt we will see a new coherent, universal ideological reaction to globalization—because I don't believe there is one that can both truly soften the brutality of capitalism and still produce steadily rising standards of living.[9]

It is also important to note that Friedman's acceptance of the inevitability of the dominant model of globalization is heavily influenced by the creation of wealth that has benefited so many people in the United States and by our relative status as a world power under the globalization system. Evidence of this influence is present throughout the book in Friedman's triumphalist view of the "unique" and important role that the United States can and should play in the management of globalization. This attitude can be seen is the following selection:

> America does have a shared national interest to pursue in today's globalization system, and it has an enormous role to play. Put simply: As the country that benefits most from global economic integration, it is our job to make sure that globalization is sustainable and that advances are leading declines for as many people as possible, in as many countries as possible, on as many days as possible.[10]

This reading of history leads Friedman to argue for a continued paternalistic and domineering role for the United States in the arena of foreign policy. A different historical reading of the past fifty years could easily lead to a position in which people from the "first" world recognize that our "success" has been bought on the backs of the "two-thirds" world and might lead in foreign policy directions that do not privilege the role of the United States in developing new pathways of globalization.

The Lexus and the Olive Tree is representative of one of the most dangerous barriers to resisting the dominant forms of globalization and seeking pathways of transformation. By accepting the status quo as inevitable, Friedman's own work actually functions to reproduce the conditions of economic globalization through his definition of globalization as "the spread of free-market capitalism to virtually every country in the world" and his limited ability to see any way to redress the excesses of globalization except through reformation. Because he has so wholeheartedly bought into the dominant interpretation of globalization, despite his ability to see many of its pitfalls and problems, his ability to imagine alternatives is constrained. Unfortunately, Friedman's uncritical acceptance of the ideological argument that rising standards of living are a prima facie good has blinded him to the moral vacuity of the model of globalization that he has chosen to endorse through his acceptance of the neoliberal description of our social order. His own blind spots prevent him from recognizing the resistance ideologies presented in this study as concrete and viable alternatives. The ability to recognize our own blind spots is never easy, and often voices outside our paradigm are able to point out those things that we cannot see. I will assume that anyone who has come this far in the study is at least amenable to the idea that different ideological perspectives form our world and our perception of globalization in radically different ways. This recognition challenges us to be open to the perspectives and standpoints of people outside of our own experience with the hope that different eyes can help us see our own reality with more clarity.

In light of the normative criteria that I have suggested for critiquing theories of globalization, we must denounce both of the dominant theories of globalization not only as incapable of providing an adequate vision of the good life, but also as fundamentally incongruent with a democratized understanding of power, care for the planet, and the social well-being of people. If we examine the effects of these forms of globalization from the perspective of the world's underclass, we can see that people around the world are dying under the weight of their poverty—from landslides to tuberculosis to starvation.

Meanwhile, in the households of the wealthy, middle class, and working class around the world, people lounge in the comfort of climate-controlled homes and La-Z-Boy chairs watching "reality" television shows and further removing ourselves from the very real consequences of our own behavior. Ignoring the hole in the ozone layer does not negate its existence. The fact is that going about our lives as usual, oblivious or in denial to the way our behavior is affecting life on the planet, is morally irresponsible. Moral justification for the overconsumption of the global North is one of the most rampant barriers to transforming globalization as we know it. Air-conditioning, cars, air travel, refrigerators, microwaves—these forms of technology have indeed improved the quality of our lives. There is something to be said in favor of labor-saving devices. There is also something to be said in favor of the health and well-being of our planet and justice for our neighbors. A critical examination of globalization must ask whether rising standards of living really are a prima facie good. In answering this question, we must grapple with the deeper philosophical question "How much is enough?" Rising standards of living for people in poverty are certainly a necessary part of addressing the social well-being of people, but continued rising standards of living for the global elite around the world are simply a reflection of greed and avarice.

Given the embeddedness of "first" world culture in the activity of the capitalist marketplace, it is almost impossible to escape completely the dominant paradigms of globalization. Our realities are partially defined by the institutional structures in which we live our lives. Short of cashing out or abdicating our retirement funds and moving to isolated, self-sufficient homes or communities, we are unable to extricate ourselves fully from the culture of capitalism. This is one of the reasons that we "first" worlders often are paralyzed by our inability to address the problems and excesses of globalization as we know it. It is impossible to imagine creative solutions to problems that we do not see. Part of the challenge for people who recognize the moral failings of neoliberal and development globalization is to disengage from the dominant system to the extent that we are able. We must create spaces that are not dominated by these ideologies in which we can envision and enact both our resistance and our visions for transformation. The other part of the challenge lies in creating new models of political economy that transform structural injustice and support the normative criteria of this study.

Assessing the Resistance Theories of Globalization

Over the past decade, and increasingly since the "battle of Seattle," neoliberals and social equity liberals have made increasing attempts to respond to their critics. Indeed, proponents of the dominant paradigms of growth and development claim to be addressing some of the issues raised by their critics, issues such as environmental degradation and the broader participation of people. Critics of globalization must continue to examine the practices of big business and development in relation to their rhetoric of environmental concern and broader participation. A critical look at these "responses" to criticism reveals a strategy of co-optation at work in these attempts to pacify resistors. Another strategy that has become evident on the part of transnational corporations is recent advertising campaigns that attempt to attract consumer dollars through appeals to the social conscience of consumers without seriously addressing the very social issues their ads raise. Known as "cause-related" advertising, these ads attempt to influence consumer spending habits by appealing to particular social causes. One recent example was a Kenneth Cole ad campaign featuring a model with a black leather handbag and the text, "Dear pro-life advocates, Isn't it a woman's right to choose? After all, she's the one carrying it." This campaign tactic does not mean that Kenneth Cole Productions necessarily contributes money to pro-choice causes. And as Dan Bischoff points out, "Carrying out your civic duty in the form of shopping inevitably avoids any real social commitment."[11] Having judged the dominant models of globalization morally untenable, the question remains: Do the resistance theories offer visions of the good life that are compatible with the norms privileged here?

Critiquing Earthist Globalization

As we have seen, the earthist approach to globalization is rooted in the core values of mutuality, justice, and sustainability. While the dominant theories of globalization would no doubt affirm that these are indeed important values, what this study highlights is the way in which a theoretical position's core values shape its vision of the good life in distinct and morally significant ways. The fact that this position invests these values with utmost significance is evident in the public policy measures it supports. While it is easy to agree that values such as mutuality, justice, and sustainability are important, a reflection of these values in a group's behavior (as witnessed in something concrete such as public policy measures) is a far more tangible reflection of that commitment than mere rhetoric.

In examining the earthist position's concern about moral agency, we can see that its emphasis on the localization of production and the development of bioregional economies is certainly compatible with the goal of democratizing power. Likewise, its belief that moral agency ought to be exercised within the context of mutuality centralizes the importance of increased participation in decision-making, both in terms of the voices involved in the process as well as consideration of the effects of particular decisions. One of the primary considerations for moving toward the localization of both governance and production in the political economy rests on the belief that people who are affected by decision-making processes have relevant wisdom to contribute to the conversation. Transnational corporate governance negates local knowledge, livelihood, and sustainability. If the earthist alternative pathways of globalization have any chance of succeeding on a larger scale, they clearly will necessitate a transformation of corporate structures of governance as well as production operations.

Concern for the earth is clearly the central organizing principle of the earthist position. From their concern for the environmental degradation of the biosphere to their alternative visions for the future of globalization, earthist proponents present a deep theory of how an ecocentric worldview can shape alternative public policy measures. Living as if justice were humanity's calling functions as the operative moral norm in approaching not only the environmental crisis, but also every aspect of the living of their lives. Their critique of hegemonic globalization is a witness to how differently we approach our moral universe when we take seriously the fact that we are interrelated with all of creation.

Both the earthist and postcolonial positions are deeply rooted in models of community that privilege mutuality and respect for other persons as foundational principles. We have seen repeatedly how the excesses of capitalist globalization continue to manifest a distinct disregard for their effects on the lives of all people. The resistance positions reclaim respect for human dignity as a central moral concern for creating a good life. This is manifested in the earthist paradigm through the two foundational presuppositions of valuing the interdependence of life and respecting the sacred quality of creation. As we have seen, these presuppositions shape an earthist approach to the problems of globalization that privilege the integrity of creation—a quality that demands caring for the material and spiritual needs of humanity as a primary reflection of human flourishing. But the earthist notion of human flourishing extends beyond the narrowly anthropocentric vision of human well-being to a conception of human flourishing as possible only within the larger context of sustainability. In other words, human life can be understood to be flourishing only when the whole of creation is flourishing, an idea that is certainly consonant with the norm of the social well-being of people privileged here.

Moving beyond the earthist perspective, there are still important aspects of eco-justice that must be addressed by "first" world constituencies. Part of the task of developing a Christian ethical approach to globalization is calling the Christian community to accountability. Consumerism within the context of the "first" world has already been raised as a moral issue, but its role within the faith community bears further examination. From the Christian ethical perspective proposed here, behavior that does not seek to democratize power, care for the earth, and promote the social well-being of people must be decried as sin. This includes any unexamined consumer behavior that complicitly contributes to the degradation of the earth as well as the impoverishment of the "two-thirds" world and the poverty of the marginalized in our hometowns. Recognizing our behavior as sin is essential to the transformation process because it is a critical first step toward taking responsibility for our actions and changing our lifestyles.

Critiquing Postcolonial Globalization

Of the four positions, the theory of postcolonial globalization is certainly the most diffuse. As a perspective deeply rooted in postmodern discourse, postcolonialism does not seek a new grand narrative by which we should order the political and economic structures of our world. Nevertheless, the values of community, respect for culture, and communal autonomy are evident in the writings and actions of many of the leaders and organizations involved in postcolonial struggles.

Support for the democratization of power is strongly evident in postcolonial globalization because this position is deeply concerned with creating models of globalization that allow grassroots people the ability to participate in self-governance. The examples of the ongoing work of civil society in the Philippines and the struggles of the Zapatistas in Mexico witness to the centrality of transforming hierarchical political structures in ways that facilitate the involvement of local people in decision-making. Fundamentally, the work of democratizing systems of power involves a serious concern for employing a critical analysis of social systems attuned to issues of authority and control. Given the subaltern social location of postcolonialists as well as their desire to dismantle oppressive systems that limit their ability to exercise self-rule, their critique is inherently political. It is the overt political nature of this position that lends itself most strongly to supporting and furthering an agenda of democratizing power. For the proponents of postcolonial globalization, issues of power are evident in their struggle against neocolonialism in the form of corporations and multilateral institutions and the neoliberal and development ideologies that drive them. A democratization of power for the "two-thirds" world demands a rearrangement of the present political structures that guide the work of the World Trade Organization and the Bretton Woods institutions, and it also necessitates a rethinking of the capitalist ideologies that drive these institutions. Furthermore, it requires a serious transformation of the corporation.

Even though explicit attention to issues of eco-justice was not forefront in the characterization of postcolonialism presented in this study, we saw that the postcolonial vision of community is implicitly ecocentric. The description of the Shona community as deeply related and connected to all of the life forms that surround it is symbolic of the postcolonial vision of community that is deeply embedded in the physical world. Similarly, the work of civil society in the Philippines was organized around the development of a national plan for sustainable development. The cosmological consciousness that permeates this position's worldview corresponds to the moral norm of caring for the planet.

Postcolonial resistance arises from the recognition of the mistreatment and abuse of marginalized people in the global South. This concern for people's social well-being is one of the motivational factors that gave rise to this position. The threats to the lives and livelihood of the marginalized posed by corporate and development globalization have generated a theory of resistance that seeks to help grassroots people regain control over their lives. To that end, attention to the social well-being of people is evident in all three postcolonial values—community, culture, and communal autonomy. Each of these works together to create a holistic vision of society—including human and nonhuman life—that provides for the well-being of all life forms.

While the two resistance movements offer support for the moral norm of the social well-being of people, this norm offers serious challenges to people still caught up in the dominant worldview. "First" world societies must face up to the increasing problem of the disintegration of community.[12] Ethicist Elizabeth Bounds connects the crisis of community in the United States directly to the alienating qualities of advanced capitalism that currently plague our world.[13] In other words, she is arguing that many of the social changes that have contributed to a loss of community in the modern era can be traced to the effects of corporate globalization. This fact is evident in the virtual elimination of family farms and other small businesses that once formed the core of the U.S. economy. The interconnected economic and social relationships that are part and parcel of rural life are also an integral part of the development of community identity. Another example lies in the trend toward urbanization that characterized the twentieth century as increasing numbers of people left their "traditional" communities in search of work.

My concern in highlighting the disintegration of community in the "first" world is not to romanticize the past or to ignore the complicated and sometimes problematic identities of past communities. Many of those communities reflected tightly controlled constructions of gender identity and behavior as well as racial biases and provincial identities that prescribed the life "choices" available for community members and prevented positive interaction with "outsiders." I am not calling for a return to the models of community identity that predominated in our history. The proposal to rethink or reimagine globalization in new ways for the future is not intended as a strategy to return the world to some mythic, idealized notion of our past. Rather, the challenge for all civilizations and communities is to learn how to respond to the changes that develop in our own historical context and to work toward building the most just world that we can. What is sorely needed in the industrialized world is a recovery of the moral conviction that human beings are fundamentally social creatures, and an important aspect of the good life is the recognition that the social well-being of people arises from participation in community. As social beings, we need each other for friendship, support, entertainment, and companionship, among other things.

The capitalist image of *Homo economicus* as the rational economic actor who exists independently from society and family negates the importance of community by construing relationships as primarily adversarial and competitive. To the extent that people experience the world within an atmosphere of isolation and fragmentation, their capacity to trust their own moral agency as an important and integral part of social transformation is diminished. Independent and isolated reflection on the far-reaching problems associated with globalization often renders feelings of helplessness and despair about what a single individual can do to make a difference. Collective perceptions of the futility of confronting the powers of globalization and a shared skepticism about individuals' abilities to effect social change become significant social barriers to the possibility of transformation.

While it is true that individual lifestyle changes are needed to bring about some changes in the hegemonic forms of globalization, the reality is that all of the pathways to transformation require the shared efforts of communities of resistance. Resistance is difficult and the support of a community of people who share similar values and goals can be a critically important resource and base from which change can emerge. This does not mean that there is only one definition or conception of how "community" is to be created, embodied, or sustained. What it does mean is that attention to the development and nurturing of a variety of types of community is essential to the task of transforming globalization.

Suggestions for Strengthening the Earthist and Postcolonial Positions

Clearly the way forward must incorporate elements of both of the resistance theories we have examined. In fact, one of the most important tasks in moving forward is to work toward more dialogue and strategy-building between the final two positions. Viewing these two resistance positions from a critical perspective, we can see that a serious engagement of discourse between these two ideologies could strengthen their collective task and further the possibility of transforming globalization.

The earthist position could benefit from the more critical political awareness that marks the postcolonial position. A heightened awareness of how structures of domination continue to reproduce behavior that is destructive to the earth community could serve to generate more politically active public policy initiatives.[14] Additionally, many of the earthist strategies of localization are incumbent upon voluntary disengagement from the dominant society and elective participation in an alternative culture. These strategies, particularly in the global North, require a certain amount of class privilege for people to participate precisely because they are voluntary. The higher prices of food bought through a CSA as well as the necessity of an up-front lump payment place this healthy and sustainable form of resistance outside the reach of many working-class people. Furthermore, alternative farming practices do not yet challenge the dominance of corporate farming in any substantial way.

The notion of voluntary simplicity also sidesteps the problem of structural injustice by making the issue one of individual choice. Earthist critiques and strategies would be greatly strengthened by a more critical structural analysis of the actions and activities that are threatening the earth. Pathways of transformation arising from a more intentional structural critique would reflect public policy measures that are more broadly accessible to all classes of people as well as strategies that directly challenge the destructive behavior of capitalist systems of production and consumption.

Likewise, the postcolonial position also could benefit from a more intentional dialogue with the earthist community. Specifically, the principle of bioregionalism offers the potential for an alternative trading paradigm that could help indebted countries disengage from the dominant international market of global capitalism. There is, in fact, already some evidence of interest in developing sustainable regional trade in the work and actions of civil society in the global South as evidenced in such documents as the Dakar Declaration.[15] We should note that the model of sustainable regional trade differs substantially from regional "free trade" initiatives. The latter are interested in creating terms of trade that benefit corporate interests, while sustainable regional trade is concerned with developing trading relationships that benefit the health and well-being of the region, including both the earth and the local people. Sustained conversation with people who hold an earthist perspective will help to ensure that any alternative regional trade that is developed will, from its inception, honor and care for the earth. The postcolonial position also may benefit by working more intentionally toward defining a positive agenda for its alternative vision of globalization rather than focusing on defining itself in opposition to an oppressive paradigm. This work has certainly already begun in the postcolonial articulation of global solidarity as a guiding principle for globalization, but a more detailed engagement of what global solidarity might entail would contribute to a more focused development of alternative pathways for the future.

Finally, we need to acknowledge the potential danger of isolationism present in some postcolonial critiques that seek to blame all problems related to globalization on the United States or the "first" world. Communities and community leaders who seek to withdraw from the world community risk an uncritical valorization of their own traditionalism without acknowledging the human reality that engaging people from other cultures is a requirement for everyone. It is certainly true that the oppressive force of the marketing of "Americanization" by corporations has overstepped the boundaries of "sharing" cultural ideas and expressions with other communities. Nevertheless, in a globalizing world, we need to move toward systems of governance and interaction that allow for genuine engagement regarding ideological differences and disagreements and for the sharing of the cultural symbols (food, clothing, music, art) of our respective societies. Only through this kind of deep engagement with pluralism will we be able to grow together and learn from one another as a human community.

Conclusion

Until we address the fundamental ideological divides that separate neoliberalism and development models of globalization from earthist and postcolonial models, the hegemonic voices will continue to exhibit the fact that the hegemonic group just do not get it. The gulf that separates the capitalist agenda from its resistors is so vast that these parties will forever be unable to meet somewhere "in the middle." When it comes to understanding the well-being of humanity as dependent on either growth and prosperity (as evidenced through wealth and power) or the self-determination of people and the well-being of the planet, there is no middle ground. These worldviews are diametrically opposed, and the moral compromise required to find a "common ground" is unacceptable. In the final analysis, it is not enough to "reform" the excesses of global capitalism. New ways must be found. Chapter 8 offers some concrete suggestions for beginning to transform the unjust forms of globalization that dominate our world today.

Notes

1. Blaine Harden, "Wowing Them with Excess in the Hamptons," *New York Times*, July 18, 2000, sec. A, p. 1.
2. This estimated annual salary is the author's calculation based on the article's information that Mr. Velasquez earns $23 an hour and works twelve hours a day, seven days a week.
3. Seth Mydans, "Before Manila's Garbage Hill Collapsed: Living Off Scavenging," *New York Times*, July 18, 2000, sec. A, p. 6.
4. See the work of the International Forum on Globalization, the Association of Social Economics, and the EZLN (Zapatista movement).
5. Genesis 2:15ff.
6. David Loy argues that the market has become a religion because it fulfills the religious role of teaching us about the world and our role in it. David R. Loy, "The Religion of the Market," *Journal of the American Academy of Religion* 65, no. 2 (summer 1997): 275.
7. Thomas L. Friedman, *The Lexus and the Olive Tree: Understanding Globalization* (New York: Farrar, Straus and Giroux, 1999), 27.
8. Ibid., 27.
9. Ibid., 273.
10. Ibid., 352.
11. Dan Bischoff, "Consuming Passions," *Ms.*, December 2000/January 2001, 60–65.
12. While this problem is not limited to the "first" world, my comments regarding the topic here will be.
13. See Elizabeth M. Bounds, *Coming Together/Coming Apart: Religion, Community, and Modernity* (New York: Routledge, 1997), esp. chaps. 1, 2, and 6.
14. This is a general critique of the earthist position. Of course, there are subsets of this group, such as the environmental justice movement, that do employ a political analysis.
15. This declaration was the result of the "Dakar 2000: From Resistance to Alternatives" conference. It is representative of many similar actions of civil society in the "two-thirds" world.

8

The Future of Globalization

Seeking Pathways of Transformation

Given the dominance of economic globalization during the last decade of the twentieth century, and now in the twenty-first century, it is harder to talk about radical alternatives to capitalism than ever before. While political scientists are still arguing about what caused the fall of the former Eastern bloc countries, mainstream economists and businesspeople are fairly adamant in their assessment that democracy and capitalism hold out the only hope for development and the elimination of poverty. The fall of the Wall has engendered a triumphalist tone among capitalists. Within this context of capitalist euphoria, alternative viewpoints are hard-pressed to get a fair hearing. The political possibility of transformation requires alternative contexts of dialogue, discernment, and activism that allow for the creativity and imagination of the human spirit to envision alternative realities.

With a sociopolitical atmosphere that either embraces neoclassical economics or approaches capitalism as an inevitability, there comes a dangerous tendency to ignore or dismiss serious critiques of globalization and capitalism as naive, utopian, or both. This study has shown that the moral stakes are high when it comes to globalization and that a more critical appraisal of all four paradigms is certainly in order. A liberationist approach to economic ethics fundamentally requires challenging liberal capitalism. One of the very foundational assumptions of liberation positions is that many of the world's current problems (e.g., massive numbers of people living in poverty, growing numbers of environmental and economic refugees, and the growing disparity between rich and poor) witness to inherent flaws in the current capitalist world order.

My own work on the subject of globalization has led me to the conclusion that it is no longer morally acceptable to talk about "economic ethics" separately from "environmental ethics" or vice versa. In the current context of our increasingly globalizing world, these two enterprises are not discrete tasks. The material ethical problems that relate to both of these subjects are so deeply interwoven that it is essential to address the problems of modernity and globalization from an organic theoretical position that recognizes the deep relations that exist between economic and ecological issues. The problems of globalization cannot begin to be solved without a shift in our theoretical approach to conceptualizing the problems because our starting point deeply affects both how we define the issue and what solutions we are able to envision.

In order to make any headway in ensuring that globalization is modeled in ways that are just and life-affirming, people must understand the complexity of the positions and the differences between the varieties of competing globalization theories. We have seen quite clearly that not all of the voices discussing globalization are saying the same thing. Intentionality in shaping the future direction of globalization requires that we pay attention to the different moral visions apparent in different theories of globalization and the sort of life they offer for us and the rest of creation. Alternative models of globalization that reflect the values of democratizing power, caring for the planet, and attending to the social well-being of people will ultimately require the combined efforts of people of goodwill around the world standing together with the Zapatistas and saying, *"Basta!"* Enough! In order to reshape globalization, local and regional communities will need to work together to develop new business plans, accountability structures, and trading partnerships that meet the environmental, social, economic, and sustainability needs of their communities. Moving the world toward a new paradigm of globalization also will require that we reimagine the spheres of economics, politics, and civil society.

Reimagining the Role of Economics

The new era of globalization called for in this study requires a fundamental rethinking of the capitalist economic paradigm that currently dominates global economic policy and practice. Reimagining the role of economics in life means a transformation of the values, the ideals, and even the very identity of corporations and business communities. I join environmentalist Paul Hawken in arguing, "The ultimate purpose of business is not, or should not be, simply to make money. Nor is it merely a system of making and selling things. The promise of business is to increase the general well-being of humankind through service, a creative invention and ethical philosophy."[1]

The notion that a business ought to be about more than making money is not a novel one. Markets and economic theories are human constructs that we have created to facilitate exchange and to ease the burden on humankind of having each community function as an isolated, self-sufficient entity. However, in the latter part of the twentieth century and the early part of the twenty-first, the dramatically changing role of transnational corporations has brought about shifts in economic and political power worldwide as well as shifts in our society regarding the meaning and value of work.

The increasing flexibility and mobility of transnational corporations is one of the most important factors contributing to the changing role of corporations in recent years. This phase began in the 1960s and '70s when large corporations located in the industrial Northeast began to search for ways to lower their production costs. At first corporations relocated their production facilities in the southeast United States where wages were lower and unions were weaker. But after several years, in the drive to continue to cut costs, business leaders again began hunting for lower-wage workers. By the 1980s the structural adjustment programs required by the International Monetary Fund and the World Bank had opened up the "two-thirds" world for direct foreign investment, and many corporations took advantage of the lower production costs available in many of these countries. These lower production costs were due to a number of factors (reduced or nonexistent environmental regulations, lower wages and often no benefits, longer work days, etc.), most related to the exploitation of workers in the "two-thirds" world.

From the perspective of the corporations (and neoclassical economists) the relocation of production facilities to sites that offer the most attractive incentives not only is infinitely logical, but is required by the ideological drive for increased efficiency, which will result in increased profit. Neoclassical ideology has no mechanism to weigh the moral relevance of toxic waste and emissions, poor safety conditions, or underpaid workers. Econometricians have yet to quantify the valuation of these factors and incorporate them into their equations. For corporations seeking to maximize their efficiency, it does not matter how a particular site comes up with the most competitive bid; in the end, lower costs increase efficiency and consequently profits.

Across the border in Mexico, *maquiladoras* sprang up almost overnight as corporations rushed to take advantage of desperate Mexican workers whose marginal status provided them with no leverage to bargain for living wages, health care, retirement benefits, safety standards, or job security.[2] Most of the *maquiladora* workers were adolescent girls whose small dexterous fingers facilitated their ability to manipulate the tiny production pieces they were assembling. The fact that the marginal working conditions of these employees resulted in loss of eyesight, loss of physical dexterity, and burnout for most employees after five or six years will never appear in any corporate annual report, nor will it be factored into any assessment of the success or failure of a given production facility. The moral obscenity that the corporate profits made on these production facilities were earned not just at the expense of these women's labor, but at the expense of their very health and livelihood, will never be acknowledged by these corporations nor by the ideology that supports them. Furthermore, the fact that much of this work is subcontracted by transnational corporations allows corporate executives to distance themselves from the material conditions of these factories and their treatment of workers and the environment either by claiming to be ignorant about the working conditions or by disavowing their responsibility for another business's workers.

As the production of goods continues to move from our local communities to unknown and often unknowable places, the very meaning of "work" is shifting in our world.[3] In many places work is no longer regarded as meaningful in and of itself; it is merely a means to an end—a way to earn money to pay the bills. The physical and philosophical shifts in labor that are being engendered by globalization have resulted in two dilemmas that the world community will have to face as we move toward establishing the good life as accessible to people from all walks of life in many different cultures and contexts.

The first dilemma can be seen on the other side of the "free trade" agreements in the countries where U.S. manufacturing and production jobs have moved. As we have seen in this study, the working conditions and wages in *maquiladoras* and other factories in the "two-thirds" world are exploitative and unjust by the measure of the good life suggested here. As human beings and as consumers, we "first" world citizens must face the reality that our consumptive behavior is directly related to the unconscionable working conditions and wages that predominate in the "two-thirds" world. The first step toward responsible action on our part is to see the relationships of accountability that are so artfully hidden by the global economy. The global production system often involves so many contractors and subcontractors that consumers have no idea how many people have played a part in producing the shirt they are wearing or the fruit or vegetables on their tables. The obfuscation of the production process is part of what allows systems of injustice to continue. Consumer responses to the gross human-rights violations that occurred in sweatshops producing Nike products in Haiti and Kathie Lee Gifford's clothing line in Honduras and New York City are an indication that people care about how their consumer goods are produced. But the current market system makes it difficult and time-consuming to be a responsible consumer. Fair trade coffee and organic produce labeling are two examples of how producers and consumers have developed systems of communication that allow consumers access to important information about the environmental and labor standards under which their food was produced. In turn, these systems allow farmers to charge prices that more accurately reflect the expenses of production.

The second dilemma can be seen in the way that the manufacturing and productive work that provided the backbone of the "working" class in the United States has been replaced over the last two decades with work in the service industry. Service is defined primarily as any work done by one person for others; while this work can include skilled labor (i.e., doctor, lawyer, or service repairperson), the proliferation of jobs in the service industry in the 1990s occurred in unskilled labor (i.e., housecleaning, restaurant jobs, or child and elder care). This shift from skilled productive labor to unskilled service labor means that a large majority of the "work" available in the United States lacks an abiding sense of meaning or purpose for workers, and very little of this work provides a living wage for workers. The low wages offered by the "new" jobs that are replacing jobs lost to "free trade" are resulting in the economic instability of the working class in the United States.

One direction in which we need to move as a human community is toward the recognition that meaningful work, safe working conditions, and a living wage are all essential requirements for our ability to live the good life. The reality is that there is an abundance of work that needs to be done. A resurgence of small-scale organic farming would provide our world with abundant opportunities for work as well as sustainable agricultural practices and more healthy food for our consumption. Many individuals work far more than the standard forty hours a week. Job responsibilities could be shared and workloads could be reduced in ways that both create more skilled jobs and allow workers more time to spend with their families and communities or for hobbies, passions, and service. For that matter, we could reduce the standard work week from forty to thirty-five or thirty hours. With the environment in the shape it is in, a multitude of reclamation projects, educational campaigns, and research endeavors could contribute to the development of more low-impact, sustainable ways of living. We also know that the need for safe, affordable housing is a common one across the globe. The problem does not lie in a lack of tasks that need to be accomplished in our world; finding meaningful work is not the problem. The problem lies in our failure as a society to recognize and prioritize the needs that will contribute to the general well-being of all people and to the earth community as a whole. As long as we continue to create economic policies that privilege profits over people, our model of globalization will reflect those values.

Let us return to Hawken's notion of the purpose of business as increasing the general well-being of humankind. If we take this definition seriously, we will need to shift the conversation from one in which the primary interest in business is to figure out how to increase growth and trade (the neoliberal preoccupation) to a conversation in which we seek to discern how markets can work toward helping to create social justice. Of course, the immediate reaction of many capitalists will be to claim that social justice is not the purpose of capitalism or of markets; in fact, as we have seen, one of the principles of neoclassical economics is that it is value-free. But what are economics or markets but human systems created to provide a mechanism for the exchange of goods? Corporations and businesses do not stand outside of human society; they are an integral part of the lives of communities. Their need to turn a profit is not in question. What is in question is the assumption that their actions exist outside of moral scrutiny or that they are not responsible to the local communities in which they operate.

In North Carolina, a heavily agricultural and manufacturing state, 19,583 jobs had been lost in manufacturing by 1999, five years after the passage of the North American Free Trade Agreement (NAFTA).[4] People who had worked for the same plant for twenty, thirty, sometimes forty years were forced to seek alternative employment in small towns bereft of viable jobs. The corporations that eviscerated the manufacturing sector of North Carolina's economy are responsible to those communities and those people who sustained them and contributed to their profitability. The choices these companies made to relocate their production facilities overseas to increase their profitability are part of an immoral system of economic priorities that is generating economic and communal instability for the sake of increased wealth production for the already wealthy. The 10, 12, and 15 percent yields of stock portfolios in the 1990s were generated on the backs of workers from around the world. While the rising numbers on our quarterly reports were intoxicating to many pension holders in the "first" world, the majority of those profits went to the world's economic elite. One of the moral questions with which we must grapple is this: How much profit is enough? What margin of return is sufficient to indicate profitability while still allowing for the ethical and humane treatment of the world's workers and our environment? It is within our right and our power as a human community to create economic systems that honor the integrity and dignity of workers and that include, as part of their mission, the task of seeking to create justice. If we understand money and markets as human constructs, they ought to have instrumental value in society, not ultimate value.

Acceptance of Hawken's definition of the purpose of business is antithetical to the prevailing globalization paradigms. Nevertheless, it is a needed corrective to an ideology of excess that disregards the major moral teachings of Christianity. The liberal culture of modernity will argue that business has nothing to do with religion. A reworked version of the separation of church and state for the corporation is the separation of church and business. Our culture has aided the development of this ideology by the increased compartmentalization of our lives that allows us to "do" religion on Sunday mornings (or some other focused time) and forget about it the rest of the week. But our faith must challenge culture, and it must challenge the excesses of globalization as well.

A transformation of globalization does not require the elimination of business, or markets, or even corporations (although it might necessitate the relocalization of corporate power). What it does require is a metamorphosis of corporate self-identity in ways that reflect the moral norms suggested in this study. An era of globalism that respects cultural diversity, the distinctive contributions that difference offers to our world, and the voices of the marginalized in decision-making calls us toward a democratization of corporations heretofore unknown in our world. While it is unclear exactly what form this kind of democratization might take, it would certainly involve a fundamental restructuring of the mission, priorities, and practices of businesses in ways that reduce the environmental impact of industrialization. It might also include the implementation of corporate accountability to local communities in the form of publicly elected boards of directors. It would certainly require recognition of local communities as stakeholders in any corporate activity that takes place within their community and affects their water, air, and land quality. In line with the earthist position, the metamorphosis of corporate identity would also likely be marked by a move away from transnationalization back toward localization in ways that allow increased interaction between businesses and communities. Many activities that have been taken over by transnational corporations, such as agriculture, do not require transnational cooperation. Perhaps we ought to rethink the role of the transnational corporation and limit the granting of charters for those activities that are possible only through large-scale production. The closer production remains to the place of consumption (for all consumer goods), the lower the environmental impact and the more accountability there is for the business to operate in socially responsible ways. While businesses and corporations have been granted the legal status of "citizens" under the law, they need to be more clearly recognized as contributing members of society whose responsibilities are more than financial. Furthermore, the absolute value of private property must be balanced by recreating systems of "commons" areas, or community-owned and -governed land, that provide important social, economic, and nutritional value to our world.

Theologically, the democratization of the corporation is grounded in the biblical vision of justice. The theo-ethical principle of justice is what challenges the absolute value of profit as a guiding norm for globalization. In the Bible, the task of calling the nation to accountability for its economic and social injustice falls to the prophets. The prophets were the social critics and social commentators of their day.[5] Exposing injustice and challenging the power of the wealthy is no more popular today than it was thirty-five hundred years ago in Israel and Judah. The scriptural message is clear: Our faith calls us not to be popular, but to be faithful. Being faithful followers of God is a lifelong calling. It is not something we can put on and take off as the fancy strikes us. Walking the walk of faith means that we care about our neighbors all the time. It means that when we make decisions as a CEO, or a stockholder, or an investor, we make those decisions with our neighbors in mind, not just with profit driving us. Furthermore, God was not just referring to the people who live next door or even in our own "neighborhoods." No, God's repeated directive that we "love our neighbors" is a metaphorical way of telling us that part of our human responsibility is to care for each other—all of us, as one interconnected, interdependent human race. From the perspective of Christian ethics, our calling to recognize, respect, and strive to maintain the interconnectedness of humanity is far more important than the interdependence of the global marketplace.

Rethinking the Role of Politics

The increased mobility of corporations has strengthened their political power and weakened state power through the mere threat of moving production facilities abroad. As labor activists Jeremy Brecher and Tim Costello have pointed out: "If Korea restricts environmental pollution, allows union organization, raises wages, and taxes corporations to pay for health and education, Nike can simply shift its footwear production to Indonesia."[6]

Another argument that the corporations make in their own defense is that, as business enterprises, they are responsible not for caring for the workers or the environment but merely for following the laws of the countries in which their facilities are located. Based on this sort of rationality corporations defend the transcendent quality of their transnationalism as they refuse to recognize any responsibility that they might have for ensuring a living wage or improving the environmental standards in the countries where they are located. The piece of the puzzle that the corporations choose to overlook in this line of defense is the extent to which the very real factor of their own mobility, which is of course based on their economic power, renders other modes of political power moot.

The traditional political power of nation-states to set environmental standards, to tax income, to require minimum wages, and to set minimal safety conditions for their workers is too frequently cast aside by debt-burdened governments desperate for the jobs and wealth creation promised by the corporations. In their bids to lure prospective investors to their countries, governments have found themselves in situations in which they felt they must offer concessions that would make their countries "competitive." The pressure from multilateral lending institutions to develop export-based economies and the poverty of their own people have put these nation-states at the mercy of the corporations. These countries no longer feel they have the "luxury" to act in morally responsible ways; they rationalize that jobs that hurt their environment are better than no jobs at all.

These regulatory concessions not only are harming the earth, the forests, the waters, and the peoples of this planet, but also are forcing local communities and nation-states to absorb traditional production costs, which in turn increases the corporation's private profits. In corporate parlance, this process is known as externalizing expenses. Instead of the notorious "trickle-down" effect, we are witnessing the "trickle-up" effect as the poorest of the poor subsidize corporations through tax concessions, environmental concessions, and labor exploitation. In the United States alone, corporate local property tax revenues dropped from 45 percent to 16 percent in the thirty years between 1957 and 1987.[7] According to David Korten, "A 1994 study by the Progressive Policy Institute of the Democratic Leadership Conference identified what it considered to be unjustified subsidies and tax benefits extended to corporations in the United States amounting to $111 billion over five years."[8]

As corporations continue to move and shift their production around the world in search of the lowest wages and most regulatory concessions, their sheer mobility reinforces the developing self-perception of their own independence and transcendence. This mobility, or the threat of it, also presents them with unacknowledged, astounding political power that is capable of coercing nation-states and local governments to act against the best interests of their constituents. But these problems are not limited to the "two-thirds" world alone. The power of corporations to influence the political process unduly to further their own economic interests over the social good of the entire community has reached startling proportions in the United States as well.

In the late 1960s and early 1970s, the business community entered a period of intense opposition from the public led by consumer advocates such as Ralph Nader and environmentalists such as Rachel Carson. This was undoubtedly due to a number of circumstances affecting the general political climate of the era, including the war in Vietnam, the civil rights movement, and the revelations of Watergate. But it was also due to the perceived negligence and indifference of corporations toward the environment, health, safety, and consumer protection.[9] The political advocacy of public interest groups resulted in the passage of a host of regulatory legislation, including the creation of regulatory bodies such as the Environmental Protection Agency (EPA), much to the dismay of the corporate world.

In response to this increase in governmental regulations, the first Business Roundtable was formed in the United States in 1972. It was composed exclusively of the CEOs of America's leading two hundred industrial, financial, and service corporations.[10] In this forum, America's foremost business leaders set aside their competitive differences in order to focus on their common concerns regarding social and economic policy in the U.S.[11] Once the group reaches consensus regarding social and economic policy goals, the managerial expertise of these business leaders kicks in as they divide their tasks and systematically coordinate a corporate lobbying agenda in which they personally participate. Political scientist Scott Bowman characterizes the Business Roundtable as "a superlobby that also functions like a legislative body insofar as it assigns responsibilities on the basis of expertise, researches numerous legislative proposals, informs its constituent members and legislators, makes recommendations on bills, drafts its own proposals, and supports or opposes legislation based on a vote of a diverse membership."[12] The Roundtable has marshaled its significant power and influence to revise federal tax policy, to affect the 1994 health-care debate, and to ensure the passage of NAFTA, among other things.[13]

It is not only through the Business Roundtable that corporations flex their political muscles. A combination of changes in the political process in the late 1960s and early 1970s weakened political party leadership, and the Federal Election Campaign Act's limitations on individual campaign contributions resulted in the increased influence of political action committees (PACs). Corporate PACs increased from 89 in 1974 to 1,467 in 1982 as corporations recognized the increased importance that PAC money represented in election campaigns.[14] Indeed, PACs have supplanted the national parties as the primary means of fund-raising for campaigns.[15]

A third area of political influence that transnational corporations have been developing over the past twenty-five years focuses on the funding of academic research and think tanks. Bowman credits the rise of corporate-funded conservative think tanks and organizations such as the Heritage Foundation, the Center for the Study of American Business, and others with playing an important role in the resurrection of free-market ideology and the ascendance of the conservative wing within the Republican Party.[16] Business interests also have gone far in promoting the ideological foundations of economic globalization by funding the establishment of law and economics programs in leading law schools that support "scholarly research advancing the premise that the unregulated marketplace produces the most efficient—and thereby the most just—society."[17]

While it is true that corporations have the right in a democratic state to express their opinions and to participate in the political process, their sheer wealth and access to political leadership has allowed their concerns and priorities to eclipse those of the well-being of the larger human and earth communities. The challenge that remains for the future is to figure out how to allow for the voices and concerns of business interests to count no more and no less than the voices and concerns of civil society.

The increased power and influence of the world's economic elite and their accompanying ideology have shifted the governance of many of our world's democracies (rule of the people) to defacto plutocracies (rule of the wealthy elite). When the wealthy elite are able to manipulate political policy-making and to effect unduly the election of sympathetic political leaders, the result is the undermining of justice and democracy for the majority.

It is clear that the democratization of power relationships in our world is both necessary and a formidable challenge. We have allowed our faith in markets to undermine democratic processes to such a degree that markets determine our political agenda more forcefully than the social well-being of people. This shift is neither inevitable nor an example of social evolution. As a human community, we must reassert the importance of democratic principles and governance and work toward renegotiating our understanding of the purpose and function of corporations and markets. We must reestablish these institutions as tools to help us care for people and the planet.

Revisioning the Role of Civil Society

A third pathway toward transformation lies in the rebuilding of community in the global North. In many parts of the world, "community" has referred and still refers to a particular group of people who are related by blood, marriage, culture, ethnicity, locale, or some other unifying factor. I will call these communities "traditional." In these communities, relationships are a given, something inherited either through birth or marriage. In addition to traditional communities, there has been another type of community, what I will call "affectional" communities. These are communities of people who end up together, sometimes voluntarily and sometimes not, and form interdependent networks of relationships that resemble those of "traditional" communities. Neither kind of community is more authentic or "better" than the other; they are merely two different ways of organizing interdependent, social relationships. Both models of community exhibit rootedness in a deep experience of human sharing and interconnection. This rootedness provides an atmosphere of support and caring that is essential for human thriving.[18]

The reality of the modern world is proof that people can live in a variety of different stages of community and relationship with others. While it is virtually impossible to live completely isolated from all human relationships, the depth and quality of those relationships can be of varying degrees. The crisis of community that marks the "first" world is a reflection of an absence of deeply rooted communal relationships that offer people the kind of support and caring necessary for human flourishing—what the authors of *Habits of the Heart* describe as "an inclusive whole, an interdependence of public and private life amid a variety of callings and a variety of people."[19]

We do not have to look too far back in our collective history to recognize the myriad ways that communities have functioned to strengthen and support the social well-being of people. Throughout history, people have relied on their families, their neighbors, and their community of faith for support, friendship, and help in times of crisis or struggle. Only within the last few decades has the increasing mobility of people begun to unravel the fabric of communal solidarity that was once a defining feature of our humanity. The trend toward urban dwelling was a phenomenon of the twentieth century caused by the rise of industrial development and manufacturing work located in and around cities and by the increasing poverty in rural America. Urban relocation often necessitated moving into a new community where one had little or no family, friends, or community. People's ability to build affectional communities in their new locales has been hampered by overwork, the pressures of child-rearing, illness, poverty, poor transportation, and stress. The irony is that these same stresses that prevent people from building new communities of support are the very same reasons that they need communities of support in the first place. The social isolation of many poor and near-poor people in the world contributes to their inability to manage effectively many of the unanticipated crises they encounter.[20]

The reality is that we do not exist as isolated individuals. We are not islands of self-sufficiency separated from the rest of our social world. Those of us who are successful are so, at least in part, because of the assistance that we have received from many people along the way. This assistance may have taken the form of parents, friends, extended family, mentors, teachers, ministers or priests, social workers, doctors, or a host of other people who have contributed to the development of our self-identity and our knowledge about the world. While these people did not make us who we are, we are who we are because of them. One of the greatest ideological barriers that we must deconstruct is the notion of the "self-made man." While it is true that there are people who are able to better their situations in life, none of these people have done so single-handedly. Social connection and relationship are a part of the nature of humanity. The social isolation that increasingly plagues our societies is a deep rift in the nature of our being that we must address if we hope to move toward the social well-being of our communities. While acknowledging the loss of "traditional" communities in the global North helps us to see our task more clearly, we also must focus on rebuilding community in the industrialized world. This rebuilding of community can come in the form of creating a wide variety of affectional communities that provide support and solidarity as a base for social relations and public policy. These communities can become loci of discourse and action that organize people around developing concrete strategies for local community development and strategies for helping local communities meet the needs of their populations.

A strongly identified sense of community also can create a strong base for challenging dominant global paradigms when communities organize to participate vocally and visibly in political and economic discourse. Currently in the industrialized world, the governmental and business sectors of society are the dominant forces in shaping and enforcing public policy initiatives. Civil society, as a mobilization of grassroots aspects of the private sphere for the public good, offers an important voice in public discourse. To the extent that these private voices are a reflection of affectional groups of people who represent newly forming communities of resistance and transformation, they can function to help provide a supportive location for continued attention to issues of social well-being while also serving to democratize the public discourse.

As this study is particularly interested in the contributions that Christian ethics can make to the globalization debates, we especially need to address the roles and responsibilities of the institutional church in moving globalization processes and strategies toward a justice- and life-oriented model of globalization and away from the dominant forms of globalization rooted in individualism and greed. The collective behavior and actions of the world Christian community of two billion people could have a significant impact on the future of globalization. An assessment of the role of Christian churches and Christian people must begin by taking a critical look inward—at our own assumptions, lifestyles, and behaviors and how they contribute to the processes we seek to fight in the name of justice.

The sins of overconsumption, indifference, and greed are so subtly woven into the fabric of our culture, and even our religion, that we often overlook or ignore them. These sins are manifested in both our individual and our communal behavior as families, communities, and nations. To the extent that our faith encourages us to focus on our intentional and individual sinful behavior at the expense of a deeper probing of the meaning of sin, we are encouraged to ignore what I believe to be the most egregious expression of sin for the globalized elite of our world. That sin is our unexamined participation in globalized systems of oppression that are killing life and destroying God's creation. Within the Christian context, we must name our complicity in economic globalization as sin because this naming holds a powerful force in our tradition. In calling Christian communities of faith to accountability, church communities and their individual members must begin to see themselves as morally responsible for participating in the transformation of globalization. Recognition of sin requires repentance and *metanoia*, or a change of heart, that can enable a transformation of the sinful behavior. The possibility of radical *metanoia* offers us hope that a shift in the direction of globalization, rooted in a change of heart, can indeed be accomplished.

Our behavior in the world, including our complicity in the processes of globalization, must be examined within the context of our faith community.

Ministers and priests must challenge congregations to examine their participation in economic processes of exploitation. Lay leaders, women's organizations, youth groups—all of our constituencies must sit together and grapple with the meaning and consequences of our consumptive lifestyles and behaviors. Christian worship is an intimate expression of a community's moral norms and sensibilities. Because our liturgical expressions are a sacred way of enacting our most central theological beliefs in the context of ritualized action, we must incorporate our struggles with these questions into the context of our worshiping community. The following prayer of confession expresses a deep wrestling with the complexities of a world that is divided between the haves and the have nots.

> I was in Green Hills Mall shopping for designer sheets,
> when a homeless child on 8th Avenue whispered,
> *I have no bed.*
> I stood at an appliance store comparing consumer reports
> on microwave ovens,
> when a Zambian child wept,
> *I have no food.*
> I hired a decorator to remodel my kitchen and to add more cupboards,
> when a Cambodian child sobbed,
> *I have no cup.*
> I dreamed of building a getaway place, a cabin in the woods,
> a country place.
> Across the water came the cry of a refugee child,
> *I have no country.*
> I bought a new big screen TV for a loved one's pleasure,
> when a war orphan murmured,
> *I have no loved ones.*[21]

While this prayer represents the struggle that we must face, it does not sentimentally romanticize the call to discipleship as one of denouncing all one's worldly possessions and marching off into the mission field. Not only is this "solution" impractical for most people, it also actually sidesteps the larger structural issues that need to be addressed in our society. Neither does the prayer castigate church members for needing sheets or buying consumer goods. What the prayer does do is call on church members to think more deeply about the context within which their consumer spending is exercised. If this liturgy is truly reflective of the moral consciousness of its community, we could expect to see a congregation whose behavior—consumer and otherwise—is radically different from the status quo. Or at the very least, we could expect to see a community that is struggling to discern how transformation might take place in our world and what role it is called to play in that transformation, both individually and communally. In the context of creating pathways for the transformation of globalization, church communities in the "first" world are called along similar lines to seek a deeper examination of their participation in the systems and structures that both reproduce economic globalization and benefit from the misfortune and poverty of others.

Conclusions

We have seen clearly that the effects of globalization differ depending on one's relative status as wealthy versus poor, "first" world versus "two-thirds" world, and formally educated versus not formally educated. With regard to the morality of each position, the standpoint of marginalized people allows them a unique vision of the moral failings of capitalism and, with it, the neoliberal and development models of globalization. In contrast, the comfortable position of those of us in the middle sectors of society often blinds us to the consequences of our own behavior.

In our world today, it is primarily the lifestyles of the wealthy and privileged "first" world constituencies that are reproducing globalization through their habits and practices. In examining who makes up this "global elite," statistics showing that the assets of the world's three wealthiest people are more than the combined GNP of all the least developed countries and their six hundred million people, often allow us as middle-class "first" world people to distance ourselves from the problem.[22] The most common rationale goes something like this: "We are not the problem, we are simple people, middle-class people, who work hard for our money and deserve any luxuries we are able to acquire." In the context of global inequality, we must remember that we are talking about relative wealth and status on a much broader scale. While the world's two hundred richest people may control $1 trillion in assets[23] and have a tremendous amount of power in shaping the engines of globalization in the form of corporations and international financial institutions, the reality is that the economic "success" of our globalizing economy is dependent on the consumer behavior of a far larger group of people. The complicity of the world's working- and middle-class people is essential to keep globalization moving forward on its current trajectory. The fact that many of the "first" world workers who lost their jobs to *maquiladoras* and "free trade" zones also shop at Wal-Mart, drink Coca-Cola, and eat at McDonald's is a witness to the complexity of our present situation. It is precisely our disposable income in the form of the daily necessities of bread and milk (or sometimes Coke and fries), as well as our penchant for electronics and entertainment, that is required by the global economy as fuel to continue its growth. In a world where 1.3 billion people live on less than $1 (U.S.) a day[24] while the median

U.S. income is $42,400,[25] the responsibility for addressing economic globalization falls on more than just the top 1 percent of the world's wealthy.[26] In relative terms, the majority of the population in the "first" world are part of the global elite who drive globalization and often benefit from its "profits."[27] Whether it is through our consumer behavior or our pension funds, most of us in the so-called "developed" world complicitly participate in the global system of capitalism in largely unexamined ways.

The truth is that the so-called "opportunities" that neoliberalism offers to the majority of the world's people living in poverty will never allow them to achieve self-sufficiency as long as the system is built on an ideology that finds the disparities that separate the people living in the Hamptons from the people living in the "Promised Land" acceptable. While it may be true that the Hampton elite did not personally murder the three Ochondra boys—Raymond, Ruel, and Ryan—the reality is that the comfort and success of the global elite around the world are a direct result of a system that offers garbage scavenging as an acceptable way of life. In such a world, we are obligated to expose this system as morally untenable and to discern our own role in perpetuating it.

This study seeks to mobilize middle-income "first" worlders, not in order to lay blame or to elicit feelings of guilt, but rather to help educate people who feel powerless about the ways in which they can begin to address the problems of inequality and oppression that plague our world. Transformation requires the participation of the majority of the world's people. It requires a rejection of the dominant paradigm not only as unsustainable, but also as a system of dominance and hierarchy that runs contrary to a moral order that values life and fosters community. It is true the earth cannot sustain continued growth and industrial capitalism in its present form, but equally important is our recognition that the human spirit cannot sustain the fragmented and atomized social order generated by the current models of globalization. A social and moral order of instrumental rationality fundamentally denies the importance and value of life *qua* life. For the majority of the world's people who are struggling to find work or keep work or who are overworked; for the children who are undernourished or undereducated or neglected; for the homeless, the refugees, and the displaced persons—for all of the marginalized people and communities who are unable to provide for their own basic needs and acquire a level of self-sufficiency—capitalist globalization offers them only smokescreens of success. It may offer the promise of small-business ownership, a micro-loan, a steady job, or a plot of land, but the number of people able to cash in on that promise is relatively low. The reality is that our current path of globalization can succeed only on the backs of a substantial constituency of low-skill, low-wage workers. Transnational corporations require an exploitable pool of labor in order to maintain the production demands of a global economy built on externalizing costs. It does not matter to the "bottom line" whether that labor comes from the global North or the global South, whether the labor pool is made up of children, young adults, or prisoners, whether the working conditions foster well-being or cause cancer. At the end of the day, corporate global economies merely require cheap labor, and the system of globalization engineered by big business brings with it a level of global poverty that provides that labor in abundance.

In the end, we must recognize that our values shape and inform our decision-making on a daily basis. Whether people support a policy of economic redistribution and political democratization or a policy of growing individual wealth will largely depend on what they believe about money, wealth, and people. In the different perspectives we have examined in this study, different groups have been motivated by differing sets of values. The two resistance positions presented here have been able to step outside of the dominant models of globalization in ways that allow them to envision the future of globalization in positive, life-affirming ways. While each of these resistance theories originates from different worldviews and even focuses on some different public policy strategies, both are supportive of the normative criteria that guide this study. Globalization will look quite different if it is able to move down the alternative pathways suggested in this study.

While the vision of the good life as reflecting democratized forms of power, intentional care of the planet, and the social well-being of people offers one way forward, we must acknowledge that there is no simple "solution" to the problems that have accompanied globalization in our world. The devastating inequality and environmental degradation wrought by the dominant forms of globalization make it clear that a healthy and sustainable life on this planet requires a transformation of dominant ideologies as well as the unsustainable habits and lifestyles of the global elite. As we continue to examine the globalizing trends and practices of our world, we must strive to ensure that many peoples and voices participate in the conversations that move us toward a new future. In our search for the good life, we must make sure that we envision a future that offers justice for all God's creation.

Notes

1. Paul Hawken, *The Ecology of Commerce: A Declaration of Sustainability* (New York: HarperCollins, 1993), 1.

2. In 1980 there were 620 *maquiladora* plants employing 119,550 workers. By 1992 this figure had risen to 2,200 factories employing more than 500,000 Mexican workers. The hourly wage in the *maquiladoras* was $1.64 compared to $16.17 in the United States. David C. Korten, *When Corporations Rule the World* (West Hartford, CT: Kumarian Press, 1995), 129.

3. Given the fact that the material production of raw goods may occur in one place, the production in another, and the finishing touches in a third—it is often impossible to label items as "made in" any particular place.

4. Jena Heath and Irwin Speizer, "NAFTA Has Cost N.C. 19,583 Jobs," *News & Observer*, Raleigh, NC, December 27, 1998, sec. A, p. 1.

5. Edward LeRoy Long Jr., *To Liberate and Redeem: Moral Reflections on the Biblical Narrative* (Cleveland, OH: Pilgrim Press, 1997), 70.

6. Jeremy Brecher and Tim Costello, *Global Village or Global Pillage: Economic Reconstruction from the Bottom Up* (Boston: South End Press, 1994), 20.

7. Korten, *When Corporations Rule the World*, 130.

8. Ibid.

9. Ibid., 143.

10. Ibid., 145. Membership included the heads of forty-two of the fifty largest Fortune 500 U.S. industrial corporations, seven of the eight largest U.S. transportation companies, and nine of the eleven largest U.S. utilities. Korten, *When Corporations Rule the World*, 144.

11. Ibid.

12. Scott Bowman, *The Modern Corporation and American Political Thought: Law, Power, and Ideology* (University Park: Pennsylvania State University Press, 1996), 153.

13. For a more detailed description of the Roundtable's activities, see ibid., 142–51.

14. Ibid., 146.

15. Ibid., 153.

16. Ibid., 150.

17. Korten, *When Corporations Rule the World*, 142.

18. This description of traditional and affectional communities is not meant to imply that disagreement and conflict do not occur within these groups, but rather to show that strong communities are a place where civil and personal strife can be met and dealt with fairly and justly.

19. As described by Larry Rasmussen in *Moral Fragments and Moral Community* (Minneapolis: Fortress, 1993), 52.

20. For a critique of the failure of current U.S. welfare policy (Personal Responsibility and Work Opportunity Reconciliation Act of 1996) to take women's social isolation into account as a significant barrier to its success, see Ellen Ott Marshall, "Liberation from the Welfare Trap?" in *Welfare Policy: Feminist Critiques*, ed. Elizabeth M. Bounds, Pamela K. Brubaker, and Mary E. Hobgood (Cleveland, OH: Pilgrim Press, 1999). For a narrative account of the ways in which social isolation contributes to the problem of homelessness in America, see Jonathan Kozol, *Rachel and Her Children: Homeless Families in America* (New York: Fawcett Columbine, 1988).

21. This "Prayer of Confession" was part of worship at Second Presbyterian Church in Nashville on February 25, 2001. This prayer was adapted from liturgy

shared at the Presbyterian Health, Education and Welfare Association's biennial meeting held in Nashville, January 2001.

22. United Nations Development Programme, "Globalization with a Human Face," *Human Development Report 1999* (New York: Oxford University Press for the United Nations Development Programme), 3.

23. Ibid., 37.

24. Ibid., 28.

25. This means that half of 2002 U.S. households had incomes higher than $42,400 and half lower. Dr. Daniel H. Weinberg, "Press Briefing on 2002 Income and Poverty Estimates," Census Bureau (September 26, 2003). Online: www.census.gov./hhes/income02/prs03asc.html.

26. While detailed attention to the racial disparities in median incomes in the United States is beyond the scope of this study, they are significant enough to bear notice. According to United for a Fair Economy, "The median black household had a net worth of only $10,000 in 1998—about 12% of the $81,700 in median wealth for whites. . . . The median Hispanic household had a net worth of only $3,000 in 1998—just 4% of whites." For the purposes of this study, this data highlights the fact that the number of black and Hispanic global elite in the United States is relatively small. This observation makes explicit a racial bias of economic globalization that warrants further study. Data taken from an email correspondence from the United for a Fair Economy Research Department on July 26, 2000.

27. Even though this analysis is focused exclusively on the relative wealth of the majority of people in the "first" world, it is also crucial to recognize the extreme poverty that exists within "first" world countries. My attention to the wealth of the global North is not intended to deny the inequalities and poverty that plague our own communities. For a good analysis of the problem of inequality in the United States, see Douglas A. Hicks, *Inequality and Christian Ethics* (Cambridge: Cambridge University Press, 2000), esp. chaps. 1 and 4.

Bibliography

Agarwal, Bina. *A Field of One's Own: Gender and Land Rights in South Asia.* Cambridge: Cambridge University Press, 1994.

Alford, C. Fred. *Think No Evil: Korean Values in the Age of Globalization.* Ithaca, NY: Cornell University Press, 1999.

Amin, Samir. *Capitalism in the Age of Globalization.* London: Zed Books, 1997.

Anderson, Sarah. *Views from the South: The Effects of Globalization and the WTO on Third World Countries.* Chicago: Food First Books, 2000.

Anderson, Sarah, and John Cavanagh, with Thea Lee and the Institute for Policy Studies. *Field Guide to the Global Economy.* New York: The New Press, 2000.

Anderson, Walter Truett, ed. *The Truth about the Truth: De-confusing and Re-constructing the Postmodern World.* New York: J. P. Tarcher, 1995.

Arrighi, Giovanni. *The Long Twentieth Century: Money, Power, and the Origin of Our Times.* London: Verso, 1994.

Artaza-Regan, Maria Paz. "In the Name of Economic Well-Being." *Christian Social Action,* June 1997, 29–32.

Ashcroft, Bill, Gareth Griffiths, and Helen Tiffin. *Key Concepts in Post-Colonial Studies.* London: Routledge, 1998.

———. *The Post-Colonial Studies Reader.* London: Routledge, 1995.

Atherton, John, ed. *Christian Social Ethics: A Reader.* Cleveland, OH: Pilgrim Press, 1994.

Baker, Dean, Gerald Epstein, and Robert Pollin. *Globalization and Progressive Economic Policy.* Amherst, MA: Cambridge University Press, 1998.

Barlow, Maude, and Tony Clarke. *MAI: The Multilateral Agreement on Investment and the Threat to American Freedom.* New York: Stoddart Publishing, 1998.

Barnet, Richard J., and John Cavanagh. *Global Dreams: Imperial Corporations and the New World Order.* New York: Touchstone, 1994.

Barnet, Richard J., and Ronald E. Muller. *Global Reach: The Power of the Multinational Corporations.* New York: Simon & Schuster, 1974.

Bell, Daniel. *The Cultural Contradictions of Capitalism.* New York: Basic Books, 1978.

Ben-David, Dan, Hakan Nordstrom, and L. Alan Winters. *Trade, Income Disparity, and Poverty.* World Trade Organization Special Studies 5. Geneva: World Trade Organization, 1999.

Beneria, Lourdes, and Martha Roldan. *The Crossroads of Class and Gender: Industrial Homework, Subcontracting, and Household Dynamics in Mexico City.* Chicago: University of Chicago Press, 1987.

Berger, Peter L. *The Capitalist Spirit: Toward a Religious Ethic of Wealth Creation.* San Francisco: Institute for Contemporary Studies, 1990.

Berry, Thomas. *The Great Work: Our Way into the Future.* New York: Bell Tower, 1999.

Berry, Wendell. *Sex, Economy, Freedom, and Community.* New York: Pantheon Books, 1992.

Bethell, Tom. *The Noblest Triumph: Property and Prosperity through the Ages.* New York: St. Martin's Press, 1999.

Beyer, Peter. *Religion and Globalization.* London: SAGE Publications, 1994.

Bischoff, Dan. "Consuming Passions." *Ms.,* December 2000/January 2001, 60–65.

Black, John. *A Dictionary of Economics.* Oxford: Oxford University Press, 1997.

Boff, Leonardo. *Cry of the Earth, Cry of the Poor.* Translated by Phillip Berryman. Maryknoll, NY: Orbis Books, 1997.

Bounds, Elizabeth M. *Coming Together/Coming Apart: Religion, Community, and Modernity.* New York: Routledge, 1997.

Bounds, Elizabeth M., Pamela K. Brubaker, and Mary E. Hobgood, eds. *Welfare Policy: Feminist Critiques.* Cleveland, OH: Pilgrim Press, 1999.

Bowman, Scott. *The Modern Corporation and American Political Thought: Law, Power, and Ideology.* University Park: Pennsylvania State University Press, 1996.

Brecher, Jeremy, John Brown Childs, and Jill Cutler. *Global Visions: Beyond the New World Order.* Boston: South End Press, 1993.

Brecher, Jeremy, and Tim Costello. *Global Village or Global Pillage: Economic Reconstruction from the Bottom Up.* Boston: South End Press, 1994.

Brecher, Jeremy, Tim Costello, and Brendan Smith. *Globalization from Below: The Power of Solidarity.* Cambridge, MA: South End Press, 2000.

Burbach, Roger. *Globalization and Its Discontents: The Rise of Postmodern Socialisms.* London: Pluto Press, 1997.

Caufield, Catherine. *Masters of Illusion: The World Bank and the Poverty of Nations.* New York: Henry Holt & Co., 1996.

Childress, James F., and John Macquarrie. *The Westminster Dictionary of Christian Ethics.* Philadelphia: Westminster, 1986.

Ching, Wong Wai. "Negotiating for a Postcolonial Identity: Theology of 'the Poor Woman' in Asia." *Journal of Feminist Studies in Religion* 16, no. 2 (2000).

Chossudovsky, Michel. *The Globalisation of Poverty: Impacts of IMF and World Bank Reforms.* London: Zed Books, 1997.

Clark, Ian. *Globalization and International Relations Theory.* Oxford: Oxford University Press, 1999.

Coats, C. David. *Old MacDonald's Factory Farm: The Myth of the Traditional Farm and the Shocking Truth about Animal Suffering in Today's Agribusiness.* New York: Continuum, 1989.

Cobb, John B., Jr. "Can a Globalized Society Be Sustainable?" *Dialog* 36, no. 1 (1997).

———. *An Earthist Challenge to Economism: A Theological Critique of the World Bank.* London: Macmillan, 1999.

Collins, Patricia Hill. *Black Feminist Thought: Knowledge, Consciousness, and the Politics of Empowerment.* New York: Routledge, 1990.

Collste, Gören. "Value Assumptions in Economic Theory." In *Studies in Ethics and Economics.* Uppsala, Sweden: Uppsala University, 1998.

Costanza, Robert. *Ecological Economics: The Science and Management of Sustainability.* New York: Columbia University Press, 1991.

Crosby, Alfred W. *Ecological Imperialism: The Biological Expansion of Europe, 900–1900.* Cambridge: Cambridge University Press, 1986.

Daly, Herman E. *Ecological Economics and the Ecology of Economics.* Cheltenham, UK: Edward Elger, 1999.

Daly, Herman E., and John B. Cobb Jr. *For the Common Good: Redirecting the Economy toward Community, the Environment, and a Sustainable Future.* Boston: Beacon Press, 1989.

Danaher, Kevin. *Fifty Years Is Enough: The Case Against the World Bank and the International Monetary Fund.* Boston: South End Press, 1994.

de Gaay Fortman, Bas, and Berma Klein Goldewijk. *God and the Goods: Global Economy in a Civilizational Perspective.* Geneva: World Council of Churches, n.d.

de Santa Ana, Julio., ed. *Sustainability and Globalization.* Geneva: WCC Publications, 1998.

Dirlik, Arif, Vinay Bahl, and Peter Gran. *History after the Three Worlds: Post-Eurocentric Historiographies.* Lanham, MD: Rowman & Littlefield, 2001.

Dornbusch, Rudiger, and F. Leslie Ch. Helmers, eds. *The Open Economy: Tools for Policymakers in Developing Countries.* New York: Oxford University Press for The World Bank, 1988.

Duchrow, Ulrich. *Alternatives to Global Capitalism: Drawn from Biblical History, Designed for Political Action.* Utrecht, Netherlands: International Books, 1995.

Edelman, Marc. *Peasants Against Globalization: Rural Social Movements in Costa Rica.* Stanford, CA: Stanford University Press, 1999.

Eisenstein, Zillah. *Global Obscenities: Patriarchy, Capitalism, and the Lure of Cyberfantasy.* New York: New York University Press, 1998.

Elfstrom, Gerard. *Moral Issues and Multinational Corporations.* New York: St. Martin's Press, 1991.

Ellison, Marvin Mahan. *The Center Cannot Hold: The Search for a Global Economy of Justice.* Washington, DC: University Press of America, 1983.

Esteva, Gustavo, and Madhu Suri Prakash. "Beyond Global Neoliberalism to Local Regeneration." *Interculture* 29, no. 2 (1996): 15–52.

———. *Grassroots Post-Modernism: Remaking the Soil of Cultures.* London: Zed Books, 1998.

Evans, Peter. *Embedded Autonomy: States and Industrial Transformation.* Princeton, NJ: Princeton University Press, 1995.

Finn, Daniel. *Just Trading: On the Ethics and Economics of International Trade.* Nashville: Abingdon Press, 1996.

Firth, Oswald, OMI. "Globalization: Christian Perspective on Economics." *Dialogue* 24 (1997): 101–24.

Friedman, Milton. *Capitalism and Freedom.* Chicago: University of Chicago Press, 1962.

Friedman, Thomas L. *The Lexus and the Olive Tree: Understanding Globalization.* New York: Farrar, Straus and Giroux, 1999.

Gebara, Ivone. *Longing for Running Water: Ecofeminism and Liberation.* Minneapolis: Fortress Press, 1999.

Giddens, Anthony. *Runaway World: How Globalization Is Reshaping Our Lives.* New York: Routledge, 2000.

Goldberg, Jeffrey. "The Crude Face of Global Capitalism." *New York Times Magazine*, October 4, 1998, 50ff.

Gray, John. *False Dawn: The Delusions of Global Capitalism.* New York: The New Press, 1998.

Greider, William. *One World, Ready or Not: The Manic Logic of Global Capitalism.* New York: Simon & Schuster, 1997.

Grossman, Richard L., and Frank T. Adams. *Taking Care of Business: Citizenship and the Charter of Incorporation.* Cambridge, MA: Charter, Ink., 1993.

Guyer, Jane I. *Money Matters: Instability, Values, and Social Payments in the Modern History of West African Communities.* Portsmouth, NH: Heinemann, 1995.

Hallman, David. *Ecotheology.* Maryknoll, NY: Orbis Books, 1994.

Haraway, Donna J. *Simians, Cyborgs, and Women: The Reinvention of Nature.* New York: Routledge, 1991.

Harding, Sandra. *Whose Science? Whose Knowledge? Thinking from Women's Lives.* Ithaca, NY: Cornell University Press, 1991.

Harrison, Bennett. *Lean and Mean: The Changing Landscape of Corporate Power in the Age of Flexibility.* New York: Basic Books, 1994.

Harrison, Beverly Wildung. *Making the Connections: Essays in Feminist Social Ethics.* Edited by Carol S. Robb. Boston: Beacon Press, 1985.

———. *Our Right to Choose: Toward a New Ethic of Abortion.* Boston: Beacon Press, 1983.

Hartsock, Nancy C. M. "The Feminist Standpoint: Developing the Ground for a Specifically Feminist Historical Materialism." In *Feminist Social Thought: A Reader.* Edited by Diana Tietjens Meyers. New York: Routledge, 1997.

———. *The Feminist Standpoint Revisited and Other Essays.* Boulder: Westview Press, 1998.
Harvey, David. *The Condition of Postmodernity: An Enquiry into the Origins of Cultural Change.* Cambridge, MA: Blackwell, 1990.
Hawken, Paul. *The Ecology of Commerce: A Declaration of Sustainability.* New York: HarperCollins, 1993.
Hayek, Friedrich von. "Individualism: True and False." In *The Essence of Hayek.* Edited by Chiaki Nishiyama and Kurt R. Leube. Stanford, CA: Hoover Institution Press, 1984.
Haynes, Jeff. *Religion, Globalization, and Political Culture in the Third World.* New York: St. Martin's Press, 1999.
Heilbroner, Robert L. *The Worldly Philosophers: The Lives, Times, and Ideas of the Great Economic Thinkers.* 6th ed. New York: Simon & Schuster, 1992.
Heilbroner, Robert L., and Lester Thurow. *Economics Explained: Everything You Need to Know about How the Economy Works and Where It's Going.* New York: Simon & Schuster, 1982.
Henderson, Hazel. *Beyond Globalization: Shaping a Sustainable Global Economy.* West Hartford, CT: Kumarian Press, 1999.
Hennessy, Rosemary, and Chrys Ingraham, eds. *Materialist Feminism: A Reader in Class, Difference, and Women's Lives.* New York: Routledge, 1997.
Henwood, Doug. *Wall Street: How It Works and for Whom.* London: Verso, 1997.
Hicks, Douglas A. *Inequality and Christian Ethics.* Cambridge: Cambridge University Press, 2000.
Hilfiker, David. "Naming Our Gods." *The Other Side* 34, no. 4 (1998): 11–15.
Hinze, Christine Firer. "Power in Christian Ethics: Resources and Frontiers for Scholarly Exploration." *The Annual of the Society of Christian Ethics* 12 (1992): 277–90.
Hofrichter, Richard. *Toxic Struggles: The Theory and Practice of Environmental Justice.* Philadelphia: New Society Publishers, 1993.
Hoogvelt, Ankie. *Globalisation and the Postcolonial World: The New Political Economy of Development.* London: Macmillan, 1997.
Hopkins, Dwight N., et al. *Religions/Globalizations: Theories and Case Studies.* Durham, NC: Duke University Press, 2001.
Houck, John W., and Oliver F. Williams. *Is the Good Corporation Dead? Social Responsibility in a Global Economy.* Lanham, MD: Rowman & Littlefield, 1996.
Hunt, E. K. *Property and Prophets: The Evolution of Economic Institutions and Ideologies.* New York: Harper & Row, 1978.
Hunt, E. K., and Howard J. Sherman. *Economics: An Introduction to Traditional and Radical Views.* 5th ed. New York: Harper & Row, 1986.
International Monetary Fund. "Globalization: Threat or Opportunity?" Washington, DC: International Monetary Fund, 2000.
———. "World Economic Outlook." Washington, DC: International Monetary Fund, 1997.
Isasi-Diaz, Ada Maria. *Mujerista Theology: A Theology for the Twenty-first Century.* Maryknoll, NY: Orbis Books, 1996.

Jameson, Fredric. *Postmodernism, or, The Cultural Logic of Late Capitalism.* Durham, NC: Duke University Press, 1991.

Jameson, Fredric, and Masao Miyoshi, eds. *The Cultures of Globalization.* Durham, NC: Duke University Press, 1998.

Johnston, Carol. *The Wealth or Health of Nations: Transforming Capitalism from Within.* Cleveland, OH: Pilgrim Press, 1998.

Kiely, Ray, and Phil Marfleet. *Globalisation and the Third World.* London: Routledge, 1998.

Klein, Naomi. "The Vision Thing: Were the DC and Seattle Protests Unfocused, or Are Critics Missing the Point?" *The Nation*, July 10, 2000, 18–21.

Kofman, Eleonore, and Gillian Youngs. *Globalization: Theory and Practice.* London: Pinter, 1996.

Korten, David C. *When Corporations Rule the World.* West Hartford, CT: Kumarian Press, 1995.

Koshy, Ninan. "The Political Dimensions and Implications of Globalization." *Voices from the Third World* 20 (1997): 26–48.

Kozol, Jonathan. *Rachel and Her Children: Homeless Families in America.* New York: Fawcett Columbine, 1988.

Krugman, Paul. *Pop Internationalism.* Cambridge, MA: MIT Press, 1996.

———. *The Return of Depression Economics.* New York: W. W. Norton, 1999.

Kung, Hans. *A Global Ethic for Global Politics and Economics.* New York: Oxford University Press, 1998.

Kurien, C. T. "Globalization—What Is It About?" *Voices from the Third World* 20 (1997): 15–25.

Kuttner, Robert. *Everything for Sale: The Virtues and Limits of Markets.* New York: Alfred A. Knopf, 1998.

Landes, David S. *The Wealth and Poverty of Nations: Why Some Are So Rich and Some So Poor.* New York: W. W. Norton, 1998.

The Latin American Provincials of the Society of Jesus. "A Letter on Neo-Liberalism in Latin America." *SEDOS* 29, no. 11 (1997): 308–11.

Latour, Bruno. *We Have Never Been Modern.* Translated by Catherine Porter. Cambridge, MA: Harvard University Press, 1993.

Leith, John H. *Introduction to the Reformed Tradition: A Way of Being the Christian Community.* Rev. ed. Atlanta: John Knox Press, 1981.

Long, Edward LeRoy, Jr. *To Liberate and Redeem: Moral Reflections on the Biblical Narrative.* Cleveland, OH: Pilgrim Press, 1997.

Loy, David R. "The Religion of the Market." *Journal of the American Academy of Religion* 65, no. 2 (1997): 275–90.

Lyotard, Jean-Francois. *The Postmodern Condition: A Report on Knowledge.* Translated by Geoff Bennington and Brian Massumi. Edited by Wlad Godzich and Jochen Schulte-Sasse. Vol. 10 of *Theory and History of Literature.* Minneapolis: University of Minnesota Press, 1984.

Mackintosh, Maureen. *Gender, Class, and Rural Transition: Agribusiness and the Food Crisis in Senegal.* London: Zed Books, 1989.

Mander, Jerry, and Edward Goldsmith, eds. *The Case Against the Global Economy and for a Turn Toward the Local.* San Francisco: Sierra Club Books, 1996.

Marglin, Stephen A. "Towards the Decolonization of the Mind." In *Dominating Knowledge: Development, Culture, and Resistance.* Edited by Frederique Apffel and Stephen A. Marglin. Oxford: Clarendon Press, 1990.

Marx, Karl. *Capital: A Critique of Political Economy.* Vol. 1. Translated by Ben Fowkes. 1867. Repr., London: Penguin Books, 1990.

McFague, Sallie. *Life Abundant: Rethinking Theology and Economy for a Planet in Peril.* Minneapolis: Fortress Press, 2001.

McKim, Donald K. *Westminster Dictionary of Theological Terms.* Louisville, KY: Westminster John Knox, 1996.

Menchu, Rigoberta. *I, Rigoberta Menchu: An Indian Woman in Guatemala.* Translated by Ann Wright. London: Verso, 1984.

Merchant, Carolyn. *Radical Ecology: The Search for a Livable World.* New York: Routledge, 1992.

Milbrath, Lester W. *Envisioning a Sustainable Society: Learning Our Way Out.* Albany: State University of New York Press, 1989.

Mies, Maria, and Vandana Shiva. *Ecofeminism.* London: Zed Books, 1993.

Mieth, Dietmar, and Marciano Vidal. *Outside the Market No Salvation?* London: SCM Press, 1997.

Mikell, Gwendolyn. *Cocoa and Chaos in Ghana.* Washington, DC: Howard University Press, 1992.

Miller, Amata. "Global Economic Structures: Their Human Implications." In *Religion and Economic Justice.* Edited by Michael Zweig. Philadelphia: Temple University Press, 1991.

Mongia, Padmini, ed. *Contemporary Postcolonial Theory: A Reader.* New York: Oxford University Press, 1996.

Mpofu, Elias. "Exploring the Self-Concept in an African Culture." *The Journal of Genetic Psychology* 155, no. 3 (1994): 341–54.

Nell, Edward J. *Making Sense of a Changing Economy: Technology, Markets, and Morals.* London: Routledge, 1996.

Neuhaus, Richard John, ed. *The Structure of Freedom: Correlations, Causes, and Cautions.* Encounter Series. Grand Rapids: Eerdmans, 1991.

Nicholson, Linda J., ed. *Feminism/Postmodernism.* New York: Routledge, 1990.

Novak, Michael. "Wealth and Virtue: The Development of Christian Economic Teaching." In *The Capitalist Spirit: Toward a Religious Ethic of Wealth Creation.* San Francisco: Institute for Contemporary Studies Press, 1990.

Nudler, Oscar, and Mark A. Lutz, ed. *Economics, Culture, and Society—Alternative Approaches: Dissenting Views from Economic Orthodoxy.* New York: Apex Press, 1996.

Oglesby, Enoch H. *Born in the Fire: Case Studies in Christian Ethics and Globalization.* New York: Pilgrim Press, 1990.

Organisation for Economic Co-operation and Development. *Open Markets Matter: The Benefits of Trade and Investment Liberalization.* Paris: Organisation for Economic Co-operation and Development, 1998.

Panikkar, K. N. "Globalization and Culture." *Voices from the Third World* 20 (1997): 49–58.

Pauw, Christoff M. "Traditional African Economies in Conflict with Western Capitalism." *Mission Studies: Journal of the International Association for Mission Studies* 14, nos. 1–2 (1997): 204–22.

Perlas, Nicanor. *Shaping Globalization: Civil Society, Cultural Power, and Threefolding.* Quezon City, Philippines: Center for Alternative Development Initiatives, 1999.

Plant, Raymond. "The Neo-Liberal Social Vision." In *The Renewal of Social Vision.* Edited by Alison and Ian Swanson Elliot. Edinburgh: Center for Theology and Public Issues, 1989.

Polanyi, Karl. *The Great Transformation: The Political and Economic Origins of Our Times.* 1944. Repr., Boston: Beacon Press, 1957.

Presbyterian Church (USA) Advisory Committee on Social Witness Policy. "Hope for a Global Future: Toward Just and Sustainable Human Development." Louisville, KY: Presbyterian Church (USA), 1996.

Prychitko, David L., ed. *Why Economists Disagree: An Introduction to the Alternative Schools of Thought.* Albany: State University of New York Press, 1998.

Quinn, Bill. *How Wal-Mart Is Destroying America and the World: And What You Can Do about It.* Berkeley, CA: Ten Speed Press, 2000.

Rasmussen, Larry L. "A Different Discipline." *Union Seminary Quarterly Review* 53, no. 3–4 (1999): 29–51.

———. *Earth Community, Earth Ethics.* Maryknoll, NY: Orbis Books, 1996.

———. "Give Us Word of the Humankind We Left to Thee: Globalization and Its Wake." Cambridge, MA: Episcopal Divinity School, 1999.

———. *Moral Fragments and Moral Community.* Minneapolis: Fortress, 1993.

———. "Power Analysis: A Neglected Agenda." The Annual of the Society of Christian Ethics 11 (1991): 3–17.

———, ed. *Reinhold Niebuhr: Theologian of Public Life.* London: Collins, 1989.

Razu, I. John Mohan. "Transnational Corporations (TNCs) as Vehicles of Globalisation Process: A Critique from Development Perspective." *Bangalore Theological Forum* 30, nos. 3–4 (1998): 33–75.

Réamonn, Páraic. "Reformed Faith and Economic Justice." *Reformed World* 46, no. 3 (1996): 97–144.

Rehmann, Jan. "'Abolition' of Civil Society? Remarks on a Widespread Misunderstanding in the Interpretation of 'Civil Society.'" *Socialism and Democracy* 13, no. 2 (1999), 1–18.

Religious Working Group on the WB and IMF. "Moral Imperatives: Addressing Structural Adjustment and Economic Reform." *Church and Society*, September/October 1998.

Rich, Bruce. *Mortgaging the Earth: The World Bank, Environmental Impoverishment, and the Crisis of Overdevelopment.* Boston: Beacon Press, 1994.

Ritzer, George. *The McDonaldization of Society: An Investigation into the Changing Character of Contemporary Social Life.* Thousand Oaks, CA: Pine Forge Press, 1996.

Robertson, Roland, and William Garrett. *Religion and Global Order.* New York: Paragon House Publishers, 1991.

Ruether, Rosemary, ed. *Women Healing Earth: Third World Women on Ecology, Feminism, and Religion.* Maryknoll, NY: Orbis Books, 1996.

Russell, Letty M., and J. Shannon Clarkson, eds. *Dictionary of Feminist Theologies.* Louisville, KY: Westminster John Knox, 1996.

Sachs, Wolfgang, ed. *The Development Dictionary: A Guide to Knowledge as Power.* London: Zed Books, 1992.

Santmire, H. Paul. *The Travail of Nature: The Ambiguous Ecological Promise of Christian Theology.* Philadelphia: Fortress Press, 1985.

Sassen, Saskia. *Globalization and Its Discontents.* New York: The New Press, 1998.

Schut, Michael. "The Great Economy/The Big Economy." *Christian Social Action,* June 1997, 33–38.

Seidman, Ann. "Man-made Starvation in Africa." In *Religion and Economic Justice.* Edited by Michael Zweig. Philadelphia: Temple University Press, 1991.

Seidman, Steven. *Contested Knowledge: Social Theory in the Postmodern Era.* Cambridge, MA: Blackwell, 1994.

———, ed. *The Postmodern Turn: New Perspectives on Social Theory.* Cambridge: Cambridge University Press, 1994.

Sen, Amartya. "Capability and Well-Being." In *The Quality of Life.* Edited by Martha Nussbaum and Amartya Sen. Oxford: Clarendon Press, 1993.

———. *Development as Freedom.* New York: Alfred A. Knopf, 1999.

Shannon, Christopher. *Conspicuous Criticism: Tradition, the Individual, and Culture in American Social Thought, from Veblen to Mills.* Baltimore: Johns Hopkins University Press, 1996.

Sherman, Amy L. *Preferential Option: A Christian and Neoliberal Strategy for Latin America's Poor.* Grand Rapids: Eerdmans, 1992.

Shiva, Vandana. *Biopiracy: The Plunder of Nature and Knowledge.* Boston: South End Press, 1997.

———. *Staying Alive: Women, Ecology, and Development.* London: Zed Books, 1989.

Shiva, Vandana, and Ingunn Moser. *Biopolitics: A Feminist and Ecological Reader on Biotechnology.* London: Zed Books, 1995.

Smith, Adam. *An Inquiry into the Nature and Causes of the Wealth of Nations.* Vol. 1. Edited by R. H. Campbell and A. S. Skinner. 1775. Repr., Oxford: Clarendon Press, 1979. Repr., Indianapolis: Liberty Fund, 1981.

———. *Theory of Moral Sentiments.* Edited by D. D. Raphael and A. L. Macfie. 1759. Repr., Oxford: University Press, 1976. Repr., Indianapolis: Liberty Fund, 1982.

Solomon, Norman. "Economics of the Jubilee: Putting Third World Debt in Context." *Church and Society,* September/October 1998, 58–67.

Soros, George. "The Capitalist Threat," *Atlantic Monthly,* February 1997, 45–58.

Sparr, Pamela, ed. *Mortgaging Women's Lives: Feminist Critiques of Structural Adjustment.* London: Zed Books, 1994.

Stackhouse, Max L. "The Global Future and the Future of Globalization." *Christian Century* 111, no. 4 (February 2–9, 1994), 109–13.

———, ed. *Christian Social Ethics in a Global Era.* Nashville: Abingdon Press, 1995.

———, ed., with Peter J. Paris. *Religion and the Powers of the Common Life.* Vol. 1 of *God and Globalization.* Harrisburg, PA: Trinity Press International, 2000.

Stackhouse, Max L., Dennis P. McCann, Shirley J. Roels, and Preston N. Williams, eds. *On Moral Business: Classical and Contemporary Resources for Ethics in Economic Life.* Grand Rapids: Eerdmans, 1995.

Strange, Susan. *Casino Capitalism.* Manchester, England: Manchester University Press, 1997.

Stiglitz, Joseph. "Address to the World Institute for Development Economics Research." Address given at the 1998 WIDER Annual Lecture, Helsinki, January 7, 1998.

———. "Towards a New Paradigm for Development: Strategies, Policies, and Processes." Address given at the 1998 Prebisch Lecture at UNCTAD, Geneva, October 19, 1998.

Sung, Jung Mo. "Evil in the Free Market Mentality." In *The Return of the Plague.* Edited by Jose Oscar and Virgil Elizondo Beozzo. London: SCM Press, 1997.

Swimme, Brian, and Thomas Berry. *The Universe Story: From the Primordial Flaring Forth to the Ecozoic Era—A Celebration of the Unfolding of the Cosmos.* San Francisco: HarperCollins, 1992.

Thomas, Caroline, and Peter Wilkin, eds. *Globalization and the South.* New York: St. Martin's Press, 1997.

Thurow, Lester C. *The Future of Capitalism: How Today's Economic Forces Shape Tomorrow's World.* New York: Penguin, 1996.

Trible, Phyllis. *Texts of Terror: Literary-Feminist Readings of Biblical Narratives.* Philadelphia: Fortress Press, 1984.

United Church of Christ Commission for Racial Justice. "Toxic Wastes and Race in the United States: A National Study of the Racial and Socioeconomic Characteristics of Communities with Hazardous Waste Sites." New York: United Church of Christ, 1987.

United Nations Development Programme. "Globalization with a Human Face." In *Human Development Report 1999.* New York: Oxford University Press for the United Nations Development Programme, 1999.

———. "A New Global Architecture." In *Human Development Report 1994.* New York: United Nations Development Programme, 1994.

Van der Ryn, Sim, and Stuart Cowan. *Ecological Design.* Washington, DC: Island Press, 1996.

van Drimmelen, Rob. *Faith in a Global Economy: A Primer for Christians.* Geneva: WCC Publications, 1998.

Vikstrom, John. "An Ethical Evaluation of Neo-Liberalism." *Ministerial Formation* no. 82 (July 1998): 14–20.

Wallach, Lori, and Michelle Sforza. *Whose Trade Organization? Corporate Globalization and the Erosion of Democracy.* Washington, DC: Public Citizen, 1999.

Waring, Marilyn. *If Women Counted: A New Feminist Economics.* San Francisco: Harper San Francisco, 1988.

Waters, Malcolm. *Globalization.* London: Routledge, 1995.

Weaver, Jace, ed. *Defending Mother Earth: Native American Perspectives on Environmental Justice.* Maryknoll, NY: Orbis Books, 1996.

Weber, Max. *The Protestant Ethic and the Spirit of Capitalism.* Translated by Talcott Parsons. 1930. Repr., London: Routledge, 1992.

Williamson, Thad. "Strategies for Meaning in the Economy." *Tikkun* 12, no. 2 (1997): 26–31, 75.

Wolfensohn, James D. "Coalitions for Change." Address given at the World Bank Annual Meeting. Washington, DC, September 28, 1999.

———. "Foundations for a More Stable Global System." Address given at the Symposium on Global Finance and Development. Tokyo, March 1, 1999.

———. "Globalization and the Human Condition." Address given at "Symposium: Celebrating the 50th Anniversary of the Aspen Institute," Aspen, CO, August 19, 2000.

———. "The Other Crisis: 1998 Annual Meetings Address." Address given at the World Bank Annual Meeting. Washington, DC, October 6, 1998.

World Bank. "The Challenge of Development." In *World Development Report.* Oxford: World Bank, Oxford University Press, 1991.

———. "Entering the 21st Century." In *World Development Report.* Oxford: World Bank, Oxford University Press, 1999/2000.

World Council of Churches. "Accelerated Climate Change: Signs of Peril, Test of Faith." New York: World Council of Churches, 1993.

———. "Christian Faith and the World Economy Today: A Study Document from the World Council of Churches." Geneva: World Council of Churches, 1992.

———. "The Poor Get Poorer and the Rich Get Richer." *Church and Society,* September/October 1998.

Yergin, Daniel, and Joseph Stanislaw. *The Commanding Heights: The Battle between Government and the Marketplace That Is Remaking the Modern World.* New York: Simon & Schuster, 1998.

Index